CUDA Fortran for Scientists and Engineers

CUDA Fortran for Scientists and Engineers
Best Practices for Efficient CUDA Fortran Programming

Gregory Ruetsch and Massimiliano Fatica

NVIDIA Corporation, Santa Clara, CA

ELSEVIER

AMSTERDAM • BOSTON • HEIDELBERG • LONDON
NEW YORK • OXFORD • PARIS • SAN DIEGO
SAN FRANCISCO • SINGAPORE • SYDNEY • TOKYO

Morgan Kaufmann is an imprint of Elsevier

Acquiring Editor: *Todd Green*
Development Editor: *Lindsay Lawrence*
Project Manager: *Punithavathy Govindaradjane*
Designer: *Matthew Limbert*

Morgan Kaufmann is an imprint of Elsevier

225 Wyman Street, Waltham, MA 02451, USA

Library of Congress Cataloging-in-Publication Data

Ruetsch, Gregory.
  CUDA Fortran for scientists and engineers : best practices for efficient
CUDA Fortran programming / Gregory Ruetsch, Massimiliano Fatica.
      pages cm
  Includes bibliographical references and index.
  ISBN 978-0-12-416970-8 (alk. paper)
  1. FORTRAN (Computer program language) I. Fatica, Massimiliano. II. Title.
III. Title: Best practices for efficient CUDA Fortran programming.
  QA76.73.F25R833   2013
  005.13'1--dc23
                                                      2013022226

British Library Cataloguing-in-Publication Data
A catalogue record for this book is available from the British Library

ISBN: 978-0-12-416970-8

Transferred to Digital Printing in 2014

For information on all MK publications visit our website at *www.mkp.com*

To Fortran programmers, who know a good thing when they see it.

Contents

PART I CUDA FORTRAN PROGRAMMING

PART III APPENDICES

Acknowledgments

Writing this book has been an enjoyable and rewarding experience for us, largely due to the interactions with the people who helped shape the book into the form you have before you. There are many people who have helped with this book, both directly and indirectly, and at the risk of leaving someone out we would like to thank the following people for their assistance.

Of course, a book on CUDA Fortran would not be possible without CUDA Fortran itself, and we would like to thank The Portland Group (PGI), especially Brent Leback and Michael Wolfe, for literally giving us something to write about. Working with PGI on CUDA Fortran has been a delightful experience.

The authors often reflect on how computations used in their theses, which required many, many hours on large-vector machines of the day, can now run on an NVIDIA graphics processing unit (GPU) in less time than it takes to get a cup of coffee. We would like to thank those at NVIDIA who helped enable this technological breakthrough. We would like to thank past and present members of the CUDA software team, especially Philip Cuadra, Mark Hairgrove, Stephen Jones, Tim Murray, and Joel Sherpelz for answering the many questions we asked them.

Much of the material in this book grew out of collaborative efforts in performance-tuning applications. We would like to thank our collaborators in such efforts, including Norbert Juffa, Patrick Legresley, Paulius Micikevicius, and Everett Phillips.

Many people reviewed the manuscript for this book at various stages in its development, and we would like to thank Roberto Gomperts, Mark Harris, Norbert Juffa, Brent Leback, and Everett Phillips for their comments and suggestions.

We would like to thank Ian Buck for allowing us to spend time at work on this endeavor, and we would like to thank our families for their understanding while we also worked at home.

Finally, we would like to thank all of our teachers. They enabled us to write this book, and we hope in some way that by doing so, we have continued the chain of helping others.

Preface

This document is intended for scientists and engineers who develop or maintain computer simulations and applications in Fortran and who would like to harness the parallel processing power of graphics processing units (GPUs) to accelerate their code. The goal here is to provide the reader with the fundamentals of GPU programming using CUDA Fortran as well as some typical examples, without having the task of developing CUDA Fortran code become an end in itself.

The CUDA architecture was developed by NVIDIA to allow use of the GPU for general-purpose computing without requiring the programmer to have a background in graphics. There are many ways to access the CUDA architecture from a programmer's perspective, including through C/C++ from CUDA C or through Fortran using The Portland Group's (PGI's) CUDA Fortran. This document pertains to the latter approach. PGI's CUDA Fortran should be distinguished from the PGI Accelerator and OpenACC Fortran interfaces to the CUDA architecture, which are directive-based approaches to using the GPU. CUDA Fortran is simply the Fortran analog to CUDA C.

The reader of this book should be familiar with Fortran 90 concepts, such as modules, derived types, and array operations. For those familiar with earlier versions of Fortran but looking to upgrade to a more recent version, there are several excellent books that cover this material (e.g., Metcalf, 2011). Some features introduced in Fortran 2003 are used in this book, but these concepts are explained in detail. Although this book does assume some familiarity with Fortran 90, no experience with parallel programming (on the GPU or otherwise) is required. Part of the appeal of parallel programming on GPUs using CUDA is that the programming model is simple and novices can get parallel code up and running very quickly.

Often one comes to CUDA Fortran with the goal of porting existing, sometimes rather lengthy, Fortran code to code that leverages the GPU. Because CUDA is a hybrid programming model, where both GPU and CPU are utilized, CPU code can be incrementally ported to the GPU. CUDA Fortran is also used by those porting applications to GPUs mainly using the directive-base OpenACC approach, but who want to improve the performance of a few critical sections of code by hand-coding CUDA Fortran. Both OpenACC and CUDA Fortran can coexist in the same code.

This book is divided into two main parts. The first part is a tutorial on CUDA Fortran programming, from the basics of writing CUDA Fortran code to some tips on optimization. The second part is a collection of case studies that demonstrate how the principles in the first part are applied to real-world examples.

This book makes use of the PGI 13.x compilers, which can be obtained from http://pgroup.com. Although the examples can be compiled and run on any supported operating system in a variety of development environments, the examples included here are compiled from the command line as one would do under Linux or Mac OS X.

Companion Site

Supplementary materials for readers can be downloaded from Elsevier:
http://store.elsevier.com/product.jsp?isbn=9780124169708.

CUDA Fortran Programming

Introduction

1

CHAPTER OUTLINE HEAD

1.1 A brief history of GPU computing

Parallel computing has been around in one form or another for many decades. In the early stages it was generally confined to practitioners who had access to large and expensive machines. Today, things are very different. Almost all consumer desktop and laptop computers have central processing units, or CPUs, with multiple cores. Even most processors in cell phones and tablets have multiple cores. The principal reason for the nearly ubiquitous presence of multiple cores in CPUs is the inability of CPU manufacturers to increase performance in single-core designs by boosting the clock speed. As a result, since about 2005 CPU designs have "scaled out" to multiple cores rather than "scaled up" to higher clock rates. Although CPUs are available with a few to tens of cores, this amount of parallelisms pales in comparison to the number of cores in a *graphics processing unit* (GPU). For example, the NVIDIA Tesla® K20X contains 2688 cores. GPUs were highly parallel architectures from their beginning, in the mid-1990s, since graphics processing is an inherently parallel task.

The use of GPUs for general-purpose computing, often referred to as GPGPU, was initially a challenging endeavor. One had to program to the graphics application programming interface (API), which proved to be very restrictive in the types of algorithms that could be mapped to the GPU. Even when such a mapping was possible, the programming required to make this happen was difficult and not intuitive for scientists and engineers outside the computer graphics vocation. As such, adoption of the GPU for scientific and engineering computations was slow.

Things changed for GPU computing with the advent of NVIDIA's CUDA® architecture in 2007. The CUDA architecture included both hardware components on NVIDIA's GPU and a software programming environment that eliminated the barriers to adoption that plagued GPGPU. Since CUDA's first appearance in 2007, its adoption has been tremendous, to the point where, in November 2010, three of the top five supercomputers in the Top 500 list used GPUs. In the November 2012 Top 500 list, the fastest computer in the world was also GPU-powered. One of the reasons for this very fast adoption of CUDA is that the programming model was very simple. CUDA C, the first interface to the CUDA architecture, is essentially C with a few extensions that can offload portions of an algorithm to run on the GPU. It is a hybrid approach where both CPU and GPU are used, so porting computations to the GPU can be performed incrementally.

In late 2009, a joint effort between The Portland Group® (PGI®) and NVIDIA led to the CUDA Fortran compiler. Just as CUDA C is C with extensions, CUDA Fortran is essentially Fortran 90 with a few extensions that allow users to leverage the power of GPUs in their computations. Many books, articles, and other documents have been written to aid in the development of efficient CUDA C applications (e.g., Sanders and Kandrot, 2011; Kirk and Hwu, 2012; Wilt, 2013). Because it is newer, CUDA Fortran has relatively fewer aids for code development. Much of the material for writing efficient CUDA C translates easily to CUDA Fortran, since the underlying architecture is the same, but there is still a need for material that addresses how to write efficient code in CUDA Fortran. There are a couple of reasons for this. First, though CUDA C and CUDA Fortran are similar, there are some differences that will affect how code is written. This is not surprising, since CPU code written in C and Fortran will typically take on a different character as projects grow. Also, there are some features in CUDA C that are not present in CUDA Fortran, such as certain aspects of textures. Conversely, there are some features in CUDA Fortran, such as the `device` variable attribute used to denote data that resides on the GPU, that are not present in CUDA C.

This book is written for those who want to use parallel computation as a tool in getting other work done rather than as an end in itself. The aim is to give the reader a basic set of skills necessary for them to write reasonably optimized CUDA Fortran code that takes advantage of the NVIDIA® computing hardware. The reason for taking this approach rather than attempting to teach how to extract every last ounce of performance from the hardware is the assumption that those using CUDA Fortran do so as a means rather than an end. Such users typically value clear and maintainable code that is simple to write and performs reasonably well across many generations of CUDA-enabled hardware and CUDA Fortran software.

But where is the line drawn in terms of the effort-performance tradeoff? In the end it is up to the developer to decide how much effort to put into optimizing code. In making this decision, we need to know what type of payoff we can expect when eliminating various bottlenecks and what effort is involved in doing so. One goal of this book is to help the reader develop an intuition needed to make such a return-on-investment assessment. To achieve this end, we discuss bottlenecks encountered in writing common algorithms in science and engineering applications in CUDA Fortran. Multiple workarounds are presented when possible, along with the performance impact of each optimization effort.

1.2 Parallel computation

Before jumping into writing CUDA Fortran code, we should say a few words about where CUDA fits in with other types of parallel programming models. Familiarity with and an understanding of other parallel programming models is not a prerequisite for this book, but for readers who do have some parallel programming experience, this section might be helpful in categorizing CUDA.

We have already mentioned that CUDA is a hybrid computing model, where both the CPU and GPU are used in an application. This is advantageous for development because sections of an existing CPU code can be ported to the GPU incrementally. It is possible to overlap computation on the CPU with computation on the GPU, so this is one aspect of parallelism.

A far greater degree of parallelism occurs within the GPU itself. Subroutines that run on the GPU are executed by many threads in parallel. Although all threads execute the same code, these threads typically operate on different data. This *data parallelism* is a fine-grained parallelism, where it is most efficient to have adjacent threads operate on adjacent data, such as elements of an array. This model of parallelism is very different from a model like Message Passing Interface, commonly known as MPI, which is a coarse-grained model. In MPI, data are typically divided into large segments or partitions, and each MPI process performs calculations on an entire data partition.

A few characteristics of the CUDA programming model are very different from CPU-based parallel programming models. One difference is that there is very little overhead associated with creating GPU threads. In addition to fast thread creation, context switches, where threads change from active to inactive and vice versa, are very fast for GPU threads compared to CPU threads. The reason context switching is essentially instantaneous on the GPU is that the GPU does not have to store state, as the CPU does when switching threads between being active and inactive. As a result of this fast context switching, it is advantageous to heavily oversubscribe GPU cores—that is, have many more resident threads than GPU cores so that memory latencies can be hidden. It is not uncommon to have the number of resident threads on a GPU an order of magnitude larger than the number of cores on the GPU. In the CUDA programming model, we essentially write a serial code that is executed by many GPU threads in parallel. Each thread executing this code has a means of identifying itself in order to operate on different data, but the code that CUDA threads execute is very similar to what we would write for serial CPU code. On the other hand, the code of many parallel CPU programming models differs greatly from serial CPU code. We will revisit each of these aspects of the CUDA programming model and architecture as they arise in the following discussion.

1.3 Basic concepts

This section contains a progression of simple CUDA Fortran code examples used to demonstrate various basic concepts of programming in CUDA Fortran.

Before we start, we need to define a few terms. CUDA Fortran is a hybrid programming model, meaning that code sections can execute either on the CPU or the GPU, or more precisely, on the *host* or *device*. The terms *host* is used to refer to the CPU and its memory, and the term *device* is used to refer to GPU and its memory, both in the context of a CUDA Fortran program. Going forward, we use the term *CPU code* to refer to a CPU-only implementation. A subroutine that executes on the device but is called from the host is called a *kernel*.

1.3.1 A first CUDA Fortran program

As a reference, we start with a Fortran 90 code that increments an array. The code is arranged so that the incrementing is performed in a subroutine, which itself is in a Fortran 90 module. The subroutine loops over and increments each element of an array by the value of the parameter b that is passed into the subroutine.

```
1   module simpleOps_m
2   contains
3     subroutine increment(a, b)
4       implicit none
5       integer, intent(inout) :: a(:)
6       integer, intent(in) :: b
7       integer :: i, n
8
9       n = size(a)
10      do i = 1, n
11         a(i) = a(i)+b
12      enddo
13
14    end subroutine increment
15  end module simpleOps_m
16
17
18  program incrementTestCPU
19    use simpleOps_m
20    implicit none
21    integer, parameter :: n = 256
22    integer :: a(n), b
23
24    a = 1
25    b = 3
26    call increment(a, b)
27
28    if (any(a /= 4)) then
29       write(*,*) '**** Program Failed ****'
30    else
31       write(*,*) 'Program Passed'
```

```
32      endif
33  end program incrementTestCPU
```

In practice, we would not accomplish such an operation in this fashion. We would use Fortran 90's array syntax within the main program to accomplish the same operation in a single line. However, for comparison to the CUDA Fortran version and to highlight the sequential nature of the operations in CPU code, we'll use this format.

The equivalent CUDA Fortran code is the following:

```
1   module simpleOps_m
2   contains
3     attributes(global) subroutine increment(a, b)
4       implicit none
5       integer, intent(inout) :: a(:)
6       integer, value :: b
7       integer :: i
8
9       i = threadIdx%x
10      a(i) = a(i)+b
11
12    end subroutine increment
13  end module simpleOps_m
14
15
16  program incrementTestGPU
17    use cudafor
18    use simpleOps_m
19    implicit none
20    integer, parameter :: n = 256
21    integer :: a(n), b
22    integer, device :: a_d(n)
23
24    a = 1
25    b = 3
26
27    a_d = a
28    call increment<<<1,n>>>(a_d, b)
29    a = a_d
30
31    if (any(a /= 4)) then
32       write(*,*) '**** Program Failed ****'
33    else
34       write(*,*) 'Program Passed'
35    endif
36  end program incrementTestGPU
```

The first difference between the Fortran 90 and CUDA Fortran code we run across is the `attributes(global)` prefix to the subroutine on line 3 of the CUDA Fortran implementation. The attribute `global` indicates that the code is to run on the device but is called from the host. (The term `global`, as with all subroutine attributes, describes the scope; the subroutine is seen from both the host and the device.)

The second major difference we notice is that the do loop on lines 10–12 of the Fortran 90 example has been replaced in the CUDA Fortran code by the statement initializing the index `i` on line 9 and the content of the loop on line 10. This difference arises out of the serial versus parallel execution of these two codes. In the CPU code, incrementing elements of the array "a" is performed sequentially in the do loop by a single CPU thread. In the CUDA Fortran version, the subroutine is executed by many GPU threads concurrently. Each thread identifies itself via the built-in `threadIdx` variable that is available in all device code and uses this variable as an index of the array. Note that this parallelism, where sequential threads modify adjacent elements of an array, is termed a *fine-grained* parallelism.

The main program in the CUDA Fortran code is executed on host. The CUDA Fortran definitions and derived types are contained in the `cudafor` module, which is used on line 17 along with the `simpleOps_m` module on line 18. As we alluded to earlier, CUDA Fortran deals with two separate memory spaces, one on the host and one on the device. Both these spaces are visible from host code, and the `device` attribute is used when declaring variables to indicate they reside in device memory—for example, when declaring the device variable `a_d` on line 22 of the CUDA Fortran code. The "_d" variable suffix is not required but is a useful convention for differentiating device from host variables in host code. Because CUDA Fortran is strongly typed in this regard, data transfers between host and device can be performed by assignment statements. This occurs on line 27, where, after the array a is initialized on the host, the data are transferred to the device memory in dynamic random-access memory (DRAM).

Once the data have been transferred to device memory in DRAM, then the kernel, or subroutine that executes on the device, can be launched, as is done on line 28. The group of parameters specified within the triple chevrons between the subroutine name and the argument list on line 28 is called the *execution configuration* and determines the number of GPU threads used to execute the kernel. We will go into the execution configuration in depth a bit later, but for now it is sufficient to say that an execution configuration of <<< 1,n >>> specifies that the kernel is executed by n GPU threads.

Although kernel array arguments such as a_d must reside in device memory, this is not the case with scalar arguments such as the second kernel argument b, which resides in host memory. The CUDA runtime will take care of the transfer of host scalar arguments, but it expects the argument to be passed by value. By default, Fortran passes arguments by reference, but arguments can be passed by value using the `value` variable attribute, as shown on line 6 of the CUDA Fortran code. The `value` attribute was introduced in Fortran 2003 as part of a mechanism for interoperating with C code.

One issue that we must contend with in a hybrid programming model such as CUDA is that of *synchronization* between the host and the device. For this program to execute correctly, we need to know that the host-to-device data transfer on line 27 completes before the kernel begins execution and that the kernel completes before the device-to-host transfer on line 29 commences. We are assured of such behavior because the data transfers via assignment statements on lines 27 and 29 are blocking or synchronous transfers. Such transfers do not initiate until all previous operations on the GPU are complete, and subsequent operations on the GPU will not begin until the data transfer is complete. The blocking nature of these data transfers is helpful in implicitly synchronizing the CPU and GPU.

The data transfers via assignment statements are blocking or synchronous operations, whereas kernel launches are nonblocking or asynchronous. Once the kernel on line 28 is launched, control immediately returns to the host. However, we are assured of the desired behavior because the data transfer in line 29 does not initiate due the blocking nature of the transfer.

There are routines that perform asynchronous transfers so that computation on the device can overlap communication between host and device as well as provide a means to synchronize the host and device, as discussed in Section 3.1.3.

1.3.2 Extending to larger arrays

The preceding example has the limitation that with the execution configuration <<< 1,n >>>, the parameter n and hence the array size must be small. This limit depends on the particular CUDA device being used. For Kepler™- and Fermi™-based products, such as the Tesla K20 and C2050 cards, the limit is n=1024, and on previous-generation cards this limit is n=512. (See Appendix A for such limits.) The way to accommodate larger arrays is to modify the first execution configuration parameter, because essentially the product of these two execution configuration parameters gives the number of GPU threads that execute the code. So, why is this done? Why are GPU threads grouped in this manner? This grouping of threads in the programming model mimics the grouping of processing elements in hardware on the GPU.

The basic computational unit on the GPU is a thread processor, also referred to simply as a *core*. In essence, a thread processor or core is a floating-point unit. Thread processors are grouped into multiprocessors, which contain a limited amount of resources used by resident threads, namely registers and shared memory. This concept is illustrated in Figure 1.1, which shows a CUDA-capable device containing a GPU with four multiprocessors, each of which contains 32 thread processors.

The analog to a multiprocessor in the programming model is a *thread block*. Thread blocks are groups of threads that are assigned to a multiprocessor and do not migrate once assigned. Multiple thread blocks can reside on a single multiprocessor, but the number of thread blocks that can simultaneously reside on a multiprocessor is limited by the resources available on a multiprocessor as well as the resources required by each thread block.

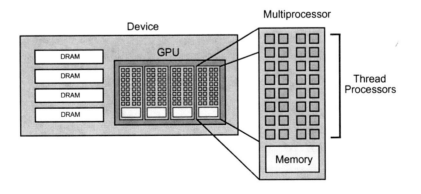

FIGURE 1.1

Hierarchy of computational units in a GPU, where thread processors are grouped together in multiprocessors.

Turning back to our example code, when the kernel is invoked, it launches a *grid* of thread blocks. The number of thread blocks launched is specified by the first parameter of the execution configuration, and the number of threads in a thread block is specified by the second parameter. So, our first CUDA Fortran program launched a grid consisting of a single thread block of 256 threads. We can accommodate larger arrays by launching multiple thread blocks, as in the following code:

```fortran
 1  module simpleOps_m
 2  contains
 3    attributes(global) subroutine increment(a, b)
 4      implicit none
 5      integer, intent(inout) :: a(:)
 6      integer, value :: b
 7      integer :: i, n
 8
 9      i = blockDim%x*(blockIdx%x-1) + threadIdx%x
10      n = size(a)
11      if (i <= n) a(i) = a(i)+b
12
13    end subroutine increment
14  end module simpleOps_m
15
16
17  program incrementTest
18    use cudafor
19    use simpleOps_m
20    implicit none
21    integer, parameter :: n = 1024*1024
22    integer, allocatable :: a(:)
23    integer, device, allocatable :: a_d(:)
24    integer :: b, tPB = 256
25
26    allocate(a(n), a_d(n))
27    a = 1
28    b = 3
29
30    a_d = a
31    call increment<<<ceiling(real(n)/tPB),tPB>>>(a_d, b)
32    a = a_d
33
34    if (any(a /= 4)) then
35       write(*,*) '**** Program Failed ****'
36    else
37       write(*,*) 'Program Passed'
38    endif
39    deallocate(a, a_d)
40  end program incrementTest
```

In the host code, we declare both host and device arrays to be allocatable. This is not needed when we use a larger array; we do this just to indicate that device arrays can be allocated and deallocated just as host arrays can. In fact, both host and device arrays can be used in the same `allocate()` and `deallocate()` statements, as on lines 26 and 39 in this example.

Aside from using allocatable arrays, this program contains only a few modifications to the CUDA Fortran code presented in Section 1.3.1. In the host code, the parameter `tPB` representing the number of threads per block is defined on line 24. When we launch a kernel with multiple thread blocks, all thread blocks in a single kernel launch must be the same size, which is specified by the second execution configuration parameter. In our example, when the number of elements in the array is not evenly divisible by the number of threads per block, we need to make sure enough threads are launched to process each element of the array, but we must also make sure we don't access the array out of bounds. The ceiling function on line 31 is used to determine the number of thread blocks required to process all array elements. In device code, the Fortran 90 `size()` intrinsic is used on line 10 to determine the number of elements in the array, which is used in the `if` condition of line 11 to make sure the kernel doesn't read or write off the end of the array.

In addition to checking for out-of-bounds memory accesses, the device code also differs from the single-block example in Section 1.3.1 in the calculation of the array index `i` on line 9. The predefined variable `threadIdx` is the index of a thread within its thread block. When we use multiple thread blocks, as is the case here, this value needs to be offset by the number of threads in previous thread blocks to obtain unique integers used to access elements of an array. This offset is determined using the predefined variables `blockDim` and `blockIdx`, which contain the number of threads in a block and the index of the block within the grid, respectively. An illustration of the way the predefined variables in device code are used to calculate the global array indices is shown in Figure 1.2.

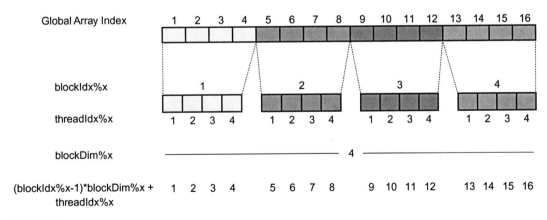

FIGURE 1.2

Calculation of the global array index in terms of predefined variables `blockDim`, `blockIdx`, and `threadIdx`. For simplicity, four thread blocks with four threads each are used. In actual CUDA Fortran code, thread blocks with much higher thread counts are used.

In both of the CUDA Fortran examples we have discussed, the kernel code accesses the x fields of the predefined variables, and as you might expect, these data types can accommodate multidimensional arrays, which we explore next.

1.3.3 Multidimensional arrays

We can easily extend our example to work on a multidimensional array. This is facilitated since the predefined variables in device code are of a derived type dim3, which contains x, y, and z fields. In terms of the host code, thus far we have specified the blocks per grid and threads per block execution configuration parameters as integers, but these parameters can also be of type dim3. Using other fields of the dim3 type, the multidimensional version of our code becomes:

```
1   module simpleOps_m
2   contains
3     attributes(global) subroutine increment(a, b)
4       implicit none
5       integer :: a(:,:)
6       integer, value :: b
7       integer :: i, j, n(2)
8
9       i = (blockIdx%x-1)*blockDim%x + threadIdx%x
10      j = (blockIdx%y-1)*blockDim%y + threadIdx%y
11      n(1) = size(a,1)
12      n(2) = size(a,2)
13      if (i<=n(1) .and. j<=n(2)) a(i,j) = a(i,j) + b
14    end subroutine increment
15  end module simpleOps_m
16
17
18
19  program incrementTest
20    use cudafor
21    use simpleOps_m
22    implicit none
23    integer, parameter :: nx=1024, ny=512
24    integer :: a(nx,ny), b
25    integer, device :: a_d(nx,ny)
26    type(dim3) :: grid, tBlock
27
28    a = 1
29    b = 3
30
31    tBlock = dim3(32,8,1)
32    grid = dim3(ceiling(real(nx)/tBlock%x), &
33                ceiling(real(ny)/tBlock%y), 1)
34    a_d = a
```

```
35    call increment<<<grid,tBlock>>>(a_d, b)
36    a = a_d
37
38    if (any(a /= 4)) then
39        write(*,*) '**** Program Failed ****'
40    else
41        write(*,*) 'Program Passed'
42    endif
43 end program incrementTest
```

After declaring the parameters nx and ny along with the host and device arrays for this two-dimensional example, we declare two variables of type dim3 used in the execution configuration on line 26. On line 31 the three components of the dim3 type specifying the number of threads per block are set; in this case each block has a 32 × 8 arrangement of threads. In the following two lines, the ceiling function is used to determine the number of blocks in the x and y dimensions required to increment all the elements of the array. The kernel is then launched with these variables as the execution configuration parameters in line 35. In the kernel code, the dummy argument a is declared as a two-dimensional array and the variable n as a two-element array, which, on lines 11 and 12, is set to hold the size of a in each dimension. An additional index j is assigned a value on line 10 in an analogous manner to i on line 9, and both i and j are checked for in-bound access before a(i,j) is incremented.

1.4 Determining CUDA hardware features and limits

There are many different CUDA-capable devices available, spanning different product lines (GeForce® and Quadro® as well as Tesla) in addition to different generations of architecture. We have already discussed the limitation of the number of threads per block, which is 1024 on Kepler and Fermi-based hardware and 512 for earlier architectures, and there are many other features and limits that vary among devices. In this section we cover the device management API, which contains routines for determining the number and types of CUDA-capable cards available on a particular system and what features and limits such cards have.

Before we go into the device management API, we should briefly discuss the notion of *compute capability*. The compute capability of a CUDA-enabled device indicates the architecture and is given in *Major.Minor* format. The *Major* component of the compute capability reflects the generation of the architecture, and the *Minor* component reflects the revision within that generation. The very first CUDA-enabled cards were of compute capability 1.0. Fermi-generation cards have compute capabilities of 2.x, and Kepler-generation cards have compute capabilities of 3.x. Some features of CUDA correlate with the compute capability; for example, double precision is available with cards of compute capability 1.3 and higher. Other features do not correlate with compute capability but can be determined through the device management API.

The device management API has routines for getting information on the number of cards available on a system as well as for selecting a card from among available cards. This API makes use of the `cudaDeviceProp` derived type for inquiring about the features of individual cards, which is demonstrated in the following program:

```fortran
1   program deviceQuery
2     use cudafor
3     implicit none
4
5     type (cudaDeviceProp) :: prop
6     integer :: nDevices=0, i, ierr
7
8     ! Number of CUDA-capable devices
9
10    ierr = cudaGetDeviceCount(nDevices)
11
12    if (nDevices == 0) then
13       write(*,"(/,'No CUDA devices found',/)")
14       stop
15    else if (nDevices == 1) then
16       write(*,"(/,'One CUDA device found',/)")
17    else
18       write(*,"(/,i0,' CUDA devices found',/)") nDevices
19    end if
20
21    ! Loop over devices
22
23    do i = 0, nDevices-1
24
25       write(*,"('Device Number: ',i0)") i
26
27       ierr = cudaGetDeviceProperties(prop, i)
28
29       ! General device info
30
31       write(*,"('  Device Name: ',a)") trim(prop%name)
32       write(*,"('  Compute Capability: ',i0,'.',i0)") &
33            prop%major, prop%minor
34       write(*,"('  Number of Multiprocessors: ',i0)") &
35            prop%multiProcessorCount
36       write(*,"('  Max Threads per Multiprocessor: ',i0)") &
37            prop%maxThreadsPerMultiprocessor
38       write(*,"('  Global Memory (GB): ',f9.3,/)") &
39            prop%totalGlobalMem/1024.0**3
40
41       ! Execution Configuration
42
43       write(*,"('  Execution Configuration Limits')")
```

```
44      write(*,"('       Max Grid Dims:  ',2(i0,' x '),i0)") &
45         prop%maxGridSize
46      write(*,"('       Max Block Dims:  ',2(i0,' x '),i0)") &
47         prop%maxThreadsDim
48      write(*,"('       Max Threads per Block: ',i0,/)") &
49         prop%maxThreadsPerBlock
50
51   enddo
52
53 end program deviceQuery
```

This code determines the number of CUDA-capable devices attached to the system from the `cudaGetDeviceCount()` routine on line 10 and then loops over each device, retrieving the device properties from the `cudaGetDeviceProperties()` routine. This code lists only a small portion of the fields available in the `cudaDeviceProp` type. A full list of the members of the `cudaDeviceProp` derived type is provided in the *CUDA Toolkit Reference Manual*, available online from NVIDIA.

We list the output of this code on a variety of Tesla devices of different compute capabilities. The first Tesla device, released in 2007, was the Tesla C870, with a compute capability of 1.0, and on a system with this device we obtain the following result:

```
One CUDA device found

Device Number: 0
   Device Name: Tesla C870
   Compute Capability: 1.0
   Number of Multiprocessors: 16
   Max Threads per Multiprocessor: 768
   Global Memory (GB):      1.500

   Execution Configuration Limits
     Max Grid Dims: 65535 x 65535 x 1
     Max Block Dims: 512 x 512 x 64
     Max Threads per Block: 512
```

Note that *the enumeration of devices is zero-based rather than unit-based*. The `Max Threads per Multiprocessor` number refers to the maximum number of *concurrent* threads that can reside on a multiprocessor. The `Global Memory` indicated in the following line of output is the amount of available memory in device DRAM. The first two lines under `Execution Configuration Limits` denote the limits in each dimension of the first two execution configuration parameters: the number and configuration of thread blocks in a kernel launch, and the number and configuration of threads in a thread block. Note that for this compute capability, grids must be a two-dimensional configuration of thread blocks, whereas thread blocks can be a three-dimensional arrangement of threads, up to the specified limits. The product of the three thread-block components specified in the execution configuration must be less than or equal to the `Max Threads per Block` limit of 512 for this device.

The next Tesla product with a higher compute capability was the Tesla C1060:

```
One CUDA device found

Device Number: 0
  Device Name: Tesla C1060
  Compute Capability: 1.3
  Number of Multiprocessors: 30
  Max Threads per Multiprocessor: 1024
  Global Memory (GB):      4.000

  Execution Configuration Limits
    Max Grid Dims: 65535 x 65535 x 1
    Max Block Dims: 512 x 512 x 64
    Max Threads per Block: 512
```

In addition to having a greater number of multiprocessors than the C870, the C1060 has a higher limit on the number of threads per multiprocessor. But perhaps the most important distinction between these devices is that the C1060 was the first Tesla device with the ability to perform double precision arithmetic. The execution configuration limits are the same as those on the C870.

The Tesla C2050 is an example of the Fermi generation of devices:

```
One CUDA device found

Device Number: 0
  Device Name: Tesla C2050
  Compute Capability: 2.0
  Number of Multiprocessors: 14
  Max Threads per Multiprocessor: 1536
  Global Memory (GB):      2.624

  Execution Configuration Limits
    Max Grid Dims: 65535 x 65535 x 65535
    Max Block Dims: 1024 x 1024 x 64
    Max Threads per Block: 1024
```

Whereas the C2050 has only 14 multiprocessors relative to the 30 of the C1060, the Fermi multiprocessor design is far more powerful than the previous multiprocessor designs. The maximum number of threads per multiprocessor has increased from previous generations. The execution configuration limits changed substantially relative to previous generations of devices. The maximum thread block size increased from 512 to 1024, and three-dimensional arrangements of thread blocks in a grid became possible, greatly facilitating the decomposition of three-dimensional problems.

The next generation of cards is the Kepler generation of devices, which have a compute capability of 3.x, such as the Tesla K20:

```
One CUDA device found

Device Number: 0
  Device Name: Tesla K20
  Compute Capability: 3.5
  Number of Multiprocessors: 13
  Max Threads per Multiprocessor: 2048
  Global Memory (GB):      4.687

  Execution Configuration Limits
    Max Grid Dims: 2147483647 x 65535 x 65535
    Max Block Dims: 1024 x 1024 x 64
    Max Threads per Block: 1024
```

With Kepler, the number of threads per multiprocessor increased again, as did the limit on the number of blocks that can be launched in the first dimension of the grid. This increased limit arose out of the desire to launch kernels with large numbers of threads using only one-dimensional thread blocks and grids. On devices with a compute capability less than 3.0, the largest number of threads that could be launched in such a fashion is 64×1024^2. For a one-to-one mapping of threads to data elements, this corresponds to a single-precision array of 256 MB. We could get around this limit by using two-dimensional grids or having each thread process multiple elements of the array, but such workarounds are no longer needed on devices of compute capability 3.0 and higher. There are many other features introduced in the Kepler architecture, which we will address in later in the book. Another Tesla device of the Kepler generation is the Tesla K10. On a system with a single Tesla K10 we obtain the following:

```
2 CUDA devices found

Device Number: 0
  Device Name: Tesla K10.G1.8GB
  Compute Capability: 3.0
  Number of Multiprocessors: 8
  Max Threads per Multiprocessor: 2048
```

```
Global Memory (GB):        4.000

Execution Configuration Limits
   Max Grid Dims: 2147483647 x 65535 x 65535
   Max Block Dims: 1024 x 1024 x 64
   Max Threads per Block: 1024

Device Number: 1
  Device Name: Tesla K10.G1.8GB
  Compute Capability: 3.0
  Number of Multiprocessors: 8
  Max Threads per Multiprocessor: 2048
  Global Memory (GB):        4.000

  Execution Configuration Limits
     Max Grid Dims: 2147483647 x 65535 x 65535
     Max Block Dims: 1024 x 1024 x 64
     Max Threads per Block: 1024
```

Each Tesla K10 contains two GPUs, each with its own 4 GB of DRAM memory. From the perspective of the CUDA Fortran programmer, a system with one K10 is no different than having two single-GPU devices in the system. We address how to program multi-GPU systems such as this in Chapter 4.

Table 1.1 summarizes some of the data from our deviceQuery code.[1] With the exception of the maximum number of thread blocks that can simultaneously reside on a multiprocessor, all of the data in Table 1.1 was obtained from members of the cudaDeviceProp derived type.

Taking the product of the number of multiprocessors on these devices and the maximum number of threads per multiprocessor, we see that in all cases the number of concurrent threads on each device can be in the tens of thousands of threads.

As noted in the table, Tesla devices of compute capability 2.0 and higher have the error-correcting code (ECC) feature, which can be turned on or off. If it is turned on, the amount of available global memory will be smaller than the numbers indicated in the table. In such cases, this reduced value will be reported, as shown in the Tesla C2050 and Tesla K20 output we just looked at. Whether ECC is enabled or disabled can be queried from the ECCEnabled field of the cudaDeviceProp type.

Although the data in Table 1.1 were obtained from particular Tesla devices, much of the data applies to other devices with the same compute capability. The only data from Table 1.1 that will vary between devices of the same compute capability are the amount of global memory and number of multiprocessors on the device.

By varying the multiprocessor count, a wide range of devices can be made using the same multiprocessor architecture. A laptop with a GeForce GT 650 M has two multiprocessors of compute capability 3.0, in contrast to the eight multiprocessors on each of the two GPUs in a Tesla K10. Despite these differences in processing power, the codes in the previous sections can run on each of these devices without any alteration. This is part of the benefit of grouping threads into thread blocks in the

---

[1] More information on these and other Tesla devices is listed in Appendix A.

Table 1.1 Characteristics of various Tesla devices.

	Tesla C870	Tesla C1060	Tesla C2050	Tesla K10	Tesla K20
Compute capability	1.0	1.3	2.0	3.0	3.5
Number of multiprocessors	16	30	14	2×8	13
Max threads per multiprocessor	786	1024	1536	2048	2048
Max thread blocks per multiprocessor	8	8	8	16	16
Max threads per thread block	512	512	1024	1024	1024
Global memory (GB)	1.5	4	3*	$2 \times 4^*$	5*

*Enabling ECC reduces available global memory.

programming model. The thread blocks are distributed to the multiprocessors by the scheduler as space becomes available. Thread blocks are independent, so the order in which they execute does not affect the outcome. This independence of thread blocks in the programming model allows the scheduling to be done behind the scenes, so the programmer need only worry about programming for threads within a thread block.

Regardless of the number of multiprocessors on a device, the number of thread blocks launched by a kernel can be quite large. Even on a laptop with a GeForce GT 650 M we obtain:

```
One CUDA device found

Device Number: 0
   Device Name: GeForce GT 650M
   Compute Capability: 3.0
   Number of Multiprocessors: 2
   Max Threads per Multiprocessor: 2048
   Global Memory (GB):      0.500

   Execution Configuration Limits
      Max Grid Dims: 2147483647 x 65535 x 65535
      Max Block Dims: 1024 x 1024 x 64
      Max Threads per Block: 1024
```

We could launch a kernel using a one-dimensional grid of one-dimensional thread blocks with 2147483647×1024 threads on the laptop GPU! Once again, the independence of thread blocks allows the scheduler to assign thread blocks to multiprocessors as space becomes available, all of which is done without intervention by the programmer.

Before spending the time to implement a full-blown version of the deviceQuery code, please note that the pgaccelinfo utility included with the PGI compilers provides this information. Sample output from pgaccelinfo on a system with a single Tesla K20 is as follows:

```
CUDA Driver Version:              5000
NVRM version: NVIDIA UNIX x86_64 Kernel Module   304.52
Sun Sep 23 20:28:04 PDT 2012

CUDA Device Number:               0
Device Name:                      Tesla K20
Device Revision Number:           3.5
Global Memory Size:               5032706048
Number of Multiprocessors:        13
Number of SP Cores:               2496
Number of DP Cores:               832
Concurrent Copy and Execution:    Yes
Total Constant Memory:            65536
Total Shared Memory per Block:    49152
Registers per Block:              65536
Warp Size:                        32
Maximum Threads per Block:        1024
Maximum Block Dimensions:         1024, 1024, 64
Maximum Grid Dimensions:          2147483647 x 65535 x 65535
Maximum Memory Pitch:             2147483647B
Texture Alignment:                512B
Clock Rate:                       705 MHz
Execution Timeout:                No
Integrated Device:                No
Can Map Host Memory:              Yes
Compute Mode:                     default
Concurrent Kernels:               Yes
ECC Enabled:                      Yes
Memory Clock Rate:                2600 MHz
Memory Bus Width:                 320 bits
L2 Cache Size:                    1310720 bytes
Max Threads Per SMP:              2048
Async Engines:                    2
Unified Addressing:               Yes
Initialization time:              44466 microseconds
Current free memory:              4951891968
Upload time (4MB):                1715 microseconds ( 962 ms pinned)
Download time:                    3094 microseconds ( 877 ms pinned)
Upload bandwidth:                 2445 MB/sec (4359 MB/sec pinned)
Download bandwidth:               1355 MB/sec (4782 MB/sec pinned)
PGI Compiler Option:              -ta=nvidia,cc35
```

The output for the PGI Compiler Option field on the last line of output relates to the flags used in the PGI Accelerator interface to CUDA. We explore compiler options for CUDA Fortran in Section 1.6.

Table 1.2 Single- and double-precision resources on various Tesla devices.

Compute capability	1.0	1.3	2.0	3.0	3.5
Representative device	Tesla C870	Tesla C1060	Tesla C2050	Tesla K10	Tesla K20
Number of multiprocessors	16	30	14	2×8	13
Single-precision cores per multiprocessor	8	8	32	192	192
Total single-precision cores	128	240	448	2×1536	2496
Double-precision cores per multiprocessor	-	1	16*	8	64
Total double-precision cores	-	30	224*	2×64	832
Max threads per multiprocessor	786	1024	1536	2048	2048

GeForce GPUs have fewer double-precision units.

1.4.1 Single and double precision

The thread processors in a multiprocessor are capable of performing single-precision floating-point arithmetic, whereas double-precision floating-point arithmetic is performed in separate double-precision cores contained within the multiprocessor. The numbers of single- and double-precision cores per multiprocessor and per device are summarized in Table 1.2.

As we mentioned, devices with a compute capability of 1.3, e.g., the Tesla C1060, were the first to support double precision. In general, both single- and double-precision resources have significantly increased with each generation of cards. The one exception to this is the double-precision capability on the Tesla K10. The Tesla K10, which has a much higher core clock than the K20, was designed to excel at single-precision performance. For double-precision performance, the Tesla K20 is the appropriate Kepler device.

We included the maximum number of threads per multiprocessor in the last row of Table 1.2 to illustrate that the number of resident threads can far exceed the computational resources on a multiprocessor in every case by more than a factor of 10. This is by design. Because context switching between GPU threads is so efficient and latencies to global memory are large, we want to oversubscribe a multiprocessor with threads to hide the large latencies to global memory.

1.4.1.1 *Accommodating variable precision*

It is often desirable to develop code using single-precision variables on a small problem size and then deploy the code on a larger problem size using double precision. Fortran 90's kind type parameters allow us to accommodate switching between single and double precision quite easily. All we have to do is to define a module with the selected kind:

```
module precision_m
  integer, parameter :: singlePrecision = kind(0.0)
  integer, parameter :: doublePrecision = kind(0.0d0)
```

```
   ! Comment out one of the lines below
   integer, parameter :: fp_kind = singlePrecision
   !integer, parameter :: fp_kind = doublePrecision
end module precision_m
```

and then use this module and the parameter `fp_kind` when declaring floating-point variables in code:

```
use precision_m
real(fp_kind), device :: a_d(n)
```

This allows us to toggle between the two precisions simply by changing the `fp_kind` definition in the precision module. (We may have to write some generic interfaces to accommodate library calls such as the NVIDIA CUDA® Fast Fourier Transform, or CUFFT, routines.)

Another option for toggling between single and double precision that doesn't involve modifying source code is through use of the preprocessor, where the precision module can be modified as:

```
module precision_m
   integer, parameter :: singlePrecision = kind(0.0)
   integer, parameter :: doublePrecision = kind(0.0d0)

#ifdef DOUBLE
   integer, parameter :: fp_kind = doublePrecision
#else
   integer, parameter :: fp_kind = singlePrecision
#endif
end module precision_m
```

Here we can compile for double precision by compiling the precision module with the compiler options `-Mpreprocess -DDOUBLE` or, if the `.CUF` file extension is used, compiling with `-DDOUBLE`.

We make extensive use of the precision module throughout this book for several reasons. The first is that it allows readers to use the example codes on whatever card they have available. It allows us to easily assess the performance characteristics of the two precisions on various codes. And finally, it is a good practice in terms of code reuse.

This technique can be extended to facilitate mixed-precision code. For example, in a code simulating reacting flow, we may want to experiment with different precisions for the flow variables and chemical species. To do so, we can declare variables in the code as follows:

```
real(flow_kind), device :: u(nx,ny,nz), v(nx,ny,nz), w(nx,ny,nz)
real(chemistry_kind), device :: q(nx,ny,nz,nspecies)
```

where `flow_kind` and `chemistry_kind` are declared as either single or double precision in the `precision_m` module.

In using this programming style, we should also define floating-point literals using a specified kind—for example:

```
real(fp_kind), parameter :: factorOfTwo = 2.0_fp_kind
```

1.5 Error handling

The return values for the host CUDA functions in the device query example, as well as all host CUDA API functions, can be used to check for errors that occurred during their execution. To illustrate such error handling, the successful execution of `cudaGetDeviceCount()` of line 10 in the `deviceQuery` example in Section 1.4 can be checked as follows:

```
ierr = cudaGetDeviceCount(nDevices)
if (ierr /= cudaSuccess) write(*,*) cudaGetErrorString(ierr)
```

The variable `cudaSuccess` is defined in the `cudafor` module that is used in this code. If there is an error, then the function `cudaGetErrorString()` is used to return a character string describing the error, as opposed to just listing the numeric error code. One error that can occur in this case is when the code is run on a machine without any CUDA-capable devices. Without a device to run on, the command cannot execute and an error is returned, without modifying the contents of `nDevices`. It is for this reason that `nDevices` is initialized to 0 when it is declared on line 6.

Error handling of kernels is a bit more complicated, since kernels are subroutines and therefore do not have a return value, and since kernels execute asynchronously with respect to the host. To aid in error checking kernel execution as well as other asynchronous operations, the CUDA runtime maintains an error variable that is overwritten each time an error occurs. The function `cudaPeekAtLastError()` returns the value of this variable, and the function `cudaGetLastError()` returns the value of the variable and resets it to `cudaSuccess`. Error checking for kernel execution can be done using the following approach:

```
call increment<<<1,n>>>(a_d, b)
ierrSync = cudaGetLastError()
ierrAsync = cudaDeviceSynchronize()
if (ierrSync /= cudaSuccess) &
   write (*,*) 'Sync kernel error:', cudaGetErrorString(ierrSync)
if (ierrAsync /= cudaSuccess) &
   write(*,*) 'Async kernel error:', cudaGetErrorString(ierrAsync)
```

which checks for both synchronous and asynchronous errors. Invalid execution configuration parameters, e.g., too many threads per thread block, would be reflected in the value of `ierrSync` returned by `cudaGetLastError()`. Asynchronous errors, which occur on the device after control is returned to the host, require a synchronization mechanism, such as `cudaDeviceSynchronize()` that blocks the host thread until all previously issued commands on the device, such as the kernel launch, have completed. Any such errors will be reflected by the return value of `cudaDeviceSynchronize()`. We could also check for asynchronous errors and reset the variable that the runtime maintains by modifying the last line as follows:

```
call increment<<<1,n>>>(a_d, b)
ierrSync = cudaGetLastError()
ierrAsync = cudaDeviceSynchronize()
if (ierrSync/= cudaSuccess) &
  write(*,*) 'Sync kernel error:', cudaGetErrorString(ierrSync)
if (ierrAsync/= cudaSuccess) write (*,*) 'Async kernel error:', &
  cudaGetErrorString(cudaGetLastError())
```

1.6 Compiling CUDA Fortran code

CUDA Fortran codes are compiled using the PGI Fortran compiler. Files with the `.cuf` or `.CUF` extension have CUDA Fortran enabled automatically, and the compiler option `-Mcuda` can be used in compiling files with other extensions to enable CUDA Fortran. In addition, because the standard PGI Fortran compiler is used, all of the features used in CPU code, such as OpenMP and SSE vectorizing features, are available for host code. Compilation of CUDA Fortran code can be as simple as issuing the command:

```
pgf90 increment.cuf
```

Behind the scenes, a multistep process takes place. The device source code is compiled into a intermediate representation called Parallel Thread eXecution (PTX). This forward-compatible PTX representation is then further compiled to executable code for different compute capabilities. The host code is compiled by the host compiler.

We can see which compute capabilities are being targeted by using the `-Mcuda=ptxinfo` compiler option. Compiling our increment example with this option generates the following output:

```
% pgf90 -Mcuda=ptxinfo increment.cuf
ptxas info    : Compiling entry function 'increment' for 'sm_10'
ptxas info    : Used 4 registers, 24+16 bytes smem
ptxas info    : Compiling entry function 'increment' for 'sm_20'
ptxas info    : Function properties for increment
    0 bytes stack frame, 0 bytes spill stores, 0 bytes spill loads
ptxas info    : Used 6 registers, 56 bytes cmem[0]
```

```
ptxas info      : Compiling entry function 'increment' for 'sm_30'
ptxas info      : Function properties for increment
    0 bytes stack frame, 0 bytes spill stores, 0 bytes spill loads
ptxas info      : Used 8 registers, 344 bytes cmem[0]
```

The output from compilation with –Mcuda=ptxinfo contains much useful information about the compilation of binary code from PTX, such as the number of registers and the amount of different types of memory utilized by the kernel, but for now let's focus on the compute capabilities that are targeted. This output indicates that binary code is generated for three compute capabilities: 1.0, 2.0, and 3.0 (denoted here by sm_10, sm_20, and sm_30). Recall that the first number in the compute capability refers to the generation of the device architecture, and the second number refers to the revision within that generation. Binary device code is compatible with any device of the same generation that has an equal or greater revision than the revision targeted by compilation. As such, this application will run on all CUDA devices of compute capabilities 1.X, 2.X, and 3.X. At runtime, the host code will select the most appropriate code to load and execute.

If we change our increment code so that the array is a double-precision floating-point array rather than an integer array, we get:

```
% pgf90 -Mcuda=ptxinfo incDP.cuf
ptxas info      : Compiling entry function 'increment' for 'sm_13'
ptxas info      : Used 5 registers, 24+16 bytes smem
ptxas info      : Compiling entry function 'increment' for 'sm_20'
ptxas info      : Function properties for increment
    0 bytes stack frame, 0 bytes spill stores, 0 bytes spill loads
ptxas info      : Used 8 registers, 56 bytes cmem[0]
ptxas info      : Compiling entry function 'increment' for 'sm_30'
ptxas info      : Function properties for increment
    0 bytes stack frame, 0 bytes spill stores, 0 bytes spill loads
ptxas info      : Used 8 registers, 344 bytes cmem[0]
```

The CUDA Fortran compiler keeps track of any compute-capability-specific features in the program, such as double-precision arithmetic, and will generate code for the lowest version of device within each generation that is legal. Since double precision was first supported in devices of compute capability 1.3, the compiler generates code for compute capabilities 1.3, 2.0, and 3.0, and hence the resulting application will run on any device that supports double precision.

In addition to containing binary code for various compute capabilities, the executable also contains PTX code. Because new compute capabilities contain new features, different versions of PTX correspond to the different compute capabilities. The version of PTX included in the executable corresponds to the highest targeted compute capability, which, in our example, would correspond to a compute capability of 3.0. This embedded PTX code can be just-in-time compiled to generate binary code for compute capabilities equal to or greater than the corresponding PTX version. So, although device binary code is compatible with devices of newer revisions of the same generation, PTX can generate code for devices of newer generations (as well as devices of equal or newer revisions of the same generation). In our example, the executable will run correctly on devices of compute capability 4.0 and higher when they become available, because device code will be generated from the embedded PTX. By default, the application will always use compatible binary code if available rather than just-in-time compile PTX, although we can force compilation of PTX through environment variables (see Section B.1.3).

The default mechanism described here for generating device binary code guarantees compatibility of CUDA Fortran applications with all appropriate devices, but there are occasions on which we would like to target a particular compute capability. The size of the resulting fat binary may be an issue. And although binary code for compute capability 3.0 will run on a device of compute capability 3.5, it might not achieve the same performance as binary code created for a compute capability of 3.5. We can target a compute capability of X.Y with the compiler option –Mcuda=ccXY. For example, we can compile our code with:

```
% pgf90 -Mcuda=cc20,ptxinfo increment.cuf
ptxas info    : Compiling entry function 'increment' for 'sm_20'
ptxas info    : Function properties for increment
    0 bytes stack frame, 0 bytes spill stores, 0 bytes spill loads
ptxas info    : Used 6 registers, 56 bytes cmem[0]
```

The resultant executable will run on any device of compute capability 2.X using the binary code and in addition will run correctly on a machine with a device of compute capability 3.X due to just-in-time compilation of PTX code. We can also target architectures using the name of the generation. For example, compiling with –Mcuda=fermi is equivalent to –Mcuda=cc20.

Aside from generating PTX information and targeting specific device architectures, there are many other arguments to the –Mcuda compiler option. A list of such arguments can be generated with pgf90 –Mcuda –help. The output of this command includes:

```
    emu              Enable emulation mode
    tesla            Compile for Tesla architecture
    cc1x             Compile for compute capability 1.x
    fermi            Compile for Fermi architecture
    cc2x             Compile for compute capability 2.x
    kepler           Compile for Kepler architecture
    cc3x             Compile for compute capability 3.x
    cuda4.0          Use CUDA 4.0 Toolkit compatibility
    cuda4.1          Use CUDA 4.1 Toolkit compatibility
    cuda4.2          Use CUDA 4.2 Toolkit compatibility
    cuda5.0          Use CUDA 5.0 Toolkit compatibility
    fastmath         Use fast math library
    [no]flushz       Enable flush-to-zero mode on the GPU
    keepgpu          Keep kernel source files
    keepbin          Keep CUDA binary files
    keepptx          Keep PTX portable assembly files
    maxregcount:<n>  Set maximum number of registers to use on the GPU
    nofma            Don't generate fused mul-add instructions
    ptxinfo          Print informational messages from PTXAS
    [no]rdc          Generate relocatable device code
```

In addition to specifying the compute architecture, we can compile CUDA code to run on the host CPU using the -Mcuda=emu option. This allows us to develop CUDA Fortran code on a system without a CUDA-enabled device and use a host debugger in kernel code. However, the execution in emulation mode is very different in that typically a single thread block executes at a time, so race conditions may not be exposed in emulation.

CUDA Fortran ships with several versions of the CUDA Toolkit libraries. The available CUDA libraries can be determined from the pgf90 -Mcuda -help output. The default version is typically the second most recent version—in this case, the CUDA 4.2 Toolkit libraries.

CUDA has a set of fast but less accurate intrinsics for single-precision functions such as sin() and cos(), which can be enabled by -Mcuda=fastmath. The option -Mcuda=maxregcount:N can be used to limit the number of registers used per thread to N. The keepgpu, keepbin, and keepptx options dump the kernel source, CUDA binary, and PTX, respectively, to files in the local directory.

Though not CUDA specific, other compiler options are the -v and -V. Compiling with the -v option provides verbose output of the compilation and linking steps. The -V option can be used to verify the version of the PGI compiler or to select the compiler version from among those installed on the machine given the appropriate argument, e.g., -V12.10 for the 12.10 version of the PGI compilers.

1.6.1 Separate compilation

CUDA Fortran has always allowed host code to launch kernels that are defined in multiple modules, whether these modules are in the same or different files. The host code needs to simply use each of the modules that contain kernels that are launched.

Likewise, sharing device data between modules is relatively straightforward and available on GPUs of any compute capability. For example, if the file b.cuf contains a simple module b_m containing the device data b_d:

```
1  module b_m
2    integer, device :: b_d
3  end module b_m
```

and the file a.cuf contains the module a_m with a kernel that uses (in the Fortran 90 sense) module b_m:

```
1  module a_m
2    integer, device :: a_d
3  contains
4    attributes(global) subroutine aPlusB()
5      use b_m
6      implicit none
7      a_d = a_d + b_d
8    end subroutine aPlusB
9  end module a_m
```

which is in turn used by the host code `aPlusB.cuf`:

```
1  program twoPlusThree
2    use a_m
3    use b_m
4    implicit none
5    integer :: a
6
7    a_d = 2
8    b_d = 3
9    call aPlusB<<<1,1>>>()
10   a = a_d
11   write(*,"('2+3=',i0)") a
12 end program twoPlusThree
```

then the entire application can be compiled and run with the following sequence of commands:

```
% pgf90 -c b.cuf
% pgf90 -c a.cuf
% pgf90 aPlusB.cuf a.o b.o
aPlusB.cuf:
% ./a.out
2+3=5
```

Sharing device data across modules is straightforward, but using device routines across modules became available as of the 13.3 compilers. This aspect of separate compilation is only possible on devices with compute capabilities of 2.0 or higher and requires the 5.0 or higher version of the CUDA Toolkit. To illustrate using device code across modules, we use the following example. The file d.cuf defines the module d_m, which contains the device data d_d as well as the routine negateD():

```
1  module d_m
2    integer, device :: d_d
3  contains
4    attributes(device) subroutine negateD()
5      d_d = -d_d
6    end subroutine negateD
7  end module d_m
```

Routines declared with `attributes(device)` are something we haven't seen before. Such routines are executed on the device, similar to kernels, but are called from device code (kernels and other `attributes(device)` code) rather than host code, such as in the kernel cMinusD() on line 7 of the file c.cuf:

```
 1  module c_m
 2     integer, device :: c_d
 3  contains
 4     attributes(global) subroutine cMinusD()
 5        use d_m
 6        implicit none
 7        call negateD()
 8        c_d = c_d + d_d
 9     end subroutine cMinusD
10  end module c_m
```

Note that no execution configuration is provided when calling the routine negateD(), as is done when launching a kernel. It is called in the same manner as any Fortran 90 subroutine or function. We do not launch a kernel when calling an attributes(device) function, because the function is executed by existing device threads when the call is encountered. We should point out that all the predefined variables (threadIdx, blockIdx, blockDim, and gridDim) available in kernels are also available in code declared with attributes(device), which we don't use in this simple code executed by a single device thread. The host code in this example is:

```
 1  program twoMinusThree
 2     use c_m
 3     use d_m
 4     implicit none
 5     integer :: c
 6
 7     c_d = 2
 8     d_d = 3
 9     call cMinusD<<<1,1>>>()
10     c = c_d
11     write(*,"('2-3=',i0)") c
12  end program twoMinusThree
```

If we try to compile the files d.cuf and c.cuf as we did b.cuf and a.cuf in the previous code, we obtain the following error:

```
% pgf90 -c d.cuf
% pgf90 -c c.cuf
PGF90-S-0155-Illegal call of a device routine from another module
- negated (c.cuf: 7)
  0 inform,  0 warnings,  1 severes, 0 fatal for cminusd
```

To make device routines accessible across modules, we need to use the -Mcuda=rdc, or *relocatable device code*, option for both the compilation and linking stages:

```
% pgf90 -Mcuda=rdc -c d.cuf
% pgf90 -Mcuda=rdc -c c.cuf
% pgf90 -Mcuda=rdc cMinusD.cuf c.o d.o
cMinusD.cuf:
% ./a.out
2-3=-1
```

When using the option –Mcuda=rdc one does not have to explicitly specify a compute capability greater than 2.0 or the CUDA 5 Toolkit, the CUDA Fortran compiler is aware of the architecture and toolkit version required for features such as these and implicitly includes the necessary options. Using the –Mcuda=ptxinfo option indicates that compute capabilities 2.0 and 3.0 are targeted by default when compiling with –Mcuda=rdc:

```
$ pgf90 -Mcuda=rdc,ptxinfo -c c.cuf
ptxas info : 16 bytes gmem, 8 bytes cmem[14]
ptxas info : Compiling entry function 'c_m_cminusd_' for 'sm_20'
ptxas info : Function properties for c_m_cminusd_
    0 bytes stack frame, 0 bytes spill stores, 0 bytes spill loads
ptxas info : Used 8 registers, 32 bytes cmem[0]
ptxas info : 16 bytes gmem
ptxas info : Compiling entry function 'c_m_cminusd_' for 'sm_30'
ptxas info : Function properties for c_m_cminusd_
    0 bytes stack frame, 0 bytes spill stores, 0 bytes spill loads
ptxas info : Used 8 registers, 320 bytes cmem[0]
```

Performance Measurement and Metrics

2

CHAPTER OUTLINE HEAD

A prerequisite to performance optimization is a means to accurately time portions of a code and subsequently describe how to use such timing information to assess code performance. In this chapter we first discuss how to time kernel execution using CPU timers, CUDA events, and the Command Line Profiler as well as the `nvprof` profiling tool. We then discuss how timing information can be used to determine the limiting factor of kernel execution. Finally, we discuss how to calculate performance metrics, especially those related to bandwidth, and how such metrics should be interpreted.

2.1 Measuring kernel execution time

There are several ways to measure kernel execution time. We can use traditional CPU timers, but in doing so we must be careful to ensure correct synchronization between host and device for such measurements to be accurate. The CUDA event API routines, which are called from host code, can be used to calculate kernel execution time using the device clock. Finally, we discuss how the Command Line Profiler and the `nvprof` profiling tool can be used to give this timing information.

2.1.1 **Host-device synchronization and CPU timers**

Care must be taken in timing GPU routines using traditional CPU timers. From the host perspective, kernel execution as well as many CUDA Fortran API functions are nonblocking or asynchronous: They return control back to the calling CPU thread prior to completing their work on the GPU. For example, consider the following code segment:

```
1  a_d = a
2  call increment<<<1,n>>>(a_d, b)
3  a = a_d
```

Once the `increment` kernel is launched in line 2, control returns to the CPU. By contrast, the data transfers before and after the kernel launch are synchronous or blocking. Such data transfers do not begin until all previously issued CUDA calls have completed, and subsequent CUDA calls will not begin until the transfer has completed.[1] Since the kernel execution is asynchronous with respect to the host thread, using a CPU timer before and after the call statement would simply record the kernel launch. To accurately time the kernel execution with host code timers, we need to explicitly synchronize the CPU thread using `cudaDeviceSynchronize()`:

```
1  a_d = a
2  t1 = myCPUTimer()
3  call increment<<<1,n>>>(a_d, b)
4  istat = cudaDeviceSynchronize()
5  t2 = myCPUTimer()
6  a = a_d
```

The function `cudaDeviceSynchronize()` blocks the calling host thread until all CUDA calls previously issued by the host thread are completed, which is required for correct measurement of `increment`. It is a best practice to call `cudaDeviceSynchronize()` before any timing call. For example, inserting a `cudaDeviceSynchronize()` before line 2 would be well advised, even though not required, because we might change the transfer at line 1 to an asynchronous transfer and forget to add the synchronization call.

An alternative to using the function `cudaDeviceSynchronize()` is to set the environment variable CUDA_LAUNCH_BLOCKING to 1, which turns kernel invocations into synchronous function calls. However, this would apply to all kernel launches of a program and would therefore serialize any CPU code with kernel execution.

2.1.2 **Timing via CUDA events**

One problem with host-device synchronization points such as those produced by the function `cudaDeviceSynchronize()` and the environment variable CUDA_LAUNCH_BLOCKING is that

---

[1] Note that asynchronous versions of data transfers are available using the `cudaMemcpy*Async()` routines, which are discussed in Section 3.1.3.

they stall the GPU's processing pipeline. Unfortunately, such synchronization points are required using CPU timers. Luckily, CUDA offers a relatively lightweight alternative to using CPU timers via the CUDA event API. The CUDA event API provides calls that create and destroy events, record events (via a GPU timestamp), and convert timestamp differences into a floating-point value in units of milliseconds.

CUDA events make use of the concept of CUDA streams, about which we should say a few words before we discuss CUDA event code. A CUDA stream is simply a sequence of operations that are performed in order on the device. Operations in different streams can be interleaved and in some cases overlapped—a property that can be used to hide data transfers between the host and the device, which we discuss in detail later. Up to now, all operations on the GPU have occurred in the default stream, or stream 0.

Typical use of the event API is shown here:

```
1   type(cudaEvent) :: startEvent, stopEvent
2   real :: time
3   integer :: istat
4
5   istat = cudaEventCreate(startEvent)
6   istat = cudaEventCreate(stopEvent)
7
8   a_d = a
9   istat = cudaEventRecord(startEvent, 0)
10  call increment<<<1,n>>>(a_d, b)
11  istat = cudaEventRecord(stopEvent, 0)
12  istat = cudaEventSynchronize(stopEvent)
13  istat = cudaEventElapsedTime(time, startEvent, stopEvent)
14  a = a_d
15
16  if (any(a/= 4)) then
17    write(*,*) '**** Program Failed ****'
18  else
19    write(*,*) '  Time for kernel execution (ms): ', time
20  endif
21
22  istat = cudaEventDestroy(startEvent)
23  istat = cudaEventDestroy(stopEvent)
```

CUDA events are of type cudaEvent and are created and destroyed with cudaEventCreate() and cudaEventDestroy(). In this code, cudaEventRecord() is used to place the start and stop events into the default stream, stream 0. The device will record a timestamp for the event when it reaches that event in the stream. The cudaEventElapsedTime() function returns the time elapsed between the recording of the start and stop events on the GPU. This value is expressed in milliseconds and has a resolution of approximately half a microsecond. Because cudaEventRecord() is non-blocking, we require a synchronization before the call to cudaEventElapsedTime() to ensure that `stopEvent` has been recorded, which is the reason for the `cudaEventSynchronize()` call on line 12. `cudaEventSynchronize()` blocks CPU execution until the specified event has been recorded on the GPU.

For very simple kernels (such as our increment example), there can be some inaccuracy in timing using CUDA events resulting from CPU-side jitter. In such cases the more accurate results can be obtained from CUDA events by simply adding a no-op kernel just before the first CUDA event call so that the `cudaEventRecord()` and subsequent kernel call will be queued up on the GPU.

2.1.3 Command Line Profiler

Timing information can also be obtained from the Command Line Profiler. This approach does not require instrumentation of code, as needed with CUDA events. It doesn't even require recompilation of the source code with special flags. Profiling can be enabled by setting the environment variable `COMPUTE_PROFILE` to 1, as is done when profiling in CUDA C code. Several other environment variables control what is being profiled and where the output is directed. A discussion of these environment variables is included in Section B.1.2, but for now we discuss the output of the simple case where only `COMPUTE_PROFILE` is set to 1. The output from the Command Line Profiler is sent to the file `cuda_profile_0.log` by default; it contains basic information, such as the method name, the GPU and CPU execution times, and the occupancy for kernel executions. For example, here is the profiler output for the multidimensional array increment code in Section 1.3.3:

```
# CUDA_PROFILE_LOG_VERSION 2.0
# CUDA_DEVICE 0 Tesla K20
# CUDA_CONTEXT 1
# TIMESTAMPFACTOR fffff693dc2e2f28
method,gputime,cputime,occupancy
method=[memcpyHtoD] gputime=[382.304] cputime=[712.000]
method=[memcpyHtoD] gputime=[1.632] cputime=[8.000]
method=[increment] gputime=[153.472] cputime=[24.000]
    occupancy=[1.000]
method=[memcpyDtoH] gputime=[433.504] cputime=[1787.000]
```

The first four lines of output contain header information, including the device number and name on which the code is executed. The fifth line indicates the fields that are displayed below for each executed method. By default these are the name of the method being executed, the time in microseconds as reported by the GPU, the time in microseconds as reported by the CPU, and the occupancy, which is reported only for kernel executions. *Occupancy* is the ratio of actual concurrent threads per multiprocessor to the maximum possible concurrent threads per multiprocessor. We discuss occupancy in detail in Section 3.5.1. The following lines display the profiling results for each method. There are two host-to-device data transfers; the first is for the array transfer, and the second is a transfer of kernel parameters and arguments that is implicitly performed by the CUDA runtime. These are followed by the kernel `increment` launch, which is then followed by the device-to-host data transfer of the resultant array.

The gputime field in the profiler output is straightforward to interpret—the time in microseconds as recorded by the GPU—but some care needs to be taken in interpreting the cputime. For nonblocking methods such as kernels, the value reported by cputime is only the CPU overhead to launch the method, in which case the wall clock time is cputime + gputime. For blocking methods such as these data transfers, cputime includes both gputime and the CPU overhead, so it is equivalent to wall clock time. In addition to launch overhead, the timing of the first called method also includes overhead associated with device initialization.

Note that the times for the data transfers are larger than the times for the kernel execution. This is partly because we are using a very simple kernel, but data transfers over the PCIe bus are often a performance bottleneck. In the following chapter on optimization, we discuss how we can minimize and hide such transfers.

As mentioned earlier, there are several environment variables in addition to COMPUTE_PROFILE that determine what is measured and how the output is configured. For a discussion of these, see Section B.1.2.

2.1.4 The nvprof profiling tool

An alternative to the Command Line Profiler is the nvprof application contained in the CUDA 5 Toolkit distribution. The Command Line Profiler and nvprof are mutually exclusive, so COMPUTE_PROFILE must be set to 0 when we use nvprof. Aside from that caveat, using nvprof is as simple as running it with your CUDA application command as an argument. Once again using our multidimensional increment code, we obtain the following output when executing nvprof ./a.out:

```
======== NVPROF is profiling a.out...
======== Command: a.out
 Program Passed
======== Profiling result:
Time(%)  Time     Calls    Avg        Min        Max       Name
44.56    385.19us  2      192.59us    1.31us    383.88us   [CUDA memcpy HtoD]
37.93    327.84us  1      327.84us   327.84us   327.84us   [CUDA memcpy DtoH]
17.51    151.36us  1      151.36us   151.36us   151.36us   increment
```

In this output, all calls to each method are summarized in one line, such as the two host-to-device data copies. Separate output for each call can be obtained using the --print-gpu-trace option.

Before leaving the discussion of the Command Line Profiler and nvprof, we should mention that we have discussed these tools in the context of "tracing" execution, meaning collecting timeline data. We can also use these tools to "profile" execution, meaning collecting hardware counters. A list of hardware counters we can profile can be obtained from executing nvprof --query-events. The collection of hardware counters is more intrusive than collecting timeline data, and as a result certain otherwise concurrent operations may be serialized.

For more information on nvprof or the Command Line Profiler, see the *CUDA Profiler Users Guide*, provided with the CUDA 5 Toolkit.

2.2 Instruction, bandwidth, and latency bound kernels

Now having the ability to time kernel execution, we can talk about how to determine the limiting factor of a kernel's execution. There are several ways to do this. One option is to use the profiler's hardware counters, but the counters used for such an analysis likely change from generation to generation of hardware. Instead, in this section we describe a method that is more general in that the same procedure will work regardless of the generation of the hardware. In fact, this method can be applied to CPU platforms as well as GPUs. For this method, multiple versions of the kernel are created; they expose the memory- and math-intensive aspects of the full kernel. Each kernel is timed, and a comparison of these times can reveal the limiting factor of kernel execution. This process is best understood by going through an example. The following code contains three kernels:

- A base kernel, which performs the desired overall operation
- A memory kernel, which has the same device memory access patterns as the base kernel but no math operations
- A math kernel, which performs the math operations of the base kernel without accessing global memory

```
1   module kernel_m
2   contains
3     attributes(global) subroutine base(a, b)
4       real :: a(*), b(*)
5       integer :: i
6       i = (blockIdx%x-1)*blockDim%x + threadIdx%x
7       a(i) = sin(b(i))
8     end subroutine base
9
10    attributes(global) subroutine memory(a, b)
11      real :: a(*), b(*)
12      integer :: i
13      i = (blockIdx%x-1)*blockDim%x + threadIdx%x
14      a(i) = b(i)
15    end subroutine memory
16
17    attributes(global) subroutine math(a, b, flag)
18      real :: a(*)
19      real, value :: b
20      integer, value :: flag
21      real :: v
22      integer :: i
23      i = (blockIdx%x-1)*blockDim%x + threadIdx%x
24      v = sin(b)
25      if (v*flag == 1) a(i) = v
26    end subroutine math
```

```
27  end module kernel_m
28
29  program limitingFactor
30    use cudafor
31    use kernel_m
32    implicit none
33    integer, parameter :: n=8*1024*1024, blockSize = 256
34    real :: a(n)
35    real, device :: a_d(n), b_d(n)
36
37    b_d = 1.0
38    call base<<<n/blockSize,blockSize>>>(a_d, b_d)
39    call memory<<<n/blockSize,blockSize>>>(a_d, b_d)
40    call math<<<n/blockSize,blockSize>>>(a_d, 1.0, 0)
41    a = a_d
42    write(*,*) a(1)
43  end program limitingFactor
```

For the math kernel, care must be taken to trick the compiler because it can detect and eliminate operations that don't contribute to stores in device memory. So, we need to put stores inside conditionals that always evaluate to false, as is done on line 25 in the preceding code. The conditional should be dependent not only on a flag passed into the subroutine but also on an intermediate result; otherwise, the compiler could move the entire operation into the conditional.

If we run this code on a Tesla C2050 while using the Command Line Profiler, we get the following output for the three kernels:

```
method=[base] gputime=[850.912] cputime=[5.000] occupancy=[1.000]
method=[memory] gputime=[625.920] cputime=[6.000] occupancy=[1.000]
method=[math] gputime=[784.384] cputime=[5.000] occupancy=[1.000]
```

Comparing gputime for the various kernels, we observe a fair amount of overlap of math and memory operations, since the sum of the gputime for the base and memory kernels is greater than the gputime for the base kernel. But because the math kernel is 92% of the base kernel time and the memory kernel is 73% of the base kernel time, the limiting factor for performance in this case is the math operations. If full precision is not needed, the math kernel can be sped up by using the fast math intrinsics, which calculate the sin() function in hardware, simply by recompiling with the -Mcuda=fastmath option. The result is:

```
method=[base] gputime=[635.424] cputime=[7.000] occupancy=[1.000]
method=[memory] gputime=[626.336] cputime=[7.000] occupancy=[1.000]
method=[math] gputime=[261.280] cputime=[7.000] occupancy=[1.000]
```

As expected, the time for the math kernel goes down considerably and along with it the base kernel time. The base kernel is now memory bound, because the memory and base kernels run in almost the same amount of time: The math operations are nearly entirely hidden by memory operations. At this point further improvement can only come from optimizing device memory accesses, if possible.

Running this code on a K20 and profiling its execution, we observe a different picture:

```
method=[base]   gputime=[529.568]  cputime=[7.000]  occupancy=[1.000]
method=[memory] gputime=[473.792]  cputime=[7.000]  occupancy=[1.000]
method=[math]   gputime=[273.344]  cputime=[8.000]  occupancy=[1.000]
```

Comparing the Tesla K20 and C2050 profiler output, we see that in addition to the kernels running faster on the K20, the base kernel is more memory bound on the K20 than on the C2050. We expect that compiling with the –Mcuda=fastmath option would not increase overall performance, percentage-wise, as much on the K20 as it does on the C2050, which we observe from the profiler output:

```
method=[base]   gputime=[481.632]  cputime=[7.000]  occupancy=[1.000]
method=[memory] gputime=[474.816]  cputime=[6.000]  occupancy=[1.000]
method=[math]   gputime=[210.624]  cputime=[8.000]  occupancy=[1.000]
```

Once again, with the –Mcuda=fastmath option, the base kernel is memory bound, and further improvement can only come from optimizing device memory accesses. Deciding whether or not we can improve memory accesses motivates the next section on memory bandwidth. But before we jump into bandwidth metrics, we need to tie up some loose ends regarding this technique of modifying source code to determine the limiting factor of a kernel. When there is very little overlap of math and memory operations, a kernel is likely latency bound. This often occurs when the occupancy is low; there simply are not enough threads on the device at one time for any overlap of operations. The remedy for this situation can often be a modification to the execution configuration.

The reason for using the profiler for time measurement in this analysis is twofold. The first is that it requires no instrumentation of the host code. (We have already written two additional kernels, so this is welcome.) The second is that we want to make sure that the occupancy is the same for all our kernels. When we remove math operations from a kernel, we likely reduce the number of registers used (which can be checked using the –Mcuda=ptxinfo flag). If the register usage varies enough, the occupancy, or fraction of actual to maximum number of threads resident on a multiprocessor, can change, which will affect runtimes. In our example, the occupancy is everywhere 1.0, but if this is not the case, we can lower the occupancy by allocating dynamic shared memory in the kernel via a third argument to the execution configuration. This optional argument is the number of bytes of dynamically allocated shared memory that are used for each thread block. We talk more about shared memory in Section 3.3.3, but for now all we need to know is that shared memory can be reserved for a thread block simply by providing the number of bytes per thread block as a third argument to the execution configuration.

2.3 Memory bandwidth

Returning to the example code in Section 2.2, we are left with a memory-bound kernel after using the fast math intrinsics to reduce time spent on evaluation of sin(). At this stage we ask how well the memory system is used and whether there is room for improvement. To answer this question, we need to calculate the memory bandwidth.

Bandwidth—the rate at which data can be transferred—is one of the most important gating factors for performance. Almost all changes to code should be made in the context of how they affect bandwidth. Bandwidth can be dramatically affected by the choice of memory in which data are stored, how the data are laid out, and the order in which they are accessed, as well as other factors.

In evaluating memory efficiency, both the theoretical peak memory bandwidth and the observed or effective memory bandwidth are used. When a code is memory bound and the effective bandwidth is much lower than the peak bandwidth, optimization efforts should focus on increasing the effective bandwidth.

2.3.1 Theoretical peak bandwidth

The theoretical peak memory bandwidth can be calculated from the memory clock and the memory bus width. Both these quantities can be queried through the device management API, as illustrated in the following code that calculates the theoretical peak bandwidth for all attached devices:

```
 1  program peakBandwidth
 2    use cudafor
 3    implicit none
 4
 5    integer :: i, istat, nDevices=0
 6    type (cudaDeviceProp) :: prop
 7
 8    istat = cudaGetDeviceCount(nDevices)
 9    do i = 0, nDevices-1
10       istat = cudaGetDeviceProperties(prop, i)
11       write(*,"(' Device Number: ',i0)") i
12       write(*,"('   Device name: ',a)") trim(prop%name)
13       write(*,"('   Memory Clock Rate (KHz): ', i0)") &
14            prop%memoryClockRate
15       write(*,"('   Memory Bus Width (bits): ', i0)") &
16            prop%memoryBusWidth
17       write(*,"('   Peak Memory Bandwidth (GB/s): ', f6.2)") &
18            2.0 * prop%memoryClockRate * &
19            (prop%memoryBusWidth / 8) * 1.e-6
20       write(*,*)
21    enddo
22  end program peakBandwidth
```

In the peak memory bandwidth calculation, the factor of 2 . 0 appears due to the double data rate of the RAM per memory clock cycle, the division by eight converts the bus width from bits to bytes, and the factor of 1 . e-6 handles the kilohertz-to-hertz and byte-to-gigabyte conversions.[2]

Running this code on a variety of Tesla hardware, we obtain:

```
Device Number:  0
  Device name:  Tesla  C870
  Memory  Clock  Rate  (KHz):  800000
  Memory  Bus  Width  (bits):  384
  Peak  Memory  Bandwidth  (GB/s):    76.80
```

```
Device Number:  0
  Device name:  Tesla  C1060
  Memory  Clock  Rate  (KHz):  800000
  Memory  Bus  Width  (bits):  512
  Peak  Memory  Bandwidth  (GB/s):  102.40
```

```
Device Number:  0
  Device name:  Tesla  C2050
  Memory  Clock  Rate  (KHz):  1500000
  Memory  Bus  Width  (bits):  384
  Peak  Memory  Bandwidth  (GB/s):  144.00
```

```
Device Number:  0
  Device name:  Tesla  K10.G1.8GB
  Memory  Clock  Rate  (KHz):  2500000
  Memory  Bus  Width  (bits):  256
  Peak  Memory  Bandwidth  (GB/s):  160.00
Device Number:  1
  Device name:  Tesla  K10.G1.8GB
  Memory  Clock  Rate  (KHz):  2500000
  Memory  Bus  Width  (bits):  256
  Peak  Memory  Bandwidth  (GB/s):  160.00
```

---

[2]Note that some calculations use $1,024^3$ instead of 10^9 for the byte-to-gigabyte conversion. Whichever factor you use, it is important to use the same factor in calculating theoretical and effective bandwidth so that the comparison is valid.

```
Device Number: 0
  Device name: Tesla K20
  Memory Clock Rate (KHz): 2600000
  Memory Bus Width (bits): 320
  Peak Memory Bandwidth (GB/s): 208.00
```

For devices with error-correcting code (ECC) memory, such as the Tesla C2050, K10, and K20, we need to take into account that when ECC is enabled, the peak bandwidth will be reduced.

2.3.2 Effective bandwidth

Effective bandwidth is calculated by timing specific program activities and by knowing how data are accessed by the program. To do so, use this equation:

$$BW_{\text{Effective}} = \frac{(R_B + W_B)/10^9}{t}$$

Here, $BW_{\text{Effective}}$ is the effective bandwidth in units of GB/s, R_B is the number of bytes read per kernel, W_B is the number of bytes written per kernel, and t is the elapsed time given in seconds.

It is helpful to obtain the effective bandwidth for a simple copy kernel, such as the memory() kernel in the limiting factor code in Section 2.2, on a variety of devices. Table 2.1 lists the best effective bandwidth obtained from a simple copy kernel among runs using different array sizes and launched with different execution configurations, with both ECC on and off on devices that support ECC.[3] Such numbers can be used as a more realistic upper limit to memory bandwidth than the theoretical peak bandwidth.

Returning to the example in Section 2.2, where a read and write are performed for each of the 8×1024^2 elements, the following calculation is used to determine effective bandwidth on the C2050 (with ECC on) for the base method when using the -Mcuda=fastmath option:

$$BW_{\text{Effective}} = \frac{(8 \times 1024^2 \times 4 \times 2)/10^9}{635 \times 10^{-6}} = 106 \text{ GB/s}$$

The number of elements is multiplied by the size of each element (4 bytes for a float), multiplied by 2 (because of the read and write), divided by 10^9 to obtain the total GB of memory transferred. The profiler results for the base kernel give a GPU time of 635 μs, which results in an effective bandwidth of roughly 106 GB/s. We could compare this result to the theoretical peak bandwidth for the C2050 of 144 GB/s, but this does not account for ECC effects. Instead we use the appropriate number of 107 GB/s from Table 2.1. As a result, we do not expect to obtain any further substantial speedups for this code on this device.

To obtain the effective bandwidth for this kernel on the Tesla K20, once again with ECC on, we simply substitute the profiler time for the base kernel of 481 μs into the preceding formula to obtain a value of 139 GB/s. Compared to the value of 145 GB/s from Table 2.1, we once again do not expect to obtain any further substantial speedups for this code on this device.

---

[3]A discussion of how to toggle ECC on and off can be found in the nvidia-smi section of Appendix B.

Table 2.1 Effective bandwidth for a simple copy kernel. Block size and array length were modified to obtain the best result in each case.

	Effective Bandwidth for Copy (GB/s)			
	Tesla C870	Tesla C1060	Tesla C2050	Tesla K20
ECC off	65	78	119	164
ECC on	-	-	107	145

2.3.3 Actual data throughput vs. effective bandwidth

It is possible to estimate the data throughput using the profiler counters. We must be cautious in comparing such calculated throughput to values obtained from the effective bandwidth calculation described in Section 2.3.2. One difference is that the profiler measures transactions using a subset of the GPUs multiprocessors and then extrapolates that number to the entire GPU, thus reporting an estimate of the data throughput.

Another distinction to be aware of is whether the counters used represent the actual data throughput or the requested data throughput. This distinction is important because the minimum memory transaction size is larger than most word sizes, and as a result the actual data transfer throughput will be equal to or larger than that of requested data throughput. The effective bandwidth is calculated based on the data relevant to the algorithm and therefore corresponds to the requested data throughput. Both actual and requested data throughput values are useful. The actual data throughput shows how close the code is to reaching the hardware limit, and the comparison of the effective bandwidth with the actual throughput indicates how much bandwidth is wasted by suboptimal memory access patterns.

The difference between actual data throughput and effective bandwidth is not an issue in the example codes used thus far, since all the data accesses have been using contiguous data. But when we access memory in a strided fashion, which we explore in Chapter 3, the values for actual data throughput and effective bandwidth can diverge.

Optimization

3

CHAPTER OUTLINE HEAD

In the previous chapter we discussed how we can use timing information to determine the limiting factor of kernel execution. Many science and engineering codes turn out to be bandwidth bound, which is why we devote the majority of this relatively long chapter to memory optimization. CUDA-enabled devices have many different memory types, and to program effectively, we need to use these memory types efficiently.

Data transfers can be broken down in to two main categories: data transfers between host and device memories, and data transfers between different memories on the device. We begin our discussion with optimizing transfers between the host and device. We then discuss the different types of memories on the device and how they can be used effectively. To illustrate many of these memory optimization techniques, we then go through an example of optimizing a matrix transpose kernel.

In addition to memory optimization, in this chapter we also discuss factors in deciding how we should choose execution configurations so that the hardware is efficiently utilized. Finally, we discuss instruction optimizations.

3.1 Transfers between host and device

The peak bandwidth between device memory and the GPU is much higher (208 GB/s on the NVIDIA Tesla K20, for example) than the peak bandwidth between host memory and device memory (16 GB/s on PCIe x16 Gen3, and 8 GB/s on PCIe x16 Gen2). Hence, for best overall application performance, it is important to minimize data transfers between host and device whenever possible and, when such transfers are necessary, make sure they are optimized.

When initially writing or porting an application to CUDA Fortran, typically a few critical sections of code are converted to CUDA Fortran kernels. If these code sections are isolated, they will require data transfers to and from the host, and overall performance will likely be gated by these data transfers. At this stage it is helpful to assess performance with and without such transfers. The overall time including data transfers is an accurate assessment of the current code performance, and the time without such transfers indicates where performance may be when more of the code is written to run on the device. We shouldn't spend time at this point optimizing transfers between the host and device, because as more host code is converted to kernels, many of these intermediate data transfers will disappear. Of course, there will always be some transfers required between the host and device, and we need to make sure these are performed as efficiently as possible, but optimizing data transfers that will eventually be removed from the code is not time well spent.

There may be some operations that do not demonstrate any speed-up when run on the device in terms of execution time. If executing the operation on the host would require extra transfers between the host and device, it may be advantageous overall to perform the operation on the device.

There are other circumstances in which data transfers between the host and device can be avoided. Intermediate data structures can be created in device memory, operated on by the device, and destroyed without ever being mapped by the host or copied to host memory.

Up to this point, we have discussed how to avoid transfers between the host and device whenever possible. In the remainder of this section we discuss how to efficiently perform necessary transfers between the host and device. This includes using pinned host memory, batching small transfers together, and performing data transfers asynchronously.

3.1.1 Pinned memory

When memory is allocated for variables that reside on the host, pageable memory is used by default. Pageable memory can be swapped out to disk to allow the program to use more memory than is available in RAM on the host system. When data is transferred between the host and the device, the direct memory access (DMA) engine on the GPU must target page-locked or *pinned* host memory. Pinned memory cannot be swapped out and is therefore always available for such transfers. To accommodate data transfers from pageable host memory to the GPU, the host operating system first allocates a temporary pinned host buffer, copies the data to the pinned buffer, and then transfers the data to the device, as illustrated in Figure 3.1. The pinned memory buffer may be smaller than the pageable memory holding the host data, in which case the transfer occurs in multiple stages. Pinned memory buffers are similarly

Pageable Data Transfer   **Pinned Data Transfer**

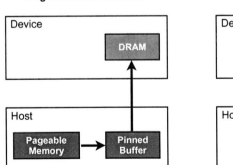 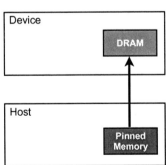

FIGURE 3.1

Depiction of host-to-device data transfer from pageable host memory (left) and pinned host memory (right). For pageable host memory, data is transferred to a temporary pinned memory buffer on the host before being transferred to the device. By using pinned memory from the outset, as on the right, the extra host data copy is eliminated.

used with transfers from the device to the host. The cost of the transfer between pageable memory and pinned host buffer can be avoided if we declare the host arrays to use pinned memory.

In CUDA Fortran, use of pinned memory is denoted using the `pinned` variable qualifier, and such memory must be declared allocatable via the `allocatable` variable qualifier. It is possible for the `allocate` statement to fail to allocate pinned memory, in which case a pageable memory allocation will be attempted. The following code demonstrates the allocation of pinned memory with error checking and demonstrates the speed-up we can expect with pinned memory:

```
1    program BandwidthTest
2
3      use cudafor
4      implicit none
5
6      integer, parameter :: nElements = 4*1024*1024
7
8      ! host arrays
9      real(4) :: a_pageable(nElements), b_pageable(nElements)
10     real(4), allocatable, pinned :: a_pinned(:), b_pinned(:)
11
12     ! device arrays
13     real(4), device :: a_d(nElements)
14
15     ! events for timing
16     type (cudaEvent) :: startEvent, stopEvent
17
18     ! misc
19     type (cudaDeviceProp) :: prop
20     real(4) :: time
21     integer :: istat, i
22     logical :: pinnedFlag
23
24     ! allocate and initialize
25     do i = 1, nElements
26        a_pageable(i) = i
27     end do
28     b_pageable = 0.0
29
30     allocate(a_pinned(nElements), b_pinned(nElements), &
31          STAT=istat, PINNED=pinnedFlag)
32     if (istat /= 0) then
33        write(*,*) 'Allocation of a_pinned/b_pinned failed'
34        pinnedFlag = .false.
35     else
36        if (.not. pinnedFlag) write(*,*) 'Pinned allocation failed'
37     end if
38
39     if (pinnedFlag) then
```

```
40        a_pinned = a_pageable
41        b_pinned = 0.0
42     endif
43
44     istat = cudaEventCreate(startEvent)
45     istat = cudaEventCreate(stopEvent)
46
47     ! output device info and transfer size
48     istat = cudaGetDeviceProperties(prop, 0)
49
50     write(*,*)
51     write(*,*) 'Device: ', trim(prop%name)
52     write(*,*) 'Transfer size (MB): ', 4*nElements/1024./1024.
53
54     ! pageable data transfers
55     write(*,*)
56     write(*,*) 'Pageable transfers'
57
58     istat = cudaEventRecord(startEvent, 0)
59     a_d = a_pageable
60     istat = cudaEventRecord(stopEvent, 0)
61     istat = cudaEventSynchronize(stopEvent)
62
63     istat = cudaEventElapsedTime(time, startEvent, stopEvent)
64     write(*,*) '  Host to Device bandwidth (GB/s): ', &
65          nElements*4/time/1.e+6
66
67     istat = cudaEventRecord(startEvent, 0)
68     b_pageable = a_d
69     istat = cudaEventRecord(stopEvent, 0)
70     istat = cudaEventSynchronize(stopEvent)
71
72     istat = cudaEventElapsedTime(time, startEvent, stopEvent)
73     write(*,*) '  Device to Host bandwidth (GB/s): ', &
74          nElements*4/time/1.e+6
75
76     if (any(a_pageable /= b_pageable)) &
77          write(*,*) '*** Pageable transfers failed ***'
78
79     ! pinned data transfers
80     if (pinnedFlag) then
81        write(*,*)
82        write(*,*) 'Pinned transfers'
83
84        istat = cudaEventRecord(startEvent, 0)
85        a_d = a_pinned
86        istat = cudaEventRecord(stopEvent, 0)
87        istat = cudaEventSynchronize(stopEvent)
88
```

```
89      istat = cudaEventElapsedTime(time, startEvent, stopEvent)
90      write(*,*) ' Host to Device bandwidth (GB/s): ', &
91          nElements*4/time/1.e+6
92
93      istat = cudaEventRecord(startEvent, 0)
94      b_pinned = a_d
95      istat = cudaEventRecord(stopEvent, 0)
96      istat = cudaEventSynchronize(stopEvent)
97
98      istat = cudaEventElapsedTime(time, startEvent, stopEvent)
99      write(*,*) ' Device to Host bandwidth (GB/s): ', &
100         nElements*4/time/1.e+6
101
102     if (any(a_pinned /= b_pinned)) &
103         write(*,*) '*** Pinned transfers failed ***'
104   end if
105
106   write(*,*)
107
108   ! cleanup
109   if (allocated(a_pinned)) deallocate(a_pinned)
110   if (allocated(b_pinned)) deallocate(b_pinned)
111   istat = cudaEventDestroy(startEvent)
112   istat = cudaEventDestroy(stopEvent)
113
114 end program BandwidthTest
```

The allocation of pinned memory is performed on line 30 with the optional keyword arguments for STAT and PINNED, which can be checked to see if any allocation was made and if so, whether the allocation resulted in pinned memory, as is done on lines 32–37.

The data transfer rate can depend on the type of host system as well as the GPU. For example, on an Intel Xeon E5540 system with a Tesla K20, the code results in:

```
Device: Tesla K20
Transfer size (MB):     16.00000

Pageable transfers
  Host to Device bandwidth (GB/s):    1.659565
  Device to Host bandwidth (GB/s):    1.593377

Pinned transfers
  Host to Device bandwidth (GB/s):    5.745055
  Device to Host bandwidth (GB/s):    6.566322
```

whereas on an Intel Xeon E5-2667 system, also with a Tesla K20, we have:

```
Device: Tesla K20m
Transfer size (MB):        16.00000

Pageable transfers
   Host to Device bandwidth (GB/s):        3.251782
   Device to Host bandwidth (GB/s):        3.301395

Pinned transfers
   Host to Device bandwidth (GB/s):        6.213710
   Device to Host bandwidth (GB/s):        6.608200
```

The transfer rates for the pinned data transfers between these two systems are similar. However, the transfer rates for pageable data transfers between host and device are greatly affected by the host system due to the implicit host-side copy from pageable memory to the pinned buffer.

We can verify whether pinned host memory was used in a transfer between host and device from the Command Line Profiler by specifying the option memtransferhostmemtype in the profiler configuration file. For example, profiling our BandwidthTest code results in:

```
# CUDA_PROFILE_LOG_VERSION 2.0
# CUDA_DEVICE 0 Tesla K20
# CUDA_CONTEXT 1
# TIMESTAMPFACTOR fffff69b0066e8b8
method,gputime,cputime,occupancy,memtransferhostmemtype
method=[ memcpyHtoD ] gputime=[ 9018.912 ] cputime=[ 9937.000 ]
      memtransferhostmemtype=[ 0 ]
method=[ memcpyDtoH ] gputime=[ 9216.160 ] cputime=[ 10160.000 ]
      memtransferhostmemtype=[ 0 ]
method=[ memcpyHtoD ] gputime=[ 2786.464 ] cputime=[ 3127.991 ]
      memtransferhostmemtype=[ 1 ]
method=[ memcpyDtoH ] gputime=[ 2501.312 ] cputime=[ 2555.000 ]
      memtransferhostmemtype=[ 1 ]
```

where a value of 0 for memtransferhostmemtype indicates pageable memory and a value of 1 indicates pinned memory.

Pinned memory should not be overused, since excessive use can reduce overall system performance. How much is too much is difficult to tell in advance, so, as with all optimizations, test the applications and the systems they run on for optimal performance parameters.

3.1.2 Batching small data transfers

An overhead is associated with every data transfer between host and device, whether using pageable or pinned memory. The impact of this overhead on overall transfer rate can be large for small data transfers, and as a result we can gain efficiency by batching small transfers together.

We can gain an understanding of how to batch multiple data transfers together by running the code in Section 3.1.1 for various array sizes. Figures 3.2 and 3.3 show the transfer rates for pageable and pinned data transfers on the two systems in Section 3.1.1 for transfer sizes ranging from a few kilobytes to nearly a gigabyte. If we are performing multiple transfers of a size that is on the steep part of these curves, then batching these individual transfers together may provide substantial reduction in overall transfer time.

3.1.2.1 *Explicit transfers using* cudaMemcpy()

CUDA Fortran may break up implicit data transfers via assignment statements into several transfers. The chance of this happening has been greatly reduced with recent compiler versions, but it may still occur. (We can determine the number of transfers from a single assignment statement by using the Command Line Profiler.) To avoid this, we can explicitly specify a single transfer of contiguous data via the cudaMemcpy() function. We could, for example, replace the implicit data transfer on line 59 in the code above with:

```
istat = cudaMemcpy(a_d, a_pageable, nElements)
```

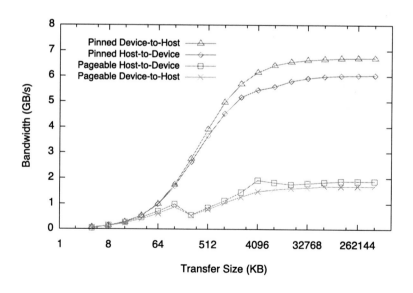

FIGURE 3.2

Host-to-device and device-to-host bandwidth for pageable and pinned memory versus transfer size on an Intel Xeon E5440 system with a Tesla K20.

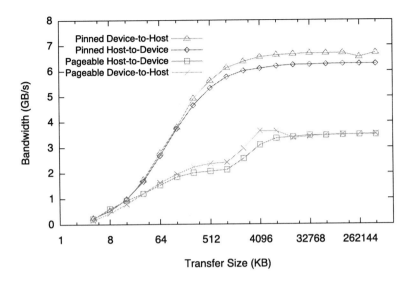

FIGURE 3.3

Host-to-device and device-to-host bandwidth for pageable and pinned memory versus transfer size on an Intel Xeon E5-2667 system with a Tesla K20.

The arguments of `cudaMemcpy()` are the destination array, source array, and number of elements[1] to be transferred. Since CUDA Fortran is strongly typed, there is no need to specify the direction of transfer. The compiler is able to detect where the data in each of the first two arguments reside based on whether the `device` qualifier was used in its declaration and will perform the appropriate data transfer. However, if we desire, there is an optional fourth argument that specifies the direction of transfer, which can take on the values `cudaMemcpyHostToDevice`, `cudaMemcpyDeviceToHost`, `cudaMemcpyDeviceToDevice`. When we use this optional fourth argument, the compiler is more forgiving in terms of ignoring the variable type of the first two arguments. In this case, the number of elements refers to the number of elements of the source array.

Assignment statements can be used in CUDA Fortran to transfer array sections between device and host, as in:

```
a_d(n1_l:n1_u, n2_l:n2_u) = a(n1_l:n1_u, n2_l:n2_u)
```

Such operations are generally broken up into multiple separate transfers. A more efficient way of performing such transfers is using the routine `cudaMemcpy2D()`. The following code section shows how to perform the same array-section transfer as the previous assignment statement using `cudaMemcpy2D()`:

---

[1] Specifying the number of elements here differs from the third argument of the CUDA C `cudaMemcpy()` call where the number of bytes to be transferred is specified.

```
istat = cudaMemcpy2D(a_d(n1_l, n2_l), n, &
                     a(n1_l, n2_l), n, &
                     n1_u-n1_l+1, n2_u-n2_l+1)
```

The first and third arguments are the first element of the destination and source arrays, respectively. The second and fourth arguments are the leading dimensions of these arrays, which we have assumed to be n, and the final two arguments are the size of the subarray in terms of the number of elements in each dimension. There is also an analogous cudaMemcpy3D() routine for transferring three-dimensional array sections.

3.1.3 Asynchronous data transfers *(advanced topic)*

Data transfers in either direction between the host and device using assignment statements or the function cudaMemcpy() are blocking transfers; that is, control is returned to the host thread only after the data transfer is complete. The cudaMemcpyAsync() function is a nonblocking variant in which control is returned immediately to the host thread. In contrast to assignment statements or cudaMemcpy(), *the asynchronous transfer version requires pinned host memory*, and it contains an additional argument, a stream ID. A stream is simply a sequence of operations that are performed in order on the device. Operations in different streams can be interleaved and in some cases overlapped—a property that can be used to hide data transfers between the host and the device.

Asynchronous data transfers enable overlap of data transfers with computation in two different ways. On all CUDA-enabled devices, it is possible to overlap host computation with asynchronous data transfers and with device computations. For example, the following code segment demonstrates how host computation in the routine cpuRoutine() is performed while data is transferred to the device and a kernel is executed.

```
istat = cudaMemcpyAsync(a_d, a_h, nElements, 0)
call kernel<<<gridSize,blockSize>>>(a_d)
call cpuRoutine(b)
```

The first three arguments of cudaMemcpyAsync are the same as the three arguments to cudaMemcpy. The last argument is the stream ID, which in this case uses the default stream, stream 0. The kernel also uses the default stream. Because the kernel is in the same stream as the asynchronous data transfer, it will not begin execution until the memory copy completes; therefore, no explicit synchronization is needed. Because the memory copy and the kernel both return control to the host immediately, the host subroutine cpuRoutine() can overlap their execution.

In the preceding example, the memory copy and kernel execution occur sequentially. On devices capable of "concurrent copy and execution," it is possible to overlap kernel execution on the device with data transfers between the host and the device. Whether a device has this capability or not can be determined from the deviceOverlap field of a cudaDeviceProp variable and is also indicated in the output of pgaccelinfo. On devices that have this capability, the overlap once again requires pinned host memory, and, in addition, the data transfer and kernel must use different, nondefault streams (streams with nonzero stream IDs). Nondefault streams are required for this overlap because memory copy, memory set functions, and kernel calls that use the default stream begin only after all preceding calls on the device (in any stream) have completed, and no operation on the device (in any stream) commences until they are finished. In the following code:

```
istat = cudaStreamCreate(stream1)
istat = cudaStreamCreate(stream2)
istat = cudaMemcpyAsync(a_d, a, n, stream1)
call kernel<<<gridSize,blockSize,0,stream2>>>(b_d)
```

two streams are created and used in the data transfer and kernel executions as specified in the last arguments of the cudaMemcpyAsync() call and the kernel execution configuration.[2]

Cases in which operations on data in a kernel are point-wise, meaning they are independent of other data, are good candidates for *pipelining* data transfers and kernel executions: Data can be broken into sections and transferred in multiple stages, where multiple kernels are launched to operate on each section as it arrives, and each section's results are transferred back to the host when the relevant kernel completes. The following full code listing demonstrates this technique of breaking up data transfers and kernels in order to hide transfer time:

```
1  ! This code demonstrates strategies hiding data transfers via
2  ! asynchronous data copies in multiple streams
3
4  module kernels_m
5  contains
6    attributes(global) subroutine kernel(a, offset)
7      implicit none
8      real :: a(*)
9      integer, value :: offset
10     integer :: i
11     real :: c, s, x
12
13     i = offset + threadIdx%x + (blockIdx%x-1)*blockDim%x
14     x = i; s = sin(x); c = cos(x)
15     a(i) = a(i) + sqrt(s**2+c**2)
16   end subroutine kernel
17 end module kernels_m
18
19 program testAsync
20   use cudafor
21   use kernels_m
```

---

[2]The last two arguments in the execution configuration are optional. The third argument of the execution configuration relates to shared memory use in the kernel, which we discuss later in this chapter.

```
22    implicit none
23    integer, parameter :: blockSize = 256, nStreams = 4
24    integer, parameter :: n = 4*1024*blockSize*nStreams
25    real, pinned, allocatable :: a(:)
26    real, device :: a_d(n)
27    integer(kind=cuda_stream_kind) :: stream(nStreams)
28    type (cudaEvent) :: startEvent, stopEvent, dummyEvent
29    real :: time
30    integer :: i, istat, offset, streamSize = n/nStreams
31    logical :: pinnedFlag
32    type (cudaDeviceProp) :: prop
33
34    istat = cudaGetDeviceProperties(prop, 0)
35    write(*,"(' Device: ', a,/)") trim(prop%name)
36
37    ! allocate pinned  host memory
38    allocate(a(n), STAT=istat, PINNED=pinnedFlag)
39    if (istat /= 0) then
40       write(*,*) 'Allocation of a failed'
41       stop
42    else
43       if (.not. pinnedFlag) &
44            write(*,*) 'Pinned allocation failed'
45    end if
46
47    ! create events and streams
48    istat = cudaEventCreate(startEvent)
49    istat = cudaEventCreate(stopEvent)
50    istat = cudaEventCreate(dummyEvent)
51    do i = 1, nStreams
52       istat = cudaStreamCreate(stream(i))
53    enddo
54
55    ! baseline case - sequential transfer and execute
56    a = 0
57    istat = cudaEventRecord(startEvent,0)
58    a_d = a
59    call kernel<<<n/blockSize, blockSize>>>(a_d, 0)
60    a = a_d
61    istat = cudaEventRecord(stopEvent, 0)
62    istat = cudaEventSynchronize(stopEvent)
63    istat = cudaEventElapsedTime(time, startEvent, stopEvent)
64    write(*,*) 'Time for sequential ', &
65         'transfer and execute (ms): ', time
66    write(*,*) '  max error: ', maxval(abs(a-1.0))
67
68    ! asynchronous version 1: loop over {copy, kernel, copy}
```

```
69   a = 0
70   istat = cudaEventRecord(startEvent,0)
71   do i = 1, nStreams
72      offset = (i-1)*streamSize
73      istat = cudaMemcpyAsync( &
74            a_d(offset+1),a(offset+1),streamSize,stream(i))
75      call kernel<<<streamSize/blockSize, blockSize, &
76                    0, stream(i)>>>(a_d,offset)
77      istat = cudaMemcpyAsync( &
78            a(offset+1),a_d(offset+1),streamSize,stream(i))
79   enddo
80   istat = cudaEventRecord(stopEvent, 0)
81   istat = cudaEventSynchronize(stopEvent)
82   istat = cudaEventElapsedTime(time, startEvent, stopEvent)
83   write(*,*) 'Time for asynchronous V1 ', &
84        'transfer and execute (ms): ', time
85   write(*,*) '  max error: ', maxval(abs(a-1.0))
86
87   ! asynchronous version 2:
88   ! loop over copy, loop over kernel, loop over copy
89   a = 0
90   istat = cudaEventRecord(startEvent,0)
91   do i = 1, nStreams
92      offset = (i-1)*streamSize
93      istat = cudaMemcpyAsync( &
94            a_d(offset+1),a(offset+1),streamSize,stream(i))
95   enddo
96   do i = 1, nStreams
97      offset = (i-1)*streamSize
98      call kernel<<<streamSize/blockSize, blockSize, &
99                    0, stream(i)>>>(a_d,offset)
100  enddo
101  do i = 1, nStreams
102     offset = (i-1)*streamSize
103     istat = cudaMemcpyAsync(&
104           a(offset+1),a_d(offset+1),streamSize,stream(i))
105  enddo
106  istat = cudaEventRecord(stopEvent, 0)
107  istat = cudaEventSynchronize(stopEvent)
108  istat = cudaEventElapsedTime(time, startEvent, stopEvent)
109  write(*,*) 'Time for asynchronous V2 ', &
110       'transfer and execute (ms): ', time
111  write(*,*) '  max error: ', maxval(abs(a-1.0))
112
113  ! asynchronous version 3:
114  ! loop over copy, loop over {kernel, event},
115  ! loop over copy
```

```
116   a = 0
117   istat = cudaEventRecord(startEvent,0)
118   do i = 1, nStreams
119      offset = (i-1)*streamSize
120      istat = cudaMemcpyAsync( &
121           a_d(offset+1),a(offset+1),streamSize,stream(i))
122   enddo
123   do i = 1, nStreams
124      offset = (i-1)*streamSize
125      call kernel<<<streamSize/blockSize, blockSize, &
126                  0, stream(i)>>>(a_d,offset)
127      istat = cudaEventRecord(dummyEvent, stream(i))
128   enddo
129   do i = 1, nStreams
130      offset = (i-1)*streamSize
131      istat = cudaMemcpyAsync( &
132           a(offset+1),a_d(offset+1),streamSize,stream(i))
133   enddo
134   istat = cudaEventRecord(stopEvent, 0)
135   istat = cudaEventSynchronize(stopEvent)
136   istat = cudaEventElapsedTime(time, startEvent, stopEvent)
137   write(*,*) 'Time for asynchronous V3 ', &
138       'transfer and execute (ms): ', time
139   write(*,*) '  max error: ', maxval(abs(a-1.0))
140
141   ! cleanup
142   istat = cudaEventDestroy(startEvent)
143   istat = cudaEventDestroy(stopEvent)
144   istat = cudaEventDestroy(dummyEvent)
145   do i = 1, nStreams
146      istat = cudaStreamDestroy(stream(i))
147   enddo
148   deallocate(a)
149
150 end program testAsync
```

This code processes the array data in four ways. The first way is the sequential case whereby all data are transferred to the device (line 58), then a single kernel is launched with enough threads to process every element in the array (line 59), followed by a data transfer from device to host (line 60). The other three ways involve different strategies for overlapping asynchronous memory copies with kernel executions.

The asynchronous cases are similar to the sequential case, only there are multiple data transfers and kernel launches, which are distinguished by different streams and array offsets. For purposes of this discussion we limit the number of streams to four, although for large arrays there is no reason that a larger number of streams could not be used. Note that the same kernel is used in the sequential and asynchronous cases in the code, as an offset is sent to the kernel to accommodate the data in different streams. The difference between the first two asynchronous versions is the order in which the copies and kernels are executed. The first version (starting on line 68) loops over each stream where each stream issues a host-to-device copy, a kernel, and a device-to-host copy. The second version (starting on line 87) issues all host-to-device copies, then all kernel launches, and then all device-to-host copies. The third asynchronous version (starting on line 113) is the same as the second version except that a dummy event is recorded after each kernel is issued in the same stream as the kernel.

At this point you may be asking why we have three versions of the asynchronous case. The reason is that these variants perform differently on different hardware generations. Running this code on the NVIDIA Tesla C1060 produces:

```
Device:  Tesla  C1060

Time  for  sequential  transfer  and  execute  (ms):      12.92381
   max  error:      2.3841858E-07
Time  for  asynchronous  V1  transfer  and  execute  (ms):      13.63690
   max  error:      2.3841858E-07
Time  for  asynchronous  V2  transfer  and  execute  (ms):      8.845888
   max  error:      2.3841858E-07
Time  for  asynchronous  V3  transfer  and  execute  (ms):      8.998560
   max  error:      2.3841858E-07
```

and on the NVIDIA Tesla C2050 we get:

```
Device:  Tesla  C2050

Time  for  sequential  transfer  and  execute  (ms):      9.984512
   max  error:      1.1920929E-07
Time  for  asynchronous  V1  transfer  and  execute  (ms):      5.735584
   max  error:      1.1920929E-07
Time  for  asynchronous  V2  transfer  and  execute  (ms):      7.597984
   max  error:      1.1920929E-07
Time  for  asynchronous  V3  transfer  and  execute  (ms):      5.735424
   max  error:      1.1920929E-07
```

To decipher these results, we need to understand a bit more about how devices schedule and execute various tasks. CUDA devices contain engines for various tasks, and operations are queued up in these engines as they are issued. Dependencies between tasks in different engines are maintained, but within any engine all dependence is lost, since tasks in an engine's queue are executed in the order they are issued by the host thread. For example, the C1060 has a single copy engine and a single kernel engine. For the preceding code, timelines for the execution on the device are schematically shown in the top diagram of Figure 3.4. In this schematic we have assumed that the times required for the host-to-device transfer, kernel execution, and device-to-host transfer are approximately the same (the kernel code was chosen in order to make these times comparable on the Tesla C1060 and C2050). For the sequential kernel, there is no overlap in any of the operations, as we would expect. For the first asynchronous

C1060 Execution Timelines

Sequential Version

Asynchronous Version 1

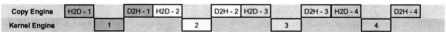

Asynchronous Versions 2 and 3

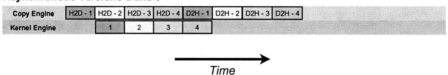

Time

C2050 Execution Timelines

Sequential Version

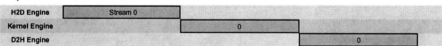

Asynchronous Versions 1 and 3

Asynchronous Version 2

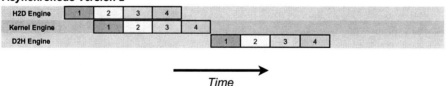

Time

FIGURE 3.4

Timelines of data transfers and kernel executions for sequential and three asynchronous strategies on Tesla C1060 and C2050. The C1060 has a single copy engine, whereas the C2050 has separate device-to-host and host-to-device copy engines. Data transfers are executed in the order they are issued from the host within each engine. As a result, different strategies achieve overlap on these different architectures.

version of our code, the order of execution in the copy engine is H2D stream(1), D2H stream(1), H2D stream(2), D2H stream(2), and so forth. This is why we do not see any speed-up when we use the first asynchronous version on the C1060: Tasks were issued to the copy engine in an order that precludes any overlap of kernel execution and data transfer. For versions two and three, however, where all the host-to-device transfers are issued before any of the device-to-host transfers, overlap is possible, as indicated by the lower execution time. From our schematic, we would expect the execution of versions two and three to be 8/12 of the sequential version, or 8.7 ms, which is what is observed in the preceding timing.

On the C2050, two features interact to cause different behavior than that observed on the C1060. The C2050 has two copy engines, one for host-to-device transfers and another for device-to-host transfers, in addition to a single kernel engine. Having two copy engines explains why the first asynchronous version achieves good speed-up on the C2050: The device-to-host transfer of data in stream(i) does not block the host-to-device transfer of data in stream(i+1), as it did on the C1060, because these two operations are in different engines on the C2050, which is schematically shown in the bottom diagram of Figure 3.4. From the schematic we would expect the execution time to be cut in half relative to the sequential version, which is roughly what is observed in the timings listed earlier. This does not explain the performance degradation observed in the second asynchronous approach, however, which is related to the C2050's support to concurrently run multiple kernels. When multiple kernels are issued back-to-back, the scheduler tries to enable concurrent execution of these kernels and, as a result, delays a signal that normally occurs after each kernel completion (which is responsible for kicking off the device-to-host transfer) until all kernels complete. So, although there is overlap between host-to-device transfers and kernel execution in the second version of our asynchronous code, there is no overlap between kernel execution and device-to-host transfers. From Figure 3.4 we would expect an overall time for the second asynchronous version to be 9/12 of the time for the sequential version, or 7.5 ms, which is what we observe from the timings above. This situation can be rectified by recording a dummy CUDA event between each kernel, which will inhibit concurrent kernel execution but enable overlap of data transfers and kernel execution, as is done in the third asynchronous version.

3.1.3.1 *Hyper-Q*

Devices of compute capability 3.5 (the highest compute capability at the time this book was written), such as the Tesla K20, contain a feature called *Hyper-Q*. Previous CUDA architectures had a single work queue, which introduced the serializations in the copy engines and kernel executions observed above. Hyper-Q introduces 32 independent work queues. In our asynchronous code example, with Hyper-Q each stream is managed by its own hardware work queue. As a result, operations in one stream will not block operations on other streams. Running the code on the NVIDIA Tesla K20, we obtain:

```
Device: Tesla K20

Time for sequential transfer and execute (ms):      7.963808
   max error:    1.1920929E-07
Time for asynchronous V1 transfer and execute (ms):     5.608096
   max error:    1.1920929E-07
Time for asynchronous V2 transfer and execute (ms):     5.646880
   max error:    1.1920929E-07
Time for asynchronous V3 transfer and execute (ms):     5.506816
   max error:    1.1920929E-07
```

where we observe that each asynchronous method achieves roughly the same performance. You may have noticed that the relative speed-up between the synchronous and asynchronous versions on the K20 isn't as large as the relative speed-up obtained by the optimal asynchronous version on the C2050. This is due to the fact that on the K20 the kernel executes in considerably less time than the data transfers, as shown in profiler output:

```
method=[ memcpyHtoDasync ] gputime=[ 712.608 ] cputime=[ 19.000 ]
method=[ kernel ] gputime=[ 442.816 ] cputime=[ 29.000 ]
        occupancy=[ 1.000 ]
method=[ memcpyDtoHasync ] gputime=[ 1295.520 ] cputime=[ 9.000 ]
```

On the C2050 the data transfers and kernels execute in roughly the same amount of time, yielding a larger relative speed-up. We could modify the kernel to achieve a similar relative speed-up on the K20 as obtained on the C2050, but the point here is the effort involved in getting the best speed-up. Hyper-Q eliminates the need for the programmer to optimally schedule work from multiple streams on the K20, whereas tailoring the order in which asynchronous copies and kernels are issued was required on the C1060 and C2050 to get the best results.

3.1.3.2 *Profiling asynchronous events*

A good way to examine asynchronous performance is via the profiler, using a configuration file containing the following:

```
conckerneltrace
timestamp
gpustarttimestamp
gpuendtimestamp
streamid
```

Unlike hardware counters, these items will not serialize execution on the device, thus inhibiting the behavior we are trying to measure. We should note that turning on profiling in the preceding code will effectively accomplish what inserting a `cudaEventRecord()` between kernel calls accomplishes, so in this case the measurement does modify what is being measured.

Before leaving the topic of overlapping kernel execution with asynchronous data transfers, we should note that the kernel chosen for this example is a very obfuscated way of calculating the value 1.0. This was chosen so that transfer time between host and device would be comparable to kernel execution time, at least for the C1060 and C2050. If we used simpler kernels, such as ones discussed up to this point, such overlaps would be difficult to detect because kernel execution time is so much smaller than data transfer time.

3.2 Device memory

Up to this point in this chapter, we have focused on efficient means of getting data to and from device DRAM. More precisely, these data are stored in global memory, which resides in DRAM. Global memory is accessible by both the device and the host and can exist for the lifetime of the application. In addition to global memory, there are other types of data stored in DRAM that have different scopes, lifetimes, and caching behaviors. There are also several memory types that exist on the chip itself. In this section, we discuss these different memory types and how they can best be used.

The various memory types in CUDA are represented in Figure 3.5. In device DRAM there are global, local, constant, and texture memories. On-chip there are registers, shared memory, and various caches (L1, constant, and texture). We go into detail and provide examples for each of these memories later in this chapter, but for now we provide these short summaries.

Global memory is the device memory that is declared with the device attribute in host code. It can be read and written from both host and device. It is available to all threads launched on the device and persists for the lifetime of the application (or until deallocated, if declared allocatable).

Local variables defined in device code are stored in on-chip registers, provided there are sufficient registers available. If there are insufficient registers, data are stored off-chip in *local memory*. (The adjective *local* in local memory refers to scope, not physical locality.) Both register memory and local memory have per-thread access.

Shared memory is memory that is accessible by all threads in a thread block. It is declared in device code using the shared variable qualifier. It can be used to share data loads and stores and to avoid global memory access patterns that are inefficient.

Constant memory can be read and written from host code but is read-only from threads in device code. It is declared using the constant qualifier in a Fortran module and can be used in any code

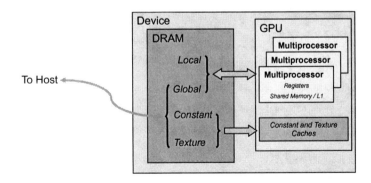

FIGURE 3.5

Schematic of device memory types in DRAM and on-chip.

Table 3.1 Device memory characteristics.

Memory	Location	Cached	Device Access	Scope	Lifetime
Register	On-chip	N/A	R/W	One thread	Thread
Local	DRAM	Fermi, Kepler	R/W	One thread	Thread
Shared	On-chip	N/A	R/W	All threads in block	Thread block
Global	DRAM	Fermi, Kepler*	R/W	All threads and host	Application
Constant	DRAM	Yes	R	All threads and host	Application
Texture	DRAM	Yes	R	All threads and host	Application

*The Tesla K10, K20 and K20X cache globals only in the L2 cache.

contained in the module as well as any code that uses the module. Constant data is cached on the chip and is most effective when threads that execute at the same time access the same value.

Texture memory is similar to constant memory in that it is read-only by device code and is also cached on the GPU. It is simply a different pathway for accessing global memory and is sometimes helpful in avoiding poor global memory access patterns by device code.

Table 3.1 summarizes the characteristics of all the device memory types.

3.2.1 Declaring data in device code

Before we discuss how to use the different types of memory efficiently, we should mention a few points regarding how data is declared in device code. For the most part, data declaration in device code is the same as in host code or regular Fortran 90. There are a few notable exceptions, however.

In declaring data in device code, we need to be aware that because the host and device have separate memory spaces, and because by default Fortran passes arguments by reference, kernel arguments either must be on the device or, in the case of host scalar arguments, must have the `value` attribute.

A second issue is that CUDA Fortran does not support the `save` attribute in device code, either explicitly or implicitly. Since variables initialized at the time of declaration implicitly get the `save` attribute, initialization of variables at declaration is not allowed in device code in CUDA Fortran. Of course, variables with the `parameter` attribute are allowed and must be assigned values at the time of declaration, since the compiler converts these to literals in the code. The following snippet of code illustrates these ideas:

```
attributes(global) subroutine increment(array, incVal)
  integer :: array(*)
  integer, value :: incVal
  integer :: otherVal=1       ! illegal
  integer, parameter :: anotherVal = 2  ! OK
```

3.2.2 **Coalesced access to global memory**

Perhaps the single most important performance consideration in programming for the CUDA architecture is coalescing global memory accesses. Before we go into how global memory is accessed, we need to refine our programming model a bit. We have discussed how threads are grouped into thread blocks, which are assigned to multiprocessors on the device. There is a further grouping of threads into *warps*, or groups of 32 threads, which is the actual grouping of threads that gets calculated in single-instruction, multiple-thread (SIMT) fashion. Each instruction on the device is issued to a warp of threads, and execution of instructions is performed by each thread in a warp in lockstep. Different warps in a thread block may be executing different instructions of the device code, and all of this activity is coordinated behind the scenes by the scheduler on each multiprocessor. For our purposes, we just need to know that instructions get simultaneously executed on a group of threads called a *warp*. Grouping of threads into warps is relevant not only to computation but also to global memory accesses. Global memory loads and stores by threads of a half-warp (for devices of compute capability 1.x) or of a warp (for devices of compute capability 2.0 and higher) are coalesced by the device into as little as one transaction when certain access requirements are met. To understand these access requirements and how they evolved with different Tesla architectures, we run some simple experiments on Tesla cards representing different compute capabilities. We do this in single and double precision (when possible).

We run two experiments that are variants of our increment kernel used in the Introduction—one with an array offset or misaligned access of the array and the other performing strided access in a similar fashion. The code that performs this is:

```
1   module kernels_m
2     use precision_m
3   contains
4     attributes(global) subroutine offset(a, s)
5       real(fp_kind) :: a(*)
6       integer, value :: s
7       integer :: i
8       i = blockDim%x*(blockIdx%x-1)+threadIdx%x + s
9       a(i) = a(i)+1
10    end subroutine offset
11
12    attributes(global) subroutine stride(a, s)
13      real(fp_kind) :: a(*)
14      integer, value :: s
15      integer :: i
16      i = (blockDim%x*(blockIdx%x-1)+threadIdx%x) * s
17      a(i) = a(i)+1
18    end subroutine stride
19  end module kernels_m
20
21  program offsetNStride
22    use cudafor
23    use kernels_m
```

```
24
25     implicit none
26
27     integer, parameter :: nMB = 4   ! transfer size in MB
28     integer, parameter :: n = nMB*1024*1024/fp_kind
29     integer, parameter :: blockSize = 256
30     ! array dimensions are 33*n for stride cases
31     real(fp_kind), device :: a_d(33*n), b_d(33*n)
32     type(cudaEvent) :: startEvent, stopEvent
33     type(cudaDeviceProp) :: prop
34     integer :: i, istat
35     real(4) :: time
36
37
38     istat = cudaGetDeviceProperties(prop, 0)
39     write(*,'(/,"Device: ",a)') trim(prop%name)
40     write(*,'("Transfer size (MB): ",i0)') nMB
41
42     if (kind(a_d) == singlePrecision) then
43        write(*,'(a,/)') 'Single Precision'
44     else
45        write(*,'(a,/)') 'Double Precision'
46     endif
47
48     istat = cudaEventCreate(startEvent)
49     istat = cudaEventCreate(stopEvent)
50
51     write(*,*) 'Offset, Bandwidth (GB/s):'
52     call offset<<<n/blockSize,blockSize>>>(b_d, 0)
53     do i = 0, 32
54        a_d = 0.0
55        istat = cudaEventRecord(startEvent,0)
56        call offset<<<n/blockSize,blockSize>>>(a_d, i)
57        istat = cudaEventRecord(stopEvent,0)
58        istat = cudaEventSynchronize(stopEvent)
59
60        istat = cudaEventElapsedTime(time, startEvent, &
61             stopEvent)
62        write(*,*) i, 2*n*fp_kind/time*1.e-6
63     enddo
64
65     write(*,*)
66     write(*,*) 'Stride, Bandwidth (GB/s):'
67     call stride<<<n/blockSize,blockSize>>>(b_d, 1)
68     do i = 1, 32
69        a_d = 0.0
70        istat = cudaEventRecord(startEvent,0)
```

```
71          call stride<<<n/blockSize,blockSize>>>(a_d, i)
72          istat = cudaEventRecord(stopEvent,0)
73          istat = cudaEventSynchronize(stopEvent)
74          istat = cudaEventElapsedTime(time, startEvent, &
75               stopEvent)
76          write(*,*) i, 2*n*fp_kind/time*1.e-6
77       enddo
78
79       istat = cudaEventDestroy(startEvent)
80       istat = cudaEventDestroy(stopEvent)
81
82    end program offsetNStride
```

3.2.2.1 *Misaligned access*

We begin by looking at results of the misaligned access for single precision data, which is shown in Figure 3.6. When an array is allocated in device memory, either explicitly or implicitly, the array is aligned with a 256-byte segment of memory. Global memory can be accessed via 32-, 64-, or 128-byte transactions that are aligned to their size. The best performance is achieved when threads in a warp (or half-warp) access data in as few memory transactions as possible, as is the case with the zero offset in Figure 3.6. In such cases, the data requested by a warp (or half-warp) of threads is coalesced into a single 128-byte (or 64-byte) transaction, where all words in the transaction have been requested. For the

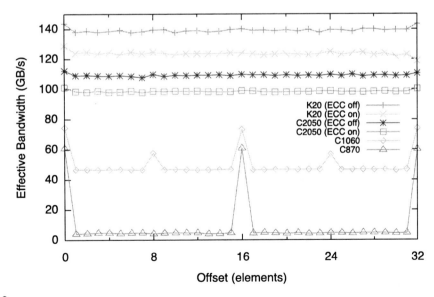

FIGURE 3.6

Effective bandwidth versus offset for single-precision data for the array increment kernel.

C870 and other cards with a compute capability of 1.0, this performance also requires that contiguous threads in a half-warp access contiguous words in a 64-byte segment of memory.

For misaligned accesses, the performance varies greatly for different compute capabilities. For the C870 with compute capability 1.0, any misaligned access by a half-warp of threads (or aligned access where the threads of the half-warp do not access memory in sequence) results in 16 separate 32-byte transactions. Since only 4 bytes are requested per 32-byte transaction, we would expect the effective bandwidth to be reduced by a factor of eight, which is roughly what we see in Figure 3.6 for offsets that are not a multiple of 16 elements, corresponding to one half-warp of threads.

For the C1060, which has a compute capability of 1.3, misaligned accesses are less problematic. Basically, the misaligned accesses of contiguous data are serviced in a few transactions that "cover" the requested data. There is still a performance penalty relative to the aligned case due to both unrequested data being transferred and some overlap of data requested by different half-warps. We analyze the three performance levels in the C1060 in detail in a moment, but first we give the algorithm that determines the type of transfers that occur. The exact algorithm used to determine the number and type of transactions by a half-warp of threads on a C1060 is:

- Find the memory segment that contains the address requested by the lowest numbered active thread. Segment size is 32 bytes for 8-bit data, 64 bytes for 16-bit data, and 128 bytes for 32-, 64-, and 128-bit data.
- Find all other active threads for which the requested address lies in the same segment, and reduce the transaction size if possible:

  - If the transaction is 128 bytes and only the lower or upper half is used, reduce the transaction size to 64 bytes.
  - If the transaction is 64 bytes and only the lower or upper half is used, reduce the transaction size to 32 bytes.

- Carry out the transaction and mark the serviced threads as inactive.
- Repeat until all threads in the half-warp are serviced.

We now apply this algorithm to our offset example, looking at what happens for offsets of zero, one, and eight.

We begin with the optimal case corresponding to zero offset. The access patterns by the first two half-warps of data are shown in Figure 3.7. In this figure, the two rows of boxes represent the same 256-byte segment of memory, with the alignments of various transaction sizes shown at the top. For each half-warp of threads, the data requested results in a single 64-byte transaction. Although only two half-warps are shown, the same occurs for all half-warps. No unrequested data is transferred, and no data is transferred twice, so this is the optimal case as though reflected in the plot of Figure 3.6. Note that any offset that is a multiple of 16 elements will have the same performance, since this just shifts the diagram by one 64-byte segment.

Shifting the access pattern by one results in the worst case for the C1060. The access pattern and resulting transactions for the first two half-warps are shown in Figure 3.8. For the first half-warp, even though only 64 bytes are requested, the entire 128-byte segment is transferred. This happens because the data requested by the first half warp lies in both lower and upper halves of the 128-byte segment; the transaction can't be reduced. The second half-warp of threads accesses data across two 128-byte segments, where the transaction in each segment can be reduced. Note that for these two half-warps,

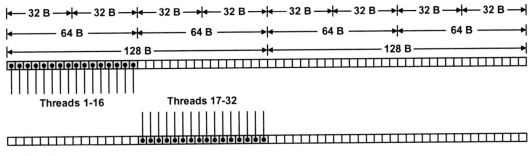

FIGURE 3.7

Diagram of transactions of two half-warps on a C1060 for the case of aligned accesses, or zero offset, of single-precision data. The 32-, 64-, and 128-byte segments are shown at the top, and two rows of boxes representing the same memory are shown beneath. The first row is used to depict the access by the first half-warp of threads, and the second row is use to depict the accesses by the second half-warp of threads. This is the optimal situation where the requests by each half-warp result in a 64-byte transaction, for a total of 128 bytes transferred for the two half-warps, with no unrequested data and no duplication of data.

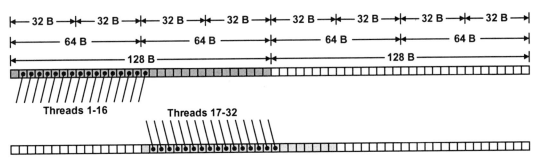

FIGURE 3.8

Diagram of transactions of two half warps on a C1060 for the case of misaligned single-precision data with an offset of one element. Two rows of boxes representing the same memory are shown beneath. The first row is used to depict the access by the first half-warp of threads, and the second row is use to depict the accesses by the second half-warp of threads. The requests by these two half-warps are serviced by three transactions totaling 224 bytes.

there are both unrequested data transferred and some data transferred twice. Also, this pattern repeats itself for subsequent pairs of half-warps, so the 32-byte transaction for the second half-warp will overlap with the 128-byte transaction of the third half-warp. For the two half-warps, 224 bytes are transferred, in comparison to 128 bytes transferred for the aligned or zero-offset case. Based on this, we would expect an effective bandwidth of slightly over half of the zero-offset case, which we see in Figure 3.6. The same number of transactions occurs for offsets of 2–7, 9–15, 17–23, and 25–31, along with the same effective bandwidth.

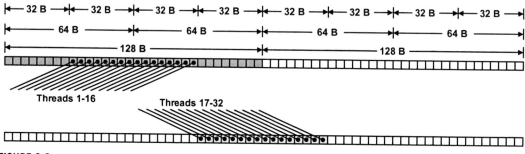

FIGURE 3.9

Diagram of transactions of two half-warps on a C1060 for the case of misaligned single-precision data with an offset of eight elements. Two rows of boxes representing the same memory are shown beneath. The first row is used to depict the access by the first half-warp of threads, and the second row is use to depict the accesses by the second half-warp of threads. The requests by these two half-warps are serviced by three transactions totaling 192 bytes.

The final case for misaligned accesses we consider for the C1060 is when the offset is 8 or 24 elements, as depicted in Figure 3.9. This is similar to the offset by one element case, except that the request from the second half-warp of threads is serviced by two 32-byte transactions rather then one 64-byte and one 32-byte transaction. This results in 192 elements being transferred for these two half-warps and a resulting effective bandwidth that should be roughly 2/3 of the aligned effective bandwidth, which we see from Figure 3.6.

For the C2050, the situation is very different than the preceding cases because of the caching of global memory introduced in the Fermi architecture. Also, memory transactions are issued per warp of threads rather than per half-warp. On the Fermi architecture, each multiprocessor has 64 KB of memory that is divided up between shared memory and L1 cache, either as 16 KB shared memory and 48 KB L1 cache, or vice versa. This L1 cache uses 128-byte cache lines. When a cache line is brought into the L1 cache on a multiprocessor, it can be used by any warp of threads resident on that multiprocessor. So, whereas some nonrequested data may be brought into the L1 cache, there should be far less duplication of data being brought on the chip. We can see this in the results of Figure 3.6, where there is little performance penalty for any offset—so little that the performance penalty due to misaligned accesses is actually smaller than the performance penalty due to ECC.

The effective bandwidth variation due to misaligned accesses on the K20 is similar to that of the C2050, where we see a slight performance penalty when global memory access is misaligned. On the K20, the L1 cache is used for local memory only, but global memory is cached in L2, which is an on-chip cache shared by all multiprocessors. Once again, the penalty for misaligned accesses is small—much less than the effect of ECC.

The preceding discussion for single-precision data also applies to double-precision data, as can shown in Figure 3.10, with the exception that the C870 does not support double-precision data and hence is not represented. On both the NVIDIA Tesla C2050 and K20, there once again is only a slight performance degradation for misaligned accesses. On the NVIDIA Tesla C1060, since the request by a half-warp of

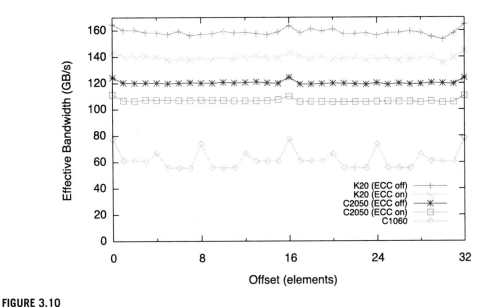

FIGURE 3.10

Effective bandwidth versus offset for double-precision data using the array increment kernel.

threads for double-precision data spans 128 bytes, there are some additional combinations of segments that can serve such requests relative to the single-precision case. These are depicted in Figure 3.11, which shows the transactions for requests of a half-warp of threads with offsets of 0 through 16.

Before we move on to the discussion of strided global memory access, we should mention here that enabling ECC can result in larger penalties when accesses are misaligned for more complicated kernels on devices of compute capability 2.0. For example, if we use an out-of-place increment operation in our kernel, b(i)=a(i)+1, rather than the in-place operation, a(i)=a(i)+1, then, on a C2050 with ECC on, we observe a substantial decrease in performance, as indicated for the case of single-precision data in Figure 3.12. As a general rule, it is always best to code such that accesses are aligned whenever possible, but this is especially true on the Tesla C2050 when ECC is on. For accesses that are naturally offset, such as those that occur in finite difference operations, on-chip shared memory can be used to facilitate aligned accesses, which will be discussed later in this chapter. On the Tesla K20 we see no such performance degradation for the out-of-place kernel when ECC is enabled, as shown in Figure 3.13, since the ECC implementation on Kepler GPUs has been improved.

3.2.2.2 *Strided access*

The same rules for coalescing that we discussed in the misaligned data access kernel also apply to the strided access kernel. The difference is that a request by a half-warp or warp of threads no longer accesses contiguous data and can span many segments of memory. The results for a stride of up to 32 elements is shown in Figure 3.14 for single-precision data, both with ECC on and off on devices with ECC.

As with the misaligned data access performance, the C870 has the most restrictive conditions for coalescing data, where any stride other than one results in data requested by a half-warp of threads being

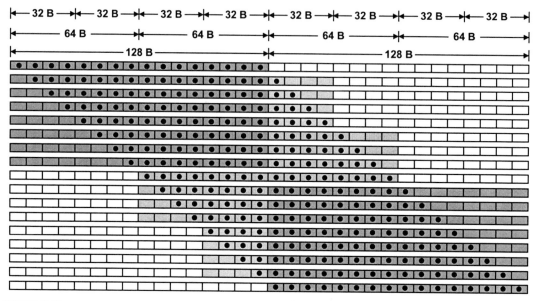

FIGURE 3.11

Transactions resulting from a half-warp of threads for contiguous double-precision data on a C1060 with offsets from 0 to 16, represented by the different rows. For double-precision data, the same access pattern occurs for even an odd number of half-warps, unlike the case of single-precision data.

serviced by 16 separate 32-byte transactions. Correspondingly, we observe an effective bandwidth of approximately 53 GB/s for unit stride and under 10 GB/s for any other offset.

For the C1060, the reduction in effective bandwidth with larger stride is more gradual because more segments are transferred as the stride increases. For large strides, a half-warp of threads is serviced by 16 separate 32-byte transactions on the C1060, the same as on the C870.

For the C2050, despite the larger effective bandwidth at unit stride, the performance at large strides is lower than the C1060 due to 128-byte L1 cache lines on the C2050 rather than 32-byte segments being transferred on the C1060. We can avoid this situation by turning off caching of global loads in the L1 cache via the compiler option –Mcuda=noL1. The results are shown in Figure 3.15 for single-precision data and Figure 3.16 for double-precision data. When strides of eight and four are reached for single- and double- precision data, respectively, segments smaller than 128 bytes are transferred when the L1 cache is disabled, resulting in a higher effective bandwidth.

On the K20, only local variables are cached in L1, so, in effect, the option –Mcuda=noL1 is on implicitly, as shown in Figure 3.17. Similarly to the C2050 with the L1 cache disabled for global loads, when a stride of eight is reached, smaller segments of data are transferred, and we observe the effective bandwidth taper more slowly.

This discussion of coalescing global loads is fairly long and involved. We went into detail because coalescing of data is one of the most important aspects of achieving good performance in CUDA Fortran.

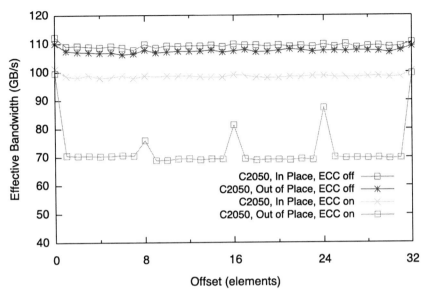

FIGURE 3.12

Effective bandwidth on the Tesla C2050 for in-place and out-of-place increment operations on single-precision data with ECC on and off. On the C2050, with ECC off, in-place and out-of-place have similar performance. However, with ECC enabled, the out-of-place operation has a performance penalty for offset accesses. It is best practice on the C2050 to make sure accesses are aligned whenever possible if ECC is enabled.

Looking back at the discussion, there are a few major themes that should be kept in mind. The first is that with newer GPU architectures, not only has the raw performance (i.e., peak bandwidth) increased, but restrictions and barriers to getting good performance have been removed. In devices of compute capability 1.0 (e.g., C870), aligned data access is critical to achieving good performance. In devices of compute capability 3.5 (e.g., K20), the misaligned accesses result in a negligible performance penalty.

Although alignment of data access is not an issue on recent CUDA architectures, accessing data with large strides results in poor effective bandwidth on all devices. This is not a new aspect of high-performance computing; data locality has always been an important issue in application performance tuning. The best way to deal with striding through memory is to avoid it whenever possible. However, there are cases in which it cannot be avoided, such as when accessing elements in multidimensional arrays along a dimension other than the first dimension. In such cases there are several options we can pursue to obtain good performance. If the strided access occurs on read-only data, textures can be used. Another option is to use on-chip shared memory, which is shared by all threads in a thread block. We can bring data into shared memory in a coalesced fashion, and then access it in a strided fashion without any performance penalty. We discuss shared memory later in the chapter, but we look at texture memory next.

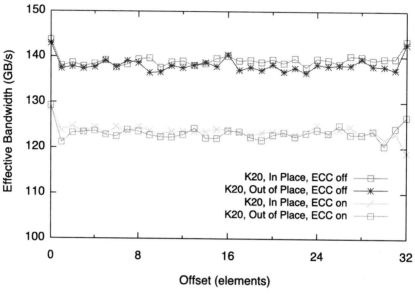

FIGURE 3.13

Effective bandwidth on the Tesla K20 for in-place and out-of-place increment operations on single-precision data with ECC on and off. Unlike the C2050 results in Figure 3.12, in-place and out-of-place bandwidth are roughly the same when ECC is either on or off.

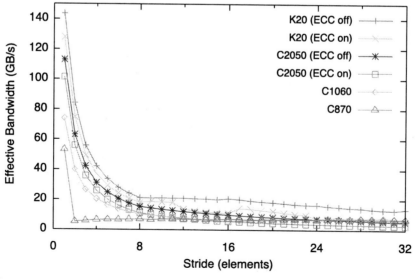

FIGURE 3.14

Effective bandwidth versus stride for single-precision data for the array increment kernel.

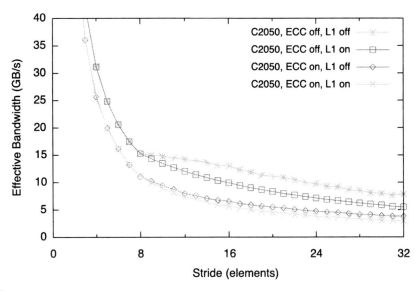

FIGURE 3.15

Effective bandwidth versus stride for single-precision data on the C2050 for cases with ECC and L1 cache on and off. The scale is adjusted to show differences at the tail of the graphs. Turning off the L1 cache results in higher effective bandwidth once a stride of eight is reached.

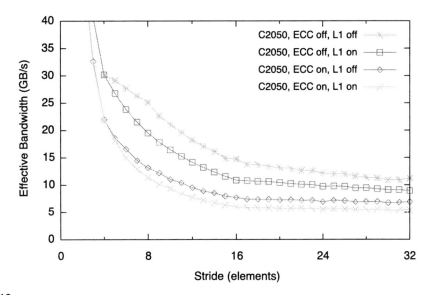

FIGURE 3.16

Effective bandwidth versus stride for double-precision data on the C2050 for cases with ECC and L1 cache on and off. The scale is adjusted to show differences at the tail of the graphs. Turning off the L1 cache results in higher effective bandwidth once a stride of four is reached.

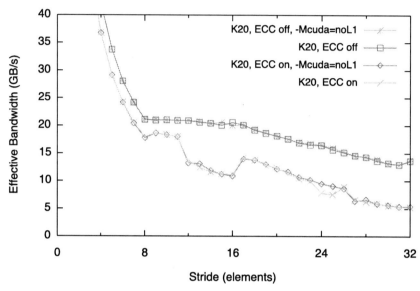

FIGURE 3.17

Effective bandwidth versus stride for single-precision data on the K20 for cases with ECC on and off, and with and without the compiler option −Mcuda=noL1. Since the K20 does not cache global variables in L1, the use of the compiler option −Mcuda=noL1 has no effect on the performance.

3.2.3 Texture memory

Textures were added to CUDA Fortran in version 12.8 of the compilers. For those familiar with textures in CUDA C, this implementation is a subset of the texture features offered in CUDA C, essentially covering the functionality offered by tex1Dfetch(). The filtering and wrapping/clamping capabilities of textures are not currently available in CUDA Fortran. In addition, only single precision is currently supported in CUDA Fortran textures.

Textures in CUDA Fortran allow us to access global memory in a read-only fashion through the texture cache. In addition to utilizing additional on-chip cache, textures may be advantageous in cases where access by sequential threads is to noncontiguous data, such as the strided data access pattern previously discussed. Such data access through textures may be advantageous because the minimum transaction size for textures is 32 bytes, as opposed to, say, the 128-byte cache line of the L1 cache on devices of compute capability 2.x. Although we can disable the caching of globals in L1 to obtain 32-byte transactions, doing so prohibits accessing other variables in global memory from using the L1 cache. In addition, textures can have more load requests in flight compared to global memory. We can see the benefit of textures from a modified version of the strided memory access kernel:

```
module kernels_m
  real, texture, pointer :: aTex(:)
```

```
 3  contains
 4    attributes(global) subroutine stride(b, a, s)
 5      real :: b(*), a(*)
 6      integer, value :: s
 7      integer :: i, is
 8      i = blockDim%x*(blockIdx%x-1)+threadIdx%x
 9      is = (blockDim%x*(blockIdx%x-1)+threadIdx%x) * s
10      b(i) = a(is)+1
11    end subroutine stride
12
13    attributes(global) subroutine strideTex(b, s)
14      real :: b(*)
15      integer, value :: s
16      integer :: i, is
17      i = blockDim%x*(blockIdx%x-1)+threadIdx%x
18      is = (blockDim%x*(blockIdx%x-1)+threadIdx%x) * s
19      b(i) = aTex(is)+1
20    end subroutine strideTex
21  end module kernels_m
22
23  program strideTexture
24    use cudafor
25    use kernels_m
26
27    implicit none
28
29    integer, parameter :: nMB = 4   ! transfer size in MB
30    integer, parameter :: n = nMB*1024*1024/4
31    integer, parameter :: blockSize = 256
32    real, device, allocatable, target :: a_d(:), b_d(:)
33    type(cudaEvent) :: startEvent, stopEvent
34    type(cudaDeviceProp) :: prop
35    integer :: i, istat, ib
36    real :: time
37
38    istat = cudaGetDeviceProperties(prop, 0)
39    write(*,'(/,"Device: ",a)') trim(prop%name)
40    write(*,'("Transfer size (MB): ",i0,/)') nMB
41
42    allocate(a_d(n*33), b_d(n))
43
44    istat = cudaEventCreate(startEvent)
45    istat = cudaEventCreate(stopEvent)
46
47    write(*,*) 'Global version'
48    write(*,*) 'Stride, Bandwidth (GB/s)'
49    call stride<<<n/blockSize,blockSize>>>(b_d, a_d, 1)
```

```
50   do i = 1, 32
51      a_d = 0.0
52      istat = cudaEventRecord(startEvent,0)
53      call stride<<<n/blockSize,blockSize>>>(b_d, a_d, i)
54      istat = cudaEventRecord(stopEvent,0)
55      istat = cudaEventSynchronize(stopEvent)
56      istat = cudaEventElapsedTime(time, startEvent, &
57          stopEvent)
58      write(*,*) i, 2*n*4/time*1.e-6
59   enddo
60
61   ! bind the texture
62   aTex => a_d
63
64   write(*,*) 'Texture version'
65   write(*,*) 'Stride, Bandwidth (GB/s)'
66   call strideTex<<<n/blockSize,blockSize>>>(b_d, 1)
67   do i = 1, 32
68      a_d = 0.0
69      istat = cudaEventRecord(startEvent,0)
70      call strideTex<<<n/blockSize,blockSize>>>(b_d, i)
71      istat = cudaEventRecord(stopEvent,0)
72      istat = cudaEventSynchronize(stopEvent)
73      istat = cudaEventElapsedTime(time, startEvent, &
74          stopEvent)
75      write(*,*) i, 2*n*4/time*1.e-6
76   enddo
77
78   ! unbind the texture
79   nullify(aTex)
80
81   istat = cudaEventDestroy(startEvent)
82   istat = cudaEventDestroy(stopEvent)
83   deallocate(a_d, b_d)
84
85 end program strideTexture
```

Textures in CUDA Fortran make use of the Fortran 90 pointer notation to "bind" a texture to a region of global memory. The texture pointer is declared on line 2 in the preceding code using both the `texture` and the `pointer` variable attributes. The kernel that uses this texture pointer is listed on lines 13–20, and the nontexture version is listed on lines 4–11. Note that the texture pointer, `aTex`, is not passed in as an argument to the kernel, and it must be declared at module scope. If a texture pointer is passed as an argument to a kernel, even if declared in the kernel with the `texture` attribute, the

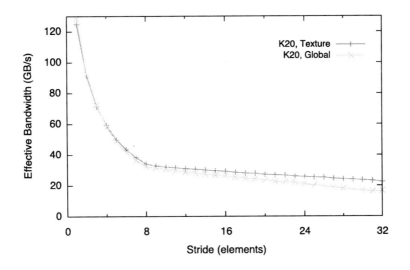

FIGURE 3.18

Effective bandwidth versus stride for single-precision data on the K20 using textures and global memory.

data will be accessed through the global memory path, not the texture path.[3] Aside from that scoping aspect, use of CUDA Fortran textures in device code is analogous to use of a global memory array, unlike CUDA C, which uses a `tex1Dfetch()` command to access the data.

Note that these kernels differ from the simple increment kernels used previously. First, since textures are read-only, these kernels must use different variables on the right- and left-hand sides of the assignment statement. Also, different indices are used to access these two arrays. We write the results in a coalesced fashion in order to highlight the effect of the strided reads.

In host code, the device data to which a texture is bound must be declared with the `target` attribute, as is done on line 32, which is standard practice with Fortran pointers. On line 62, the texture binding occurs using the pointer notation. And on line 79, the texture is unbound using the Fortran 90 `nullify()` command.

Running this code on the K20 we see slightly improved performance at large strides with the texture version, as shown in Figure 3.18. The improved performance at large strides is due to the ability of textures to have more load requests in flight than global memory.

On the K10, K20, and K20X, where the L1 cache is used only for caching local data, the texture cache is especially attractive for read-only data that is reused in the kernel. For example, the following code kernels calculate at each interior point in a 2D mesh the average of the nearest four and eight points using both global and texture memory:

---

[3]To verify use of the texture path, compile the code with `-Mcuda=keepgpu`, which dumps the generated CUDA C code. The texture fetch will be denoted in this code by `__pgi_texfetchf()`.

```
1   module kernels_m
2     real, texture, pointer :: aTex(:,:)
3     integer, parameter :: n = 2048
4     integer, parameter :: nTile = 32
5   contains
6     attributes(global) subroutine average4(b, a)
7       implicit none
8       real :: b(n,n), a(0:n+1,0:n+1)
9       integer :: i, j
10      i = blockDim%x*(blockIdx%x-1)+threadIdx%x
11      j = blockDim%y*(blockIdx%y-1)+threadIdx%y
12      b(i,j) = 0.25*( &
13                       a(i-1,j)+ &
14           a(i,j-1)+              a(i,j+1)+&
15                       a(i+1,j))
16    end subroutine average4
17
18    attributes(global) subroutine average8(b, a)
19      implicit none
20      real :: b(n,n), a(0:n+1,0:n+1)
21      integer :: i, j
22      i = blockDim%x*(blockIdx%x-1)+threadIdx%x
23      j = blockDim%y*(blockIdx%y-1)+threadIdx%y
24      b(i,j) = 0.125*( &
25           a(i-1,j-1)+a(i-1,j)+a(i-1,j+1)+ &
26           a(i,j-1)+              a(i,j+1)+&
27           a(i+1,j-1)+a(i+1,j)+a(i+1,j+1))
28    end subroutine average8
29
30    attributes(global) subroutine average4Tex(b)
31      implicit none
32      real :: b(n,n)
33      integer :: i, j
34      i = blockDim%x*(blockIdx%x-1)+threadIdx%x
35      j = blockDim%y*(blockIdx%y-1)+threadIdx%y
36      b(i,j) = 0.25*( &
37                       aTex(i-1,j)+ &
38           aTex(i,j-1)+              aTex(i,j+1)+ &
39                       aTex(i+1,j))
40    end subroutine average4Tex
41
42    attributes(global) subroutine average8Tex(b)
43      implicit none
44      real :: b(n,n)
45      integer :: i, j
46      i = blockDim%x*(blockIdx%x-1)+threadIdx%x
```

```
47        j = blockDim%y*(blockIdx%y-1)+threadIdx%y
48        b(i,j) = 0.125*( &
49             aTex(i-1,j-1)+aTex(i-1,j)+aTex(i-1,j+1)+ &
50             aTex(i,j-1)+                   aTex(i,j+1)+ &
51             aTex(i+1,j-1)+aTex(i+1,j)+aTex(i+1,j+1))
52     end subroutine average8Tex
53  end module kernels_m
```

The complete code is contained in Appendix D.1. This access pattern is very common in finite difference codes, and in Chapter 6 we will show an example of its use in solving the Laplace equation. Running this code on a Tesla K20, we obtain:

```
Device: Tesla K20

 4-point versions
   Global Bandwidth   (GB/s):      90.71741
     Max Error:          0.000000
   Texture Bandwidth (GB/s):      94.64387
     Max Error:          0.000000

 8-point versions
   Global Bandwidth   (GB/s):      58.48986
     Max Error:          0.000000
   Texture Bandwidth (GB/s):      82.60018
     Max Error:          0.000000
```

where we see a substantial improvement in bandwidth for textures in the eight-point stencil case, where data reuse is large.

3.2.4 Local memory

Local memory is thread-private memory that is stored in device DRAM. It is important to realize that the moniker *local* refers to a variable's scope (meaning thread-private) and not to its physical location, which is off-chip in device DRAM. Depending on the amount of local memory used and whether or not local memory is cached, local memory can become a performance bottleneck.

3.2.4.1 Detecting local memory use (advanced topic)

We examine under what conditions local memory is used for arrays by compiling the following set of kernels:

```
1  module localmem
2    implicit none
3  contains
```

```
 4      attributes(global) subroutine k1(a)
 5        real :: a(*), b(2)
 6        integer :: i
 7        i = blockDim%x*(blockIdx%x-1) + threadIdx%x
 8        b(1) = 1; b(2) = 2
 9        a(i) = b(2)
10      end subroutine k1
11
12      attributes(global) subroutine k2(a,j,k)
13        real :: a(*), b(2)
14        integer :: i,j,k
15        b(j) = 1.0
16        i = blockDim%x*(blockIdx%x-1) + threadIdx%x
17        a(i) = b(k)
18      end subroutine k2
19
20      attributes(global) subroutine k3(a)
21        real :: a(*), b(256)
22        integer :: i
23        b = 1.0
24        i = blockDim%x*(blockIdx%x-1) + threadIdx%x
25        a(i) = b(2)
26      end subroutine k3
27    end module localmem
```

The three kernels declare the variable b, which is thread-private data: Each thread executing the kernel has its own version of this array. In the first kernel, b contains only two elements and is accessed using static indices. In the second kernel, b is also a two-element array but is accessed by variable or dynamic indexes. In the third kernel, b is declared with 256 elements and, due to the array initialization b=1.0, is accessed in a dynamic fashion.

Feedback on the amount of local memory used can be obtained during compilation by using the -Mcuda=ptxinfo compiler option. If we compile the preceding code for devices of compute capability 1.x, we obtain the following output:

```
% pgf90 -c -Mcuda=ptxinfo,cc10 local.cuf
ptxas info    : Compiling entry function 'k1' for 'sm_10'
ptxas info    : Used 2 registers, 8+16 bytes smem

ptxas info    : Compiling entry function 'k2' for 'sm_10'
ptxas info    : Used 3 registers, 8+0 bytes lmem,
                24+16 bytes smem

ptxas info    : Compiling entry function 'k3' for 'sm_10'
```

```
ptxas info     : Used 3 registers, 1024+0 bytes lmem,
                 8+16 bytes smem, 4 bytes cmem[1]
```

In the first kernel, there is no mention of local memory in the compiler feedback; hence the array is placed in register memory. This is the ideal situation. Because register memory is not indexable, the dynamic indexing in the second kernel forces the array to be allocated in local memory, as indicated by `8+0 bytes lmem`, where the `8+0` notation refers to different stages of compilation. The array assignment in the third kernel amounts to dynamic indexing, and as a result we see `1024+0 bytes lmem`, so this array also resides in local memory.

In compiling for compute capability 2.0, we obtain:

```
% pgf90 -c -Mcuda=ptxinfo,cc20 local.cuf
ptxas info     : Compiling entry function 'k1' for 'sm_20'
ptxas info     : Function properties for k1
     0 bytes stack frame, 0 bytes spill stores, 0 bytes spill loads
ptxas info     : Used 6 registers, 40 bytes cmem[0]
ptxas info     : Compiling entry function 'k2' for 'sm_20'
ptxas info     : Function properties for k2
     8 bytes stack frame, 0 bytes spill stores, 0 bytes spill loads
ptxas info     : Used 10 registers, 56 bytes cmem[0]
ptxas info     : Compiling entry function 'k3' for 'sm_20'
ptxas info     : Function properties for k3
  1024 bytes stack frame, 0 bytes spill stores, 0 bytes spill loads
ptxas info     : Used 19 registers, 40 bytes cmem[0]
```

For compute capabilities of 2.0 and higher, local memory use is reported by the `stack frame` parameter, where we observe similar local memory usage in the second and third kernels, reported by `8 bytes stack frame` and `1024 bytes stack frame`.

Another way to determine how much local memory is used, and in addition how often it is used, is by inspecting the generated PTX code. The compiler option `-Mcuda=keepptx` can be used to save the PTX intermediate code to a file with the `.ptx` extension in the local directory. Local memory will be declared with the `.local` mnemonic—for example:

```
.local .align 8 .b8     __local_depot2[1024];
```

and will be accessed using `ld.local` or `st.local`:

```
st.local.u32    [%r16+-4], %r10;
```

Up to this point we have discussed local memory used by thread private arrays declared in device code, but local memory can also be used to hold scalar variables declared in device code when the source code exceeds register limits. Register spill loads and stores are reported along with the stack frame—for example:

```
ptxas info      : Compiling entry function 'jacobian_v1'
                  for 'sm_20'
ptxas info      : Function properties for jacobian_v1
       160 bytes stack frame, 164 bytes spill stores,
                  176 bytes spill loads
ptxas info      : Used 63 registers, 4200+0 bytes smem,
                  100 bytes cmem[0], 176 bytes cmem[2],
                  40 bytes cmem[16]
```

indicates 164 spill stores and 176 spill loads. We should note that spill loads and stores are counted statically and therefore reflect the number of load-and-store instructions in the generated code (weighted by the size of each load/store). It does not take into account how often these instructions are executed. Whether register spill loads and stores occur in a loop or not will not be reflected by these numbers.

To establish the frequency of local memory use, whether from arrays placed in local memory due to size or dynamic indexing or from register spills, we should resort to the profiler. Note that although local memory use is best avoided on devices with a compute capability of 1.x, local memory may not degrade performance on devices of compute capability 2.x and higher, since local memory is cached in the L1 cache. It is possible for local memory to be contained in L1 if there is no contention for resources there. The profiler can assist in this assessment via use of the `l1_local_load_hit` and associated counters. L1 resources can be enhanced using the `cudaFuncSetCacheConfig()` and `cudaDeviceSetCacheConfig()` functions, which we discuss in the section on L1 cache. In addition, we can disable use of the L1 cache by global variables, to allow more resources for local variables using the `-Mcuda=noL1`.

3.2.5 Constant memory

All CUDA devices have 64 KB of constant memory. Constant memory is read-only by kernels but can be read and written by the host. Constant memory is cached on-chip, which can be a big advantage on devices that do not have an L1 cache or do not or are not set up to cache globals, such as when the compiler option `-Mcuda=noL1` is used.

Accesses to different addresses in constant cache by threads in a half-warp (compute capability 1.x) or warp (compute capability 2.0 and higher) are serialized, since there is only one read port. As a result, the constant cache is most effective when all threads in a half-warp or warp access the same address. A good example of its use is for physical constants.

In CUDA Fortran, constant data must be declared in the declaration section of a module, i.e., before the `contains`, and can be used in any code in the module or any host code that includes the module. Our increment example can be written using constant memory:

```
1  module simpleOps_m
2    integer, constant :: b
3  contains
4    attributes(global) subroutine increment(a)
5      implicit none
6      integer, intent(inout) :: a(:)
7      integer :: i
8
9      i = threadIdx%x
10     a(i) = a(i)+b
11
12   end subroutine increment
13 end module simpleOps_m
14
15
16 program incrementTest
17   use cudafor
18   use simpleOps_m
19   implicit none
20   integer, parameter :: n = 256
21   integer :: a(n)
22   integer, device :: a_d(n)
23
24   a = 1
25   b = 3
26
27   a_d = a
28   call increment<<<1,n>>>(a_d)
29   a = a_d
30
31   if (any(a /= 4)) then
32      write(*,*) '**** Program Failed ****'
33   else
34      write(*,*) 'Program Passed'
35   endif
36 end program incrementTest
```

where the parameter b has been declared as a constant variable using the constant attribute on line 2.
The kernel no longer uses b as an argument and it does not need to be declared in the host code. Aside
from these changes (simplifications), the code remains the same as the code used in the introduction.

For variables declared in modules, it is very easy to experiment with constant memory. Simply
switching the variable attribute between constant and device will place the variable in constant
and global memories, respectively.

3.2.5.1 *Detecting constant memory use (advanced topic)*

As with local memory, constant memory use in kernels can be viewed when we compile via the -Mcuda=ptxinfo flag, where constant memory use is denoted by various cmem[] values. We should keep in mind that the compiler makes extensive use of constant memory. The amount of constant memory used by the compiler depends on the compute capability that is targeted. If we compile this code targeting a compute capability of 1.0 and if b is declared with the device variable attribute we obtain:

```
ptxas info    : Compiling entry function 'increment' for 'sm_10'
ptxas info    : Used 4 registers, 16+16 bytes smem, 4 bytes cmem[14]
```

and if b is declared with the constant variable attribute we obtain:

```
ptxas info    : Compiling entry function 'increment' for 'sm_10'
ptxas info    : Used 4 registers, 16+16 bytes smem, 16 bytes cmem[0]
```

When we target a compute capability of 2.0 and declare b with the device variable attribute we obtain:

```
ptxas info    : Compiling entry function 'increment' for 'sm_20'
ptxas info    : Function properties for increment
    0 bytes stack frame, 0 bytes spill stores, 0 bytes spill loads
ptxas info    : Used 8 registers, 48 bytes cmem[0], 8 bytes cmem[14]
```

and when we declare b with the constant variable attribute we obtain:

```
ptxas info    : Compiling entry function 'increment' for 'sm_20'
ptxas info    : Function properties for increment
    0 bytes stack frame, 0 bytes spill stores, 0 bytes spill loads
ptxas info    : Used 6 registers, 48 bytes cmem[0], 16 bytes cmem[2]
```

On devices of compute capability 2.0 and higher, kernel parameters are stored in constant memory, designated by cmem[0], which is one reason we see higher constant memory usage compared to compute capabilities of 1.x (where such parameters are placed in shared memory).

Devices of compute capability 2.0 and higher support the *LoaD Uniform* (LDU) instruction, which loads a variable in global memory through the constant cache if the variable is read-only in the kernel, and if an array, the index is not dependent on the threadIdx variable. This last requirement ensures that each thread in a warp is accessing the same value, resulting in optimal constant cache use. As a result, for our increment kernel the constant cache is used for b whether declared in constant memory with the constant variable attribute or in global memory when declared with the device variable attribute. We can verify this by compiling with the -Mcuda=keepptx option and examining the PTX code. When we use the device variable attribute in the declaration of b, the statement:

```
ldu.global.u32    %r8, [_simpleops_m_16];
```

indicates a uniform load of a 32-bit word in global memory through the constant cache. There are other uniform loads occurring for kernel parameters, but the _simpleops_m_16 parameter here indicates loading of user-defined module data, where simpleops_m is the module name. In contrast, when we use the constant variable attribute when declaring b, the PTX code contains:

```
ld.const.u32      %r10, [_simpleops_m_17];
```

indicating a load from constant memory. In either case, we get the benefit of constant cache. Because of the load uniform instruction, explicit use of the constant cache through the constant variable qualifier has become less important in performance tuning. In fact, relying on the load uniform instruction is beneficial for cases where the amount of data would exceed the 64 KB of constant memory reserved in DRAM. But note that register usage is smaller in this kernel when b is declared as a constant variable. In cases where register pressure is an issue, it may be beneficial to declare some read-only variables in constant memory.

3.3 On-chip memory

In this section we discuss various types of on-chip memory. Most of this section is devoted to shared memory and its use, which we save for last. Before discussing shared memory, we briefly comment on register usage and, for cards of compute capability 2.0 and higher, L1 cache.

3.3.1 L1 cache

On devices of compute capability 2.x and 3.x, there are 64 KB of on-chip memory per multiprocessor that can be configured for use between L1 cache and shared memory. On devices with compute capabilities of 2.x, there are two settings, 48 KB shared memory/16 KB L1 cache and 16 KB shared memory/48 KB L1 cache. On devices of compute capability 3.x, there are three settings, the two just mentioned as well as the 32 KB shared memory/32 KB L1 cache. By default the 48 KB shared memory setting is used.

We can configure the shared memory/L1 cache during runtime from the host, either for all kernels on the device using the runtime function cudaDeviceSetCacheConfig() and on a per-kernel basis using cudaFuncSetCacheConfig(). The former routine takes one argument, one of the preferences cudaFuncCachePreferNone, cudaFuncCachePreferShared corresponding to 48 KB shared memory and 16 KB L1 cache, cudaFuncCachePreferL1 corresponding to 16 KB shared memory and 48 KB L1 cache, and, on devices of compute capability 3.x, cudaFuncCachePreferEqual with 32 KB shared memory and 32 KB L1 cache. The cudaFuncSetCacheConfig configuration routine takes the function name for the first argument and one of the preferences as a second argument. The driver will honor the preferences whenever possible. The case where this is not honored is when more shared memory is required for a single thread block than requested by the cache configuration setting, which is why the default setting prefers a larger shared memory allocation.

The cache configuration requested and used during kernel execution can be verified using the profiler options cacheconfigrequested and cacheconfigexecuted. For example, running the increment code with these options specified in the profile configuration file, we obtain:

```
#  CUDA_PROFILE_LOG_VERSION  2.0
#  CUDA_DEVICE  0  Tesla  K20
#  CUDA_CONTEXT  1
#  TIMESTAMPFACTOR  fffff69c52860010
method , gputime , cputime , occupancy , cacheconfigexecuted ,
         cacheconfigrequested
method =[ memcpyHtoD ] gputime =[ 1.440 ] cputime =[ 9.000 ]
method =[ memcpyHtoD ] gputime =[ 0.928 ] cputime =[ 8.000 ]
method =[ increment ] gputime =[ 5.472 ] cputime =[ 521.000 ]
         occupancy =[0.125 ]
         cacheconfigrequested=[ 0 ]cacheconfigexecuted=[ 0 ]
method =[ memcpyDtoH ] gputime =[ 2.656 ] cputime =[ 60.000 ]
```

where the value of 0 represents cudaFuncCachePreferNone. Values of 1, 2, and 3 correspond to cudaFuncCachePreferShared, cudaFuncCachePreferL1, and cudaFuncCachePreferEqual, respectively.

It is best practice to change the cache configuration whenever possible as a preprocessing step in host code before kernels are launched, because changing the configuration can idle kernel execution.

For the Tesla K10, K20, and K20X, the L1 cache is used only for local memory, since variables that reside in global memory are cached only in L2 cache. For devices of compute capability 2.0, the L1 cache is used by default for variables in global as well as local memory. As we have seen from the coalescing discussion for strided access of global memory, it may be advantageous to turn L1 caching of global loads off in order to avoid 128-byte cache-line loads. This can be done per compilation unit via the flag –Mcuda=noL1.

3.3.2 Registers

Register memory is thread-private memory that is partitioned among all resident threads on a multiprocessor. All variables declared locally in device routines without the shared variable attribute are placed either in register or local memory. Scalar thread-private variables are placed in registers if there is sufficient space, and thread-private arrays may or may not be placed in registers, depending on the size of the array and how it is addressed. See Section 3.2.4 for more information on what gets placed in local memory. Because registers are on-chip and local memory is in device DRAM (although it can be cached on-chip), it is preferable for thread-private variables to reside in registers.

The number of 32-bit registers per multiprocessor has grown steadily with each generation of devices, from 8K registers for devices of compute capability 1.0 to 64K registers on devices of compute capability 3.x. See Appendix A for a description of the register properties for various devices. The number of registers per multiprocessor can be queried at runtime via the `regsPerBlock` field of the `cudaDeviceProp` derived type.

The number of registers used per thread in a kernel is controlled by the compiler. However, the programmer can limit the number of registers used in every kernel in a compilation unit by using the `-Mcuda=maxregcount:N` compiler option. Limiting the number of registers per thread can increase the number of blocks that can concurrently reside on a multiprocessor, which by itself can result in better latency hiding. However, restricting the number of registers can increase register pressure.

Register pressure occurs when there are not enough registers available for a given task. As a result, registers can spill to local memory. Due to the opposing factors of higher occupancy and register spilling, some experimentation is often needed to obtain the optimal configuration. Both register and local memory spill loads and stores for each kernel can be obtained by using the `-Mcuda=ptxinfo` compiler option. For example, compiling the constant memory version of the increment kernel, we obtain:

```
ptxas info    : Compiling entry function 'increment' for 'sm_20'
ptxas info    : Function properties for increment
    0 bytes stack frame, 0 bytes spill stores, 0 bytes spill loads
ptxas info    : Used 8 registers, 48 bytes cmem[0], 8 bytes cmem[14]
```

indicates that 8 registers are used per thread on this device for this kernel. With a maximum of 1536 threads per multiprocessor for a device of compute capability 2.0 at full occupancy, meaning 1536 threads are resident per multiprocessor, a total of 12,288 registers per multiprocessor would be used, far less than the 32K registers available. As a result we expect the kernel to run at full occupancy. Note that register spilling is not necessarily a performance issue if the spilling is contained in the on-chip L1 cache and is not forced to device memory. See the discussion in Section 3.2.4 for more information on this issue. In addition to the limits imposed by available registers on a multiprocessor, there are per-thread limits to the number of registers used: 127 registers per thread for compute capability 1.x, 63 registers per thread for compute capabilities 2.x and 3.0, and 255 registers per thread for compute capability 3.5.

In addition to information regarding register use at compile time, obtained when we compile with `-Mcuda=ptxinfo`, register usage is also provided in the Command Line Profiler with the `regperthread` option specified in the configuration file.

The compiler and hardware thread scheduler will schedule instructions as optimally as possible to avoid register memory bank conflicts. They achieve the best results when the number of threads per block is a multiple of 64. Other than following this rule, an application has no direct control over these bank conflicts.

3.3.3 Shared memory

The last on-chip memory we discuss here is shared memory. Unlike register memory and the on-chip caches, the programmer has complete control over shared memory, deciding how much shared memory to use, which variables use it, and how it is accessed. Shared memory is allocated per thread block, since all threads in the block have access to the same shared memory. Because a thread can access shared memory that was loaded from global memory by another thread within the same thread block, shared memory can be used to facilitate global memory coalescing in cases where it would otherwise not be possible.

Shared memory is declared using the `shared` variable qualifier in device code. Shared memory can be declared in several ways inside a kernel, depending on whether the amount of memory is known at compile time or at runtime. The following code illustrates various methods of using shared memory:

```fortran
1  ! This code shows how dynamically and statically allocated
2  ! shared memory are used to reverse a small array
3
4  module reverse_m
5    implicit none
6    integer, device :: n_d
7  contains
8    attributes(global) subroutine staticReverse(d)
9      real :: d(:)
10     integer :: t, tr
11     real, shared :: s(64)
12
13     t = threadIdx%x
14     tr = size(d)-t+1
15
16     s(t) = d(t)
17     call syncthreads()
18     d(t) = s(tr)
19   end subroutine staticReverse
20
21   attributes(global) subroutine dynamicReverse1(d)
22     real :: d(:)
23     integer :: t, tr
24     real, shared :: s(*)
25
26     t = threadIdx%x
27     tr = size(d)-t+1
28
29     s(t) = d(t)
30     call syncthreads()
31     d(t) = s(tr)
32   end subroutine dynamicReverse1
33
34   attributes(global) subroutine dynamicReverse2(d, nSize)
35     real :: d(nSize)
36     integer, value :: nSize
37     integer :: t, tr
```

```
38        real, shared :: s(nSize)
39
40        t = threadIdx%x
41        tr = nSize-t+1
42
43        s(t) = d(t)
44        call syncthreads()
45        d(t) = s(tr)
46      end subroutine dynamicReverse2
47
48      attributes(global) subroutine dynamicReverse3(d)
49        real :: d(n_d)
50        real, shared :: s(n_d)
51        integer :: t, tr
52
53        t = threadIdx%x
54        tr = n_d-t+1
55
56        s(t) = d(t)
57        call syncthreads()
58        d(t) = s(tr)
59      end subroutine dynamicReverse3
60    end module reverse_m
61
62
63    program sharedExample
64      use cudafor
65      use reverse_m
66
67      implicit none
68
69      integer, parameter :: n = 64
70      real :: a(n), r(n), d(n)
71      real, device :: d_d(n)
72      type(dim3) :: grid, tBlock
73      integer :: i, sizeInBytes
74
75      tBlock = dim3(n,1,1)
76      grid = dim3(1,1,1)
77
78      do i = 1, n
79        a(i) = i
80        r(i) = n-i+1
81      enddo
82
83      sizeInBytes = sizeof(a(1))*tBlock%x
84
```

```
85    ! run version with static shared memory
86    d_d = a
87    call staticReverse<<<grid,tBlock>>>(d_d)
88    d = d_d
89    write(*,*) 'Static case max error:', maxval(abs(r-d))
90
91    ! run dynamic shared memory version 1
92    d_d = a
93    call dynamicReverse1<<<grid,tBlock,sizeInBytes>>>(d_d)
94    d = d_d
95    write(*,*) 'Dynamic case 1 max error:', maxval(abs(r-d))
96
97    ! run dynamic shared memory version 2
98    d_d = a
99    call dynamicReverse2<<<grid,tBlock,sizeInBytes>>>(d_d,n)
100   d = d_d
101   write(*,*) 'Dynamic case 2 max error:', maxval(abs(r-d))
102
103   ! run dynamic shared memory version 3
104   n_d = n   ! n_d declared in reverse_m
105   d_d = a
106   call dynamicReverse3<<<grid,tBlock,sizeInBytes>>>(d_d)
107   d = d_d
108   write(*,*) 'Dynamic case 3 max error:', maxval(abs(r-d))
109
110 end program sharedExample
```

This code reverses the data in a 64-element array using shared memory. All of the kernel codes are very similar; the main difference is how the shared memory arrays are declared and how the kernels are invoked. If the shared memory array size is known at compile time, as in the staticReverse kernel, then the array is declared using that value, whether an integer parameter or literal, as is done on line 11 with s(64). In this kernel, the two indices representing the original and reverse order are calculated on lines 13 and 14, respectively. On line 16, the data are copied from global memory to shared memory. The reversal is done on line 18, where both indices t and tr are used to copy data from shared memory to global memory. Before executing line 18, where each thread accesses data in shared memory that was written by another thread, we need to make sure all threads have completed the loads to shared memory on line 16. This is accomplished by the barrier synchronization on line 17, syncthreads(). This barrier synchronization occurs between all threads in a thread block, meaning that no thread can pass this line until all threads in the same thread block have reached it. The reason shared memory is used in this example is to facilitate global memory coalescing. Optimal global memory coalescing is achieved for both reads and writes because global memory is always accessed through the index t. The reversed index tr is only used to access shared memory, which does not have the access restrictions global memory has for optimal performance. The only performance issue with shared memory is bank conflicts, which are discussed in the next section.

The other three kernels in this example use dynamic shared memory, where the amount of shared memory is not known at compile time and must be specified (in bytes) when the kernel is invoked in the optional third execution configuration parameter, as is done on lines 93, 99, and 106. The first dynamic shared memory kernel, dynamicReverse1, declares the shared memory array on line 24 using an assumed-size array syntax. The size is implicitly determined from the third execution configuration parameter when the kernel is launched. The remainder of the kernel code is identical to the staticReverse kernel.

We can use dynamic shared memory via automatic arrays, as shown in dynamicReverse2 and dynamicReverse3. In these cases, the dimension of the dynamic shared memory array is specified by an integer that is in scope. In dynamicReverse2, the subroutine argument nSize is used on line 38 to declare the shared memory array size, and in dynamicReverse3 the device variable n_d, declared in the beginning of the module, is used on line 50 to declare the shared memory array size. Note that in both these cases the amount of dynamic memory must still be specified in the third parameter of the execution configuration when the kernel is invoked.

Given these options for declaring dynamic shared memory, which one should be used? If we want to use multiple dynamic shared memory arrays, especially if they are of different types, we need to use the automatic arrays as in dynamicReverse2 and dynamicReverse3. If we were to specify multiple dynamic shared memory arrays using assumed size notation as on line 24, how would the compiler know how to distribute the total amount of dynamic shared memory among such arrays? Aside from that factor, the choice is up to the programmer; there is no performance difference between these methods of declaration.

3.3.3.1 Detecting shared memory usage (advanced topic)

Static shared memory usage per thread block is reported during compilation for each kernel when we use the -Mcuda=ptxinfo compiler option. For example, compiling our array reversal code targeting compute capability 3.0, we have:

```
ptxas info    : Compiling entry function 'staticreverse' for 'sm_30'
ptxas info    : Function properties for staticreverse
    0 bytes stack frame, 0 bytes spill stores, 0 bytes spill loads
ptxas info    : Used 10 registers, 256+0 bytes smem, 336 bytes cmem[0]

ptxas info    : Compiling entry function 'dynamicreverse1' for 'sm_30'
ptxas info    : Function properties for dynamicreverse1
    0 bytes stack frame, 0 bytes spill stores, 0 bytes spill loads
ptxas info    : Used 10 registers, 336 bytes cmem[0]

ptxas info    : Compiling entry function 'dynamicreverse2' for 'sm_30'
ptxas info    : Function properties for dynamicreverse2
    0 bytes stack frame, 0 bytes spill stores, 0 bytes spill loads
ptxas info    : Used 6 registers, 332 bytes cmem[0]

ptxas info    : Compiling entry function 'dynamicreverse3' for 'sm_30'
ptxas info    : Function properties for dynamicreverse3
    0 bytes stack frame, 0 bytes spill stores, 0 bytes spill loads
ptxas info    : Used 10 registers, 328 bytes cmem[0]
```

where only the `staticReverse` kernel indicates 256 bytes of shared memory is reserved. Note that on devices of compute capability 1.x, static shared memory is also used by the system. So, targeting devices of compute capability 1.0, we get:

```
ptxas info     : Compiling entry function 'staticreverse' for 'sm_10'
ptxas info     : Used 4 registers, 272+16 bytes smem, 4 bytes cmem[14]

ptxas info     : Compiling entry function 'dynamicreverse1' for 'sm_10'
ptxas info     : Used 4 registers, 16+16 bytes smem, 4 bytes cmem[14]

ptxas info     : Compiling entry function 'dynamicreverse2' for 'sm_10'
ptxas info     : Used 3 registers, 16+16 bytes smem, 4 bytes cmem[14]

ptxas info     : Compiling entry function 'dynamicreverse3' for 'sm_10'
ptxas info     : Used 4 registers, 16+16 bytes smem, 4 bytes cmem[14]
```

where we observe shared memory use for each kernel.

The Command Line Profiler can report both static and dynamic shared memory use when the options `stasmemperblock` and `dynsmemperblock` are placed in the configuration file. Profiling the array reversal code in this manner, we get:

```
# CUDA_PROFILE_LOG_VERSION 2.0
# CUDA_DEVICE 0 Tesla K20
# CUDA_CONTEXT 1
# TIMESTAMPFACTOR fffff69de87d2020
method,gputime,cputime,dynsmemperblock,stasmemperblock,occupancy
method=[ memcpyHtoD ] gputime=[ 1.344 ] cputime=[ 9.000 ]
method=[ memcpyHtoD ] gputime=[ 0.928 ] cputime=[ 8.000 ]
method=[ staticreverse ] gputime=[ 5.568 ] cputime=[ 9.000 ]
        dynsmemperblock=[ 0 ] stasmemperblock=[ 256 ]
        occupancy=[ 0.031 ]
method=[ memcpyDtoH ] gputime=[ 2.560 ] cputime=[ 57.000 ]
method=[ memcpyHtoD ] gputime=[ 0.928 ] cputime=[ 8.000 ]
method=[ memcpyHtoD ] gputime=[ 0.896 ] cputime=[ 7.000 ]
method=[ dynamicreverse1 ] gputime=[ 5.088 ] cputime=[ 9.000 ]
        dynsmemperblock=[ 256 ] stasmemperblock=[ 0 ]
        occupancy=[ 0.031 ]
method=[ memcpyDtoH ] gputime=[ 2.592 ] cputime=[ 57.000 ]
method=[ memcpyHtoD ] gputime=[ 0.928 ] cputime=[ 8.000 ]
method=[ dynamicreverse2 ] gputime=[ 3.904 ] cputime=[ 10.000 ]
        dynsmemperblock=[ 256 ] stasmemperblock=[ 0 ]
        occupancy=[ 0.031 ]
method=[ memcpyDtoH ] gputime=[ 2.144 ] cputime=[ 59.000 ]
method=[ memcpyHtoD ] gputime=[ 0.896 ] cputime=[ 8.000 ]
method=[ memcpyHtoD ] gputime=[ 0.928 ] cputime=[ 7.000 ]
method=[ dynamicreverse3 ] gputime=[ 4.544 ] cputime=[ 8.000 ]
        dynsmemperblock=[ 256 ] stasmemperblock=[ 0 ]
```

```
        occupancy=[  0.031  ]
method=[  memcpyDtoH  ] gputime=[  2.112  ] cputime=[  55.000  ]
```

3.3.3.2 *Shared memory bank conflicts*

To achieve high memory bandwidth for concurrent accesses, shared memory is divided into equally sized memory modules (banks) that can be accessed simultaneously. Therefore, any memory load or store of n addresses that spans n distinct memory banks can be serviced simultaneously, yielding an effective bandwidth that is n times as high as the bandwidth of a single bank.

However, if multiple addresses of a memory request map to the same memory bank, the accesses are serialized. The hardware splits a memory request that has bank conflicts into as many separate conflict-free requests as necessary, decreasing the effective bandwidth by a factor equal to the number of separate memory requests. The one exception here is when all threads in a half-warp or warp address the same shared memory location, resulting in a broadcast. Devices of compute capability 2.0 and higher have the additional ability to multicast shared memory accesses, meaning that multiple accesses to the same location by any number of threads within a warp are served simultaneously.

To minimize bank conflicts, it is important to understand how memory addresses map to memory banks and how to optimally schedule memory requests. Shared memory banks are organized such that successive 32-bit words are assigned to successive banks and each bank has a bandwidth of 32 bits per clock cycle. The bandwidth of shared memory is 32 bits per bank per clock cycle.

For devices of compute capability 1.x, the warp size is 32 threads and the number of banks is 16. A shared memory request for a warp is split into one request for the first half of the warp and one request for the second half of the warp. Note that no bank conflict occurs if only one memory location per bank is accessed by a half-warp of threads.

For devices of compute capability 2.x, the warp size is 32 threads and the number of banks is also 32. A shared memory request for a warp is not split as with devices of compute capability 1.x, meaning that bank conflicts can occur between threads in the first half of a warp and threads in the second half of the same warp.

On devices of compute capability 3.x, we have the ability to control the size of the shared memory banks. By default the shared memory bank size is 32 bits, but it can be set to 64 bits using the `cudaDeviceSetSharedMemConfig()` function with the argument `cudaSharedMemBankSizeEightByte`. Doing so can help avoid shared memory bank conflicts when we deal with double-precision data. Other arguments to this command are `cudaSharedMemBankSizeDefault` and `cudaSharedMemBankSizeFourByte`. The function `cudaDeviceGetSharedMemConfig(config)` returns in `config` the current size of the shared memory banks.

3.4 Memory optimization example: matrix transpose

In this section we present an example that illustrates many of the memory optimization techniques discussed in this chapter, as well as the performance measurements discussed in the previous chapter. The code we want to optimize is a transpose of a matrix of single-precision values that operates out of place, i.e., the input and output matrices address separate memory locations. For simplicity in presentation, we consider only square matrices for which the dimensions are integral multiples of 32 on a side.

The host code for all the transpose cases is given in Appendix D.2. The host code performs typical tasks: allocation and data transfers between host and device, launches and timings of several kernels as well as validation of their results, and deallocation of host and device memory.

In addition to performing several different matrix transposes, we run a kernel that performs a matrix copy. The performance of the matrix copy serves as an indication of what we would like the matrix transpose to achieve. For both matrix copy and transpose, the relevant performance metric is the effective bandwidth, calculated in GB/s as twice the size of the matrix (in GB), once for reading the matrix and once for storing, divided by time of execution (in seconds). We call each routine NUM_REP times and normalize the effective bandwidth accordingly.

All kernels in this study launch thread blocks of dimension 32×8, each of which transposes (or copies) a tile of size 32×32. As such, the parameters TILE_DIM and BLOCK_ROWS are set to 32 and 8, respectively. Using a thread block with fewer threads than elements in a tile is advantageous for the matrix transpose in that each thread transposes several matrix elements, four in our case, and much of the cost of calculating the indices is amortized over these elements.

One last preliminary issue we should mention is how the thread indices are mapped to array elements. We use an (x, y) coordinate system for which the origin is in the upper-left corner of the array when we interpret the array elements. This coordinate system maps seamlessly to the x and y components of our predefined variables threadIdx, blockIdx, and blockDim. Because the first index in multidimensional variables varies the quickest in Fortran, as does the x component of the predefined variables, contiguous elements are along the x-direction in this interpretation. Another choice would have been to interpret the x and y components of the predefined variables as the row and column of the matrix, which effectively transposes the problem. There is no performance advantage to either approach; the same performance bottlenecks appear, but switch from reading to writing global data.

With these above conventions in mind, we look at our first kernel, the matrix copy:

```
29    attributes(global) subroutine copySharedMem(odata, idata)
30
31       real, intent(out) :: odata(nx,ny)
32       real, intent(in) :: idata(nx,ny)
33
34       real, shared :: tile(TILE_DIM, TILE_DIM)
35       integer :: x, y, j
36
37       x = (blockIdx%x-1) * TILE_DIM + threadIdx%x
38       y = (blockIdx%y-1) * TILE_DIM + threadIdx%y
39
40       do j = 0, TILE_DIM-1, BLOCK_ROWS
41          tile(threadIdx%x, threadIdx%y+j) = idata(x,y+j)
42       end do
43
44       call syncthreads()
```

```
45
46        do j = 0, TILE_DIM-1, BLOCK_ROWS
47          odata(x,y+j) = tile(threadIdx%x, threadIdx%y+j)
48        end do
49      end subroutine copySharedMem
```

This copy kernel uses shared memory. Use of shared memory for a copy isn't necessary, but we use it here because it mimics the data access pattern used in the optimal transpose kernel. Little, if any, performance is lost due to shared memory use in the copy.

Data is copied from global to the shared memory tile on line 41 and then from the shared memory tile back to global memory on line 47. These two statements occur in loops, which are required since the number of threads in a block is smaller by a factor of TILE_DIM/BLOCK_ROWS than the number of elements in a tile. Each thread is responsible for copying four elements of the matrix. Note also that TILE_DIM needs to be used in the calculation of the matrix index y in line 38 rather than BLOCK_ROWS or blockIdx%y, whereas for the calculation of x on line 37, TILE_DIM could be replaced by blockDim%x. The looping is done in the second dimension rather than the first because each warp of threads loads contiguous elements of idata from global memory on line 41 and stores contiguous elements of odata to global memory on line 47. Therefore, both reads from idata and writes to odata are coalesced.

Note that the synchthreads() call in line 44 is technically not needed, since each element in the shared memory tile is read and written by the same thread. But the synchthreads() call is included here to mimic the behavior of its use in the transpose case. The performance of the shared memory copy kernel for different devices is listed here:

	Effective Bandwidth (GB/s)				
Routine	Tesla C870	Tesla C1060	Tesla C2050	Tesla K10	Tesla K20
copySharedMem	61.2	71.3	101.4	118.8	149.6

We should mention that all devices that support ECC have it enabled in this section.

We start our discussion of the transpose with a very simple kernel:

```
56      attributes(global) &
57          subroutine transposeNaive(odata, idata)
58
59        real, intent(out) :: odata(ny,nx)
60        real, intent(in) :: idata(nx,ny)
61
62        integer :: x, y, j
63
64        x = (blockIdx%x-1) * TILE_DIM + threadIdx%x
65        y = (blockIdx%y-1) * TILE_DIM + threadIdx%y
```

```
66
67       do j = 0, TILE_DIM-1, BLOCK_ROWS
68          odata(y+j,x) = idata(x,y+j)
69       end do
70     end subroutine transposeNaive
```

In `transposeNaive`, the reads from `idata` are coalesced, but the writes to `odata` by contiguous threads now have a stride of 1024 elements or 4096 bytes. This puts us well into the asymptote of Figure 3.14, and we expect the performance of this kernel to suffer accordingly. The observed performance of `transposeNaive` bears this out:

Routine	Effective Bandwidth (GB/s)				
	Tesla C870	Tesla C1060	Tesla C2050	Tesla K10	Tesla K20
copySharedMem	61.2	71.3	101.4	118.8	149.6
transposeNaive	3.9	3.2	18.5	6.5	54.6

The `transposeNaive` kernels performs from about 3 to 20 times worse than the `copySharedMem` kernel, depending on the architecture.

The remedy for the poor transpose performance is to avoid the large strides by using shared memory. A depiction of how shared memory is used in the transpose is presented in Figure 3.19. Using a tile of shared memory in this fashion is similar to the cache-blocking schemes used to optimize CPU code (see Garg and Sharapov, 2002 or Dowd and Severance, 1998). The kernel code corresponding to Figure 3.19 is:

```
79    attributes(global) &
80        subroutine transposeCoalesced(odata, idata)
81
82      real, intent(out) :: odata(ny,nx)
83      real, intent(in)  :: idata(nx,ny)
84      real, shared :: tile(TILE_DIM, TILE_DIM)
85      integer :: x, y, j
86
87      x = (blockIdx%x-1) * TILE_DIM + threadIdx%x
88      y = (blockIdx%y-1) * TILE_DIM + threadIdx%y
89
90      do j = 0, TILE_DIM-1, BLOCK_ROWS
91         tile(threadIdx%x, threadIdx%y+j) = idata(x,y+j)
92      end do
93
94      call syncthreads()
95
96      x = (blockIdx%y-1) * TILE_DIM + threadIdx%x
```

```
97         y = (blockIdx%x-1) * TILE_DIM + threadIdx%y
98
99         do j = 0, TILE_DIM-1, BLOCK_ROWS
100            odata(x,y+j) = tile(threadIdx%y+j, threadIdx%x)
101         end do
102      end subroutine transposeCoalesced
```

On line 91, a warp of threads reads contiguous data from `idata` into rows of the shared memory `tile`. After recalculating the array indices on line 96 and 97, a column on the shared memory `tile` is written to contiguous addresses in `odata`. Because a thread will write different data to `odata` than it has read from `idata`, the block-wise barrier synchronization `syncthreads()` on line 94 is required. Adding to our effective bandwidth table, we have:

	Effective Bandwidth (GB/s)				
Routine	Tesla C870	Tesla C1060	Tesla C2050	Tesla K10	Tesla K20
copySharedMem	61.2	71.3	101.4	118.8	149.6
transposeNaive	3.9	3.2	18.5	6.5	54.6
transposeCoalesced	36.6	23.6	51.6	65.8	90.4

The `transposeCoalesced` results are an improvement from the `transposeNaive` case, but they are still far from the performance of the `copySharedMem` kernel.

Although using shared memory has improved the transpose performance, the use of shared memory in the `transposeCoalesced` kernel is not optimal. For a shared memory tile of 32×32 elements, all elements in a column of data are from the same shared memory bank, resulting in a worst-case scenario

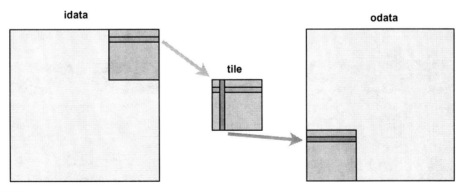

FIGURE 3.19

Depiction of how a shared memory tile is used to achieve full coalescing of global memory reads and writes. A warp of threads reads a partial row from `idata` and writes it to a row of the shared memory `tile`. The same warp of threads reads a column of the shared memory `tile` and writes it to a partial row of `odata`.

for memory bank conflicts: reading a column (C2050, K20) or half-column (C870, C1060) of data results in a 32-way or 16-way bank conflict, respectively. Luckily, the solution for this is simply to pad the first index of the shared memory array, as in line 114 of the `transposeNoBankConflict` kernel:

```
109    attributes(global) &
110        subroutine transposeNoBankConflicts(odata, idata)
111
112      real, intent(out) :: odata(ny,nx)
113      real, intent(in) :: idata(nx,ny)
114      real, shared :: tile(TILE_DIM+1, TILE_DIM)
115      integer :: x, y, j
116
117      x = (blockIdx%x-1) * TILE_DIM + threadIdx%x
118      y = (blockIdx%y-1) * TILE_DIM + threadIdx%y
119
120      do j = 0, TILE_DIM-1, BLOCK_ROWS
121         tile(threadIdx%x, threadIdx%y+j) = idata(x,y+j)
122      end do
123
124      call syncthreads()
125
126      x = (blockIdx%y-1) * TILE_DIM + threadIdx%x
127      y = (blockIdx%x-1) * TILE_DIM + threadIdx%y
128
129      do j = 0, TILE_DIM-1, BLOCK_ROWS
130         odata(x,y+j) = tile(threadIdx%y+j, threadIdx%x)
131      end do
132    end subroutine transposeNoBankConflicts
```

Removing the bank conflicts solves most of our performance issues:

	Effective Bandwidth (GB/s)				
Routine	Tesla C870	Tesla C1060	Tesla C2050	Tesla K10	Tesla K20
copySharedMem	61.2	71.3	101.4	118.8	149.6
transposeNaive	3.9	3.2	18.5	6.5	54.6
transposeCoalesced	36.6	23.6	51.6	65.8	90.4
transposeNoBankConflict	45.6	23.6	96.1	94.0	137.6

with the exception that the Tesla C1060 transpose kernel still performs well below the copy kernel. This gap in performance is due to partition camping and is related to the size of the matrix. A similar performance degradation can occur for the Tesla C870 for different matrix sizes.

3.4.1 Partition camping *(advanced topic)*

The following discussion of partition camping generally applies to devices with a compute capability less than 2.0, e.g., C870 and C1060. Partition camping can occur in devices of compute capability 2.0 and higher, but it is far less common and the effects are less severe.

Just as shared memory is divided into 16 banks of 32-bit width, global memory is divided into either six partitions (Tesla C870) or eight partitions (Tesla C1060) of 256-byte width. To use shared memory effectively on these architectures, threads within a half-warp should access different banks so that these accesses can occur simultaneously. If threads within a half-warp access shared memory though only a few banks, bank conflicts occur. To use global memory effectively, concurrent accesses to global memory by all active warps should be divided evenly among partitions. The term *partition camping* is used to describe the case when global memory accesses are directed through a subset of partitions, causing requests to queue up at some partitions while others go unused, and is analogous to shared memory bank conflicts.

Coalescing concerns global memory accesses within a half-warp, whereas partition camping concerns global memory accesses among active half-warps. Since partition camping concerns the way active thread blocks distributed among multiprocessors behave, the issue of how thread blocks are scheduled on multiprocessors is important. When a kernel is launched on devices of compute capability 1.x, the order in which blocks are assigned to multiprocessors is the natural column-major order that they occur in the blockIdx variable. Initially this assignment occurs in a round-robin fashion. Once maximum occupancy is reached, additional blocks are assigned to multiprocessors as needed; how quickly and the order in which blocks complete kernels cannot be determined.

If we return to our matrix transpose and look at how our blocks in our 1024 × 1024 matrices map to partitions on the Tesla C1060, as depicted in Figure 3.20, we immediately see that partition camping is a problem. On a Tesla C1060, with eight partitions of 256-byte width, all data in strides of 2048 bytes (or 512 single precision elements) map to the same partition. Any single-precision matrix with an integral multiple of 512 columns, such as our matrices, will contain columns whose elements map to only one partition. With tiles of 32 × 32 elements (or 128 × 128 bytes), all the data within the first two columns of tiles map to the same partition, and likewise for other pairs of tile columns (assuming the matrix is aligned to a partition segment).

Concurrent blocks will be accessing tiles row-wise in idata, which will be roughly equally distributed among partitions. However, these blocks will access tiles column-wise in odata, which will typically access global memory through one or two partitions.

To avoid partition camping, we can pad the matrix just as we did with the shared memory tile. However, padding by enough columns to eliminate partition camping can be very expensive memory-wise. Another option that is effective is basically to reinterpret how the components of blockIdx relate to the matrix.

3.4.1.1 *Diagonal reordering*

Although the programmer does not have direct control of the order in which blocks are scheduled (which is determined by the value of the automatic kernel variable blockIdx), the programmer does have flexibility in how to interpret the components of blockIdx. Given how the components blockIdx are named, i.e., x and y, we generally assume that these components refer to a Cartesian coordinate system. This does not need to be the case, however, and we can choose otherwise. Doing so essentially

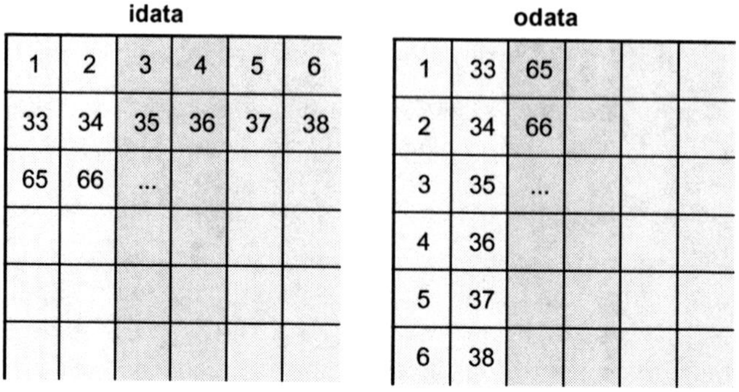

idata

odata

1	2	3	4	5	6
33	34	35	36	37	38
65	66	...			

1	33	65			
2	34	66			
3	35	...			
4	36				
5	37				
6	38				

FIGURE 3.20

Diagram of how thread blocks (numbers) are assigned to partitions (colors) for the upper-left corner of both idata and odata. For a 1024 × 1024 element matrix of single-precision data, all the elements in a column belong to the same partition on a C1060. Reading values from idata is distributed evenly among active thread blocks, but groups of 32 thread blocks will write to odata through the same partition.

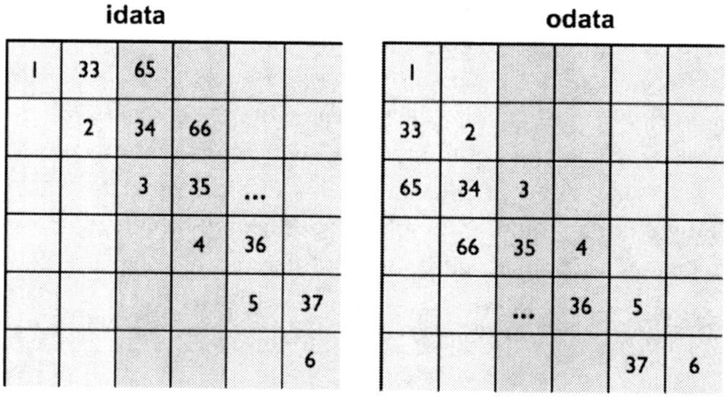

idata

odata

I	33	65			
	2	34	66		
		3	35	...	
			4	36	
				5	37
					6

I					
33	2				
65	34	3			
	66	35	4		
		...	36	5	
				37	6

FIGURE 3.21

Diagram of how thread blocks (numbers) are assigned to partitions (colors) for the upper-left corner of both idata and odata using a diagonal interpretation of the blockIdx components. Here both reads and writes are evenly distributed across partitions.

amounts to rescheduling the blocks in software, which is what we are after here: how to reschedule the blocks so that operations are evenly distributed across partitions for both input and output matrices.

One way to avoid partition camping in both reading from idata and writing to odata is to use a diagonal interpretation of the components of blockIdx: The y component represents different diagonal slices of tiles through the matrix, and the x component indicates the distance along each diagonal. Doing so results in the mapping of blocks, as depicted in Figure 3.21. The kernel that performs this transformation is:

```
142    attributes(global) &
143        subroutine transposeDiagonal(odata, idata)
144
145      real, intent(out) :: odata(ny,nx)
146      real, intent(in) :: idata(nx,ny)
147      real, shared :: tile(TILE_DIM+1, TILE_DIM)
148      integer :: x, y, j
149      integer :: blockIdx_x, blockIdx_y
150
151      if (nx==ny) then
152          blockIdx_y = blockIdx%x
153          blockIdx_x = &
154              mod(blockIdx%x+blockIdx%y-2,gridDim%x)+1
155      else
156          x = blockIdx%x + gridDim%x*(blockIdx%y-1)
157          blockIdx_y = mod(x-1,gridDim%y)+1
158          blockIdx_x = &
159              mod((x-1)/gridDim%y+blockIdx_y-1,gridDim%x)+1
160      endif
161
162      x = (blockIdx_x-1) * TILE_DIM + threadIdx%x
163      y = (blockIdx_y-1) * TILE_DIM + threadIdx%y
164
165      do j = 0, TILE_DIM-1, BLOCK_ROWS
166          tile(threadIdx%x, threadIdx%y+j) = idata(x,y+j)
167      end do
168
169      call syncthreads()
170
171      x = (blockIdx_y-1) * TILE_DIM + threadIdx%x
172      y = (blockIdx_x-1) * TILE_DIM + threadIdx%y
173
174      do j = 0, TILE_DIM-1, BLOCK_ROWS
175          odata(x,y+j) = tile(threadIdx%y+j, threadIdx%x)
176      end do
177    end subroutine transposeDiagonal
```

On lines 152 and 153, a mapping from Cartesian to diagonal coordinates is specified for our case of square matrices. After this mapping is complete, the code is the same as transposeNoBankConflicts with the exception that all occurrences of blockIdx.x are replaced with blockIdx_x and likewise for the y component. We can now add a final row to our table of results:

The transposeDiagonal kernel has brought the Tesla C1060 transpose performance close to that of the copySharedMem kernel. Note that reordering did not help performance on most of the other devices. The added computation required for the indices actually hurt performance in most cases. The Tesla K10 does show slight improvement with diagonal reordering, bringing the performance from

Routine	Effective Bandwidth (GB/s)				
	Tesla C870	Tesla C1060	Tesla C2050	Tesla K10	Tesla K20
copySharedMem	61.2	71.3	101.4	118.8	149.6
transposeNaive	3.9	3.2	18.5	6.5	54.6
transposeCoalesced	36.6	23.6	51.6	65.8	90.4
transposeNoBankConflict	45.6	23.6	96.1	94.0	137.6
transposeDiagonal	44.2	64.3	90.3	110.4	128.7

roughly 80% to 93% of the copySharedMem performance. Diagonal reordering is much more critical for the Tesla C1060, bringing performance from 33% to 90% of the copySharedMem performance.

There are a few points to remember about partition camping. On cards of compute capability less than 2.0, partition camping is problem-size-dependent. If our matrices were multiples of 386 32-bit elements per side, we would see partition camping on the C870 and not on the C1060. Partition camping is far less common and generally less severe on devices of compute capability of 2.0 and higher because the assignment of blocks to multiprocessors is hashed.

3.5   Execution configuration

Even if a kernel has been optimized so that all global memory accesses are perfectly coalesced, we still have to deal with the issue that such memory accesses have a latency of several hundred cycles. To get good overall performance, we have to ensure that there is enough parallelism on a multiprocessor so that stalls for memory accesses are hidden as much as possible. There are two ways to achieve this parallelism: through the number of concurrent threads on a multiprocessor and through the number of independent operations issued per thread. The first of these we call *thread-level parallelism* and the second is *instruction-level parallelism*.

3.5.1   Thread-level parallelism

Thread-level parallelism can be controlled to some degree by the execution configuration specified in the host code used to launch kernels. In the execution configuration, we specify the number of threads per block and the number of blocks in the kernel launch. The number of thread blocks that can reside on a multiprocessor for a given kernel is then an important consideration and can be limited by a variety of factors, some of which are given in Figure 3.22 for different generations of Tesla cards. For a more detailed table of such properties, see Appendix A. There is a limit on the number of thread blocks per multiprocessor, regardless of the thread block size or resource use. This limit is 8 thread blocks on devices with a compute capabilities of 1.x and 2.x and 16 thread blocks for devices of compute capability 3.x. There are also limits on the number of threads per block, threads per multiprocessor, register size, and available shared memory, which can limit the number of concurrent threads.

The metric *occupancy* is used to help assess the thread-level parallelism of a kernel on a multiprocessor. *Occupancy* is the ratio of the number of active warps per multiprocessor to the maximum number

	Tesla C870	Tesla C1060	Tesla C2050	Tesla K20
Computer capability	1.0	1.3	2.0	3.5
Max threads/thread block	512	512	1024	1024
Max thread blocks/multiprocessor	8	8	8	16
Max warps/multiprocessor	24	32	48	64
Threads/warp	32	32	32	32
Max threads/multiprocessor	768	1024	1536	2048
32-bit registers/multiprocessor	8K	16K	32K	64K

FIGURE 3.22

Thread block and multiprocessor limits for various CUDA architectures.

of possible active warps. Warps are used in the definition since they are the unit of threads that are executed simultaneously, but we can think of this metric in terms of threads. A higher occupancy does not necessarily lead to higher performance, since we can express a fair amount of instruction-level parallelism in kernel code. But if we rely on thread-level parallelism to hide latencies, then the occupancy should not be very small. Occupancy can be determined for all kernel launches by using the Command Line Profiler, where it is a default option.

To illustrate how choosing various execution configurations can affect performance, we can use a simple copy code listed in Appendix D.3. The kernels in this code are relatively simple, for example the first kernel we investigate is:

```
12    attributes(global) subroutine copy(odata, idata)
13      use precision_m
14      implicit none
15      real(fp_kind) :: odata(*), idata(*), tmp
16      integer :: i
17
18      i = (blockIdx%x-1)*blockDim%x + threadIdx%x
19      tmp = idata(i)
20      odata(i) = tmp
21    end subroutine copy
```

In using double precision data and targeting a Tesla K20 with the -Mcuda=cc35 compiler option, we observe the following results:

In this table, the thread block size and effective bandwidth are obtained from the output of the code, and the occupancy is obtained from the file generated by the Command Line Profiler. We use thread block sizes that are a multiple of a warp of threads, as we should always do. If we were to launch a kernel with 33 threads per block, two complete warps per block would be processed, where the results from all but one thread in the second warp are masked out.

Since the Tesla K20 has maxima of 2048 threads and 16 thread blocks per multiprocessor, kernel launches with thread block sizes of 32 and 64 cannot achieve full occupancy. The effective bandwidth

Thread Block	Occupancy	Effective Bandwidth (GB/s)
32	0.25	96
64	0.5	125
128	1.0	136
256	1.0	137
512	1.0	137
1024	1.0	133

of launches with 32 threads per block size suffer as a result, but even with half occupancy the bandwidth of the kernel execution with 64 threads per thread block comes close to the maximum observed; full occupancy is not needed to achieve good performance.

In general, more threads per block do not indicate higher occupancy. If we look at the results on the Tesla C2050, also with double-precision data, we have:

Thread Block	Occupancy	Effective Bandwidth (GB/s)
32	0.167	55
64	0.333	82
128	0.667	103
256	1.0	102
512	1.0	103
1024	0.667	98

The Tesla C2050 has maxima of 1536 threads and 8 thread blocks per multiprocessor, so, with a thread block of 1024 threads, only a single thread block can reside on a multiprocessor at one time, resulting in two-thirds occupancy. Once again, higher occupancy does not imply better performance, since the thread block of 128 threads results in two-thirds occupancy but achieves the highest bandwidth of all the runs.

3.5.1.1 *Shared memory*

Shared memory can be helpful in several situations, such as helping to coalesce or eliminate redundant access to global memory. However, it also can act as a constraint on occupancy. Our example code does not use shared memory in the kernel; however, we can determine the sensitivity of performance to occupancy by changing the amount of dynamically allocated shared memory, as specified in the third parameter of the execution configuration. By simply increasing this parameter (without modifying the kernel), it is possible to effectively reduce the occupancy of the kernel and measure its effect on performance. For example, if we launch the same copy kernel using:

```
call copy<<<grid, threadBlock, 0.9*smBytes >>>(b_d, a_d)
```

where `smBytes` is the size of shared memory per multiprocessor in bytes, then we force there to be only one concurrent thread block per multiprocessor. Doing so yields the following results on the Tesla K20 as we add to the previous table:

Thread Block	No Shared Memory		Shared Memory	
	Occupancy	Bandwidth (GB/s)	Occupancy	Bandwidth (GB/s)
32	0.25	96	0.016	8
64	0.5	125	0.031	15
128	1.0	136	0.063	29
256	1.0	137	0.125	53
512	1.0	137	0.25	91
1024	1.0	133	0.5	123

The results under the *No Shared Memory* columns are those from the previous table of K20 results. The occupancy under the *Shared Memory* column indicates that only one thread block resides at any one time on a multiprocessor when the shared memory is used, and the bandwidth numbers indicate that performance degrades as we would expect. This exercise prompts the question: What can be done in more complicated kernels where either register or shared memory use limits the occupancy? Do we have to put up with poor performance in such cases? The answer is no if we use instruction-level parallelism.

3.5.2 Instruction-level parallelism

We have already seen an example of instruction-level parallelism in this book. In the transpose example of Section 3.4, a shared-memory tile of 32×32 was used in most of the kernels. But because the maximum number of threads per block is 512 on certain devices, it is not possible to launch a kernel with 32×32 threads per block. Instead, we have to use a thread block with fewer threads and have each thread process multiple elements. In the transpose case, blocks of 32×8 threads were launched, with each thread processing four elements.

For the example in this section, we can modify the `copy` kernel to take advantage of instruction-level parallelism as follows:

```
27    attributes(global) subroutine copy_ILP(odata, idata)
28       use precision_m
29       implicit none
30       real(fp_kind) :: odata(*), idata(*), tmp(ILP)
31       integer :: i,j
32
33       i = (blockIdx%x-1)*blockDim%x*ILP + threadIdx%x
34
35       do j = 1, ILP
36          tmp(j) = idata(i+(j-1)*blockDim%x)
```

```
37        enddo
38
39        do j = 1, ILP
40            odata(i+(j-1)*blockDim%x) = tmp(j)
41        enddo
42    end subroutine copy_ILP
```

where the parameter ILP is set to 4. In this kernel, each thread copies ILP array elements, so a thread block of blockDim%x threads will copy ILP*blockDim%x elements. In addition to having each thread copy multiple elements, we group or batch all the loads together in the loop from lines 35–37 through use of a thread-private array tmp(ILP), which resides in register memory. The reason we do this *load batching* is because in CUDA a load command will not block further independent execution, but the first use of the data requested by a load will block until that load completes. The term *load-use separation* is used to describe the amount of time or the number of instructions between when a load is issued and when the requested data is used. The larger the load-use separation, the better in terms of hiding load latencies. By *load batching*, as is done in the loop from lines 35–37, we can have ILP load requests in flight per thread. We have increased the load-use separation of the first load by the other ILP-1 loads issued in the loop.

If we once again use dynamically allocated shared memory to restrict the occupancy to a single block per multiprocessor, we can append the results for ILP=4 to our table:

| | No Shared Memory | | | Shared Memory | | |
| | | | | | No ILP | ILP=4 |
Thread Block	Occupancy	Bandwidth		Occupancy	Bandwidth	Bandwidth
32	0.25	96		0.016	8	26
64	0.5	125		0.031	15	50
128	1.0	136		0.063	29	90
256	1.0	137		0.125	53	125
512	1.0	137		0.25	91	140
1024	1.0	133		0.5	123	139

Here we see greatly improved performance for low levels of occupancy, approximately a factor of three better than the kernel that does not use instruction-level parallelism. The use of instruction-level parallelism essentially increases the effective occupancy by a factor equal to ILP. For example, a block of 128 threads (occupancy 1/16) obtains a bandwidth of 90 GB/s when ILP=4, similar to the 91 GB/s obtained with a block of 512 threads (1/4 occupancy) when no instruction-level parallelism is used and similar to the 96 GB/s obtained when a block of 32 threads with no shared memory is used (also 1/4 occupancy).

Table 3.2 Native arithmetic throughput given in operations per clock cycle per multiprocessor. For a warp of 32 threads, one instruction corresponds to 32 operations, so the instruction throughput is 1/32 the operation throughput. The entry *MI* implies the operation gets translated to multiple instructions.

	Compute Capability				
Operations	1.0	1.3	2.0	3.0	3.5
32-bit iand(), ieor(), ior()	8	8	32	160	160
32-bit ishft()	8	8	16	32	64
32-bit integer add, compare	10	10	32	160	160
32-bit integer multiply, multiply-add	MI	MI	16	32	32
32-bit floating-point add, multiply, multiply-add	8	8	32	192	192
32-bit floating-point reciprocal, reciprocal square root	2	2	4	32	32
64-bit floating-point add, multiply, multiply-add	–	1	16*	8	64

*Throughput is lower for Geforce GPUs.

The approach of using a single thread to process multiple elements of a shared memory array can be beneficial even if occupancy is not an issue. This is because some operations common to each element can be performed by the thread once, amortizing the cost over the number of shared memory elements processed by the thread. We observe that at a quarter and half occupancy, the results for ILP=4 surpass those at full occupancy when shared memory isn't used to restrict the number of thread blocks per multiprocessor.

One drawback of instruction-level parallelism is that the thread-private arrays like tmp(ILP) consume registers and consequently can further add to register pressure. As a result, how much instruction-level parallelism to use is a balancing act, and some experimentation is generally needed to get optimal results.

3.6 Instruction optimization

Up to this point, we have addressed optimization from the perspective of data movement, both between the host and device and within the device. We have also spoken about ensuring that there is enough parallelism exposed to keep the device busy, either through thread-level parallelism (execution configuration and occupancy) or though instruction-level parallelism. When a code is not memory bound and there is sufficient parallelism exposed on the device, then we need to address the instruction throughput of kernels in order to increase performance.

The arithmetic throughput of various native instructions on devices of different compute capabilities is listed in Table 3.2. (A more complete version of this table can be found in the *CUDA C Programming Guide*.) Aside from type conversions, other instructions map to multiple native instructions, with the exception of certain device intrinsics.

3.6.1 **Device intrinsics**

CUDA Fortran allows access to many of the built-in device functions through the use of the cudadevice module in device code. A full list of the built-in functions available to CUDA Fortran is included in the *CUDA Fortran Programming and Reference Guide*. Here we briefly discuss as few classes of these functions.

3.6.1.1 *Directed rounding*

Directed rounding in CUDA is available through additional instructions rather than by setting a rounding mode. The suffixes _ru, _rd, _rn, and _rz imply rounding upward, downward, to the nearest even, and to zero. For example, 32-bit and 64-bit floating-point addition functions are available in various rounding modes using __fadd_[rn,rz,ru,rd] and __dadd_[rn,rz,ru,rd].

3.6.1.2 *C intrinsics*

There are some C intrinsics available through the cudadevice module that are not available in Fortran. In particular, sincos(x, s, c) calculates both sine and cosine of the argument x. This function nearly doubles the throughput relative to calling sine and cosine separately, without any loss of precision.

3.6.1.3 *Fast math intrinsics*

CUDA has a set of fast but less accurate intrinsics for 32-bit floating-point data that can be enabled per compilation unit through the -Mcuda=fastmath compiler option or selectively by using the cudadevice module and explicitly calling __fdividef(x,y), __sinf(x), __cosf(x), __tanf(x), __sincosf(x,s,c), __logf(x), __log2f(x), __log10f(x), __expf(x), __exp10f(x), and __powf(x,y).

3.6.2 **Compiler options**

We have already discussed the compiler option -Mcuda=fastmath used to invoke faster but less accurate intrinsics for 32-bit floating-point data. There are some other compiler options that affect instruction throughput.

The option -Mcuda=nofma toggles the use of fusing multiply-add instructions. If we compile the simple example code:

```
1  module mfa_m
2  contains
3    attributes(global) subroutine k(a, b, c)
4      implicit none
5      real :: a, b, c
6      c = a*b+c
7    end subroutine k
8  end module mfa_m
```

and dump the generated PTX code via the -Mcuda=keepptx option, the PTX code generated for compute capability 1.x contains the instruction:

```
mad.f32          %f4, %f2, %f3, %f1;
```

whereas the PTX generated for compute capabilities 2.0 and higher contains the instruction:

```
fma.rn.f32       %f4, %f2, %f3, %f1;
```

The MAD and FMA both combine the multiply and add operations into a single instruction, but they do so very differently. The MAD instruction truncates the mantissa of the product prior to its use in the addition, whereas the FMA instruction is an IEEE-754(2008)-compliant fused-multiply add instruction where the full-width product is used in the addition, followed by a single rounding step. Contrast this to the case where -Mcuda=nofma is specified, where for all targeted compute capabilities the PTX contains the two instructions:

```
mul.rn.f32       %f4, %f2, %f3;
add.f32          %f5, %f1, %f4;
```

The MAD or FMA instructions will execute faster than separate MUL and ADD instructions because there is dedicated hardware for those operations. But because the MUL rounds to the nearest even versus the truncation of the intermediate result in MAD, on devices of compute capability 1.x separate multiplication and addition will generally be more accurate than MAD. On devices of compute capability 2.0 and higher, however, the lack of any truncation or rounding of the product prior to the addition in FMA means that the FMA will in general yield a more accurate result than separate MUL and ADD instructions.

The option -Mcuda=[no]flushz controls single-precision denormals support. Code compiled with -Mcuda=flushz flushes denormals to zero and will generally execute faster than code with -Mcuda=noflushz where denormals are supported. The compiler option -Mcuda=fastmath implies -Mcuda=flushz. On devices of compute capability 1.x, denormals are not supported and -Mcuda=flushz is implied. On devices of compute capability 2.0 and higher, denormals are supported and are used by default.

3.6.3 Divergent warps

Another instruction optimization is minimizing the number of divergent warps. Consider the following segment of device code:

```
1      i = blockDim%x*(blockIdx%x-1) + threadIdx%x
2      if (mod(i,2) == 0) then
3        x(i) = 0
4      else
5        x(i) = 1
6      endif
```

which sets x(i) to zero or one if the index i is even or odd. Because a warp of threads executes in tandem, if a branch of a conditional is satisfied by any thread in a warp, all threads in a warp must execute that branch. The various execution paths are serialized and the instruction count per thread increases accordingly. The results for threads that do not satisfy the branch are effectively masked out, but the performance implications are that every thread in a warp executes every branch that is satisfied by one thread in the warp. In our example, because half the threads in a warp satisfy each branch, all threads execute both branches. The performance penalty is not severe for this simple example, but if there are many branches to an if or case construct or multiple levels of nesting of such control flow statements, warp divergence can become a problem. On the other hand, if a condition evaluates uniformly over a warp of threads, then at most a single branch is executed, as in the following example:

```
1      i = blockDim%x*(blockIdx%x-1) + threadIdx%x
2      if (mod((i-1)/warpsize,2) == 0) then
3        x(i) = 0
4      else
5        x(i) = 1
6      endif
```

which sets x(i) to 0 or 1 if it belongs to an even or odd warp, respectively. Here each thread only executes one branch.

3.7 Kernel loop directives

Although not strictly a performance optimization technique, *kernel loop directives*, or *CUF kernels*, can be used to simplify programming of certain operations on the device. These directives instruct the compiler to generate kernels from a region of host code consisting of tightly nested loops. Essentially, kernel loop directives allow us to inline kernels in host code.

We have used an array increment example extensively in this book. The CUF kernel version of the increment code is:

```
1    program incrementTest
2      implicit none
```

```
3    integer, parameter :: n = 1024*1024
4    integer :: a(n), i, b
5    integer, device :: a_d(n)
6    integer, parameter :: tPB = 256
7
8    a = 1
9    b = 3
10
11   a_d = a
12
13   !$cuf kernel do <<<*,tPB>>>
14   do i = 1, n
15      a_d(i) = a_d(i) + b
16   enddo
17
18   a = a_d
19
20   if (any(a /= 4)) then
21      write(*,*) '**** Program Failed ****'
22   else
23      write(*,*) 'Program Passed'
24   endif
25 end program incrementTest
```

In this code there is no kernel contained in the module. In place of an explicit device routine is the directive on line 13 that instructs the compiler to automatically generate a kernel from the do loop on lines 14–17. An execution configuration is provided on line 13, indicating that a thread block of tPB threads be used when launching the kernel. The * specified for the first execution configuration parameter leaves the compiler free to calculate the number of thread blocks to launch in order to carry out the operation in the loop. The execution configuration could have been specified as <<<*, *>>>, in which case the compiler would choose the thread block size as well as the number of thread blocks to launch. We can determine what execution configuration parameters are used in a CUF kernel launch from output of the Command Line Profiler when gridsize and threadblocksize are specified in the configuration file:

```
# CUDA_PROFILE_LOG_VERSION 2.0
# CUDA_DEVICE 0 Tesla K20
# CUDA_CONTEXT 1
# TIMESTAMPFACTOR fffff68da82e00f0
method,gputime,cputime,gridsizeX,gridsizeY,threadblocksizeX,
   threadblocksizeY,threadblocksizeZ,occupancy
method=[ memcpyHtoD ] gputime=[ 1250.176 ] cputime=[ 1593.000 ]
method=[ incrementtest_14_gpu ]
   gputime=[ 67.264 ] cputime=[ 26.000 ]
   gridsize=[ 4096, 1 ] threadblocksize=[ 256, 1, 1 ]
```

```
occupancy=[ 1.000 ]
method=[ memcpyDtoH ] gputime=[ 2111.168 ] cputime=[ 3198.000 ]
```

where an execution configuration of <<<4096,256>>> was used to launch the automatically generated kernel `incrementtest_14_gpu`.

Data management in code using CUF kernels is performed explicitly. Arrays on the `device` are declared with the `device` attribute, as on line 5, and host-to-device and device-to-host data transfers are explicitly performed on lines 11 and 18, respectively. The scalar variable `b` is a host variable that is passed by value to the generated kernel.

The two-dimensional version of our increment example using a CUF kernel is:

```
1  program incrementTest
2    implicit none
3    integer, parameter :: n = 4*1024
4    integer :: a(n,n), i, j, b
5    integer, device :: a_d(n,n)
6
7    a = 1
8    b = 3
9
10   a_d = a
11
12   !$cuf kernel do (2) <<< (*,*), (32,8) >>>
13   do j = 1, n
14      do i = 1, n
15         a_d(i,j) = a_d(i,j) + b
16      enddo
17   enddo
18
19   a = a_d
20
21   if (any(a /= 4)) then
22      write(*,*) '**** Program Failed ****'
23   else
24      write(*,*) 'Program Passed'
25   endif
26 end program incrementTest
```

In this case the do (2) specified on the directive indicates that the generated kernel will map to the two following loops. Multidimensional thread blocks and grids specified by the execution configuration in the directive map to the nested loops in an innermost to outermost fashion. For example, for the thread block of 32 × 8, the predefined kernel variable `threadIdx%x` will run from 1 to 32 and map to the i index, and `threadIdx%y` will run from 1 to 8 and map to the j index. Rather than specifying the thread block size, we could have also used <<<(*,*),(*,*)>>> or even <<<*,*>>> and have the compiler choose the thread block and grid size. Using single asterisks for the execution configuration would still result in both loops being mapped to the kernel due to the do (2) specification. Without the (2) specified after the do, only the outer loop will be mapped to threadIdx%x and the generated kernel will contain the loop over i.

3.7.1 Reductions in CUF kernels

One area where CUF kernels are very beneficial is in performing reductions. Efficient reductions in CUDA are not trivial to write, as we will see in the Monte Carlo case study. We need to reduce data both within and across thread blocks. CUF kernels do this automatically for you, as in the following code.

```
1  program reduce
2     implicit none
3     integer, parameter :: n = 1024*1024
4     integer :: i, aSum = 0
5     integer, device :: a_d(n)
6     integer, parameter :: tPB = 256
7
8     a_d = 1
9
10    !$cuf kernel do <<<*,tPB>>>
11    do i = 1, n
12       aSum = aSum + a_d(i)
13    enddo
14
15    if (aSum /= n) then
16       write(*,*) '**** Program Failed ****'
17    else
18       write(*,*) 'Program Passed'
19    endif
20 end program reduce
```

In this code the variable aSum is a scalar variable declared on the host. As such, the compiler knows to perform a reduction on the device and place the result on the host variable. This particular example performs a sum reduction, but other types of reductions can be performed.

3.7.2 Streams in CUF kernels

Up to this point we have only used the first two execution parameters in the directive for CUF kernels. We can also specify a stream in which the CUF kernel will be launched by specifying a stream ID as an optional parameter. This can be accomplished in two ways. The first is as a fourth execution configuration parameter, for example:

```
!$cuf kernel do <<< *,*,0,streamID>>>
```

with 0 as the third parameter. We can also specify the stream ID as a third parameter with the `stream` keyword:

```
!$cuf kernel do <<< *,*,stream=streamID>>>
```

3.7.3 Instruction-level parallelism in CUF kernels

In Section 3.5.2 we saw how it was possible to use instruction-level parallelism to hide latencies. We essentially had each thread process multiple elements of an array. We can achieve the same effect in CUF kernels by explicitly specifying thread block and grid parameters that are not sufficient to cover all elements of the array. The compiler will then generate a kernel where by each thread processes multiple elements. For example, if we return to our first CUF kernel code and explicitly specify the grid size in addition to the block size on the directive, we have:

```
1  program ilp
2    implicit none
3    integer, parameter :: n = 1024*1024
4    integer :: a(n), i, b
5    integer, device :: a_d(n)
6    integer, parameter :: tPB = 256
7
8    a = 1
9    b = 3
10
11   a_d = a
12
13   !$cuf kernel do <<<1024,tPB>>>
14   do i = 1, n
15      a_d(i) = a_d(i) + b
16   enddo
17
18   a = a_d
19
20   if (any(a /= 4)) then
21      write(*,*) '**** Program Failed ****'
22   else
23      write(*,*) 'Program Passed'
24   endif
25 end program ilp
```

Here the 1024 blocks of 256 threads cannot processes the 1024^2 elements if each thread processes a single element, so the compiler generates a loop that results in each thread processing four array elements.

Multi-GPU Programming

4

CHAPTER OUTLINE HEAD

There are many configurations in which multiple GPUs can be used by an application based on the number of host threads launched and whether or not resources are distributed across multiple compute nodes, as in a cluster. CUDA is compatible with any host threading model, such as OpenMP and MPI, and each host thread can access either single or multiple GPUs. In this chapter we explore two common scenarios: using multiple GPUs from a single host thread and using MPI where each MPI process uses a separate GPU. We discuss these two multi-GPU approaches in the following sections.

4.1 CUDA multi-GPU features

The CUDA 4.0 toolkit introduced a greatly simplified model for multi-GPU programming. Prior to this release, management of multiple GPUs from a single host thread required use of the driver API's push and pop context functions. As of CUDA 4.0, one does not have to deal with contexts explicitly, since switching to another device is simply done with `cudaSetDevice()`. All CUDA calls are issued to the *current* GPU, and `cudaSetDevice()` sets the current GPU. A simple example of its use is in the following code that assigns values to arrays on different devices:

```
1  module kernel
2  contains
```

```
 3     attributes(global) subroutine assign(a, v)
 4       implicit none
 5       real :: a(*)
 6       real, value :: v
 7       a(threadIdx%x) = v
 8     end subroutine assign
 9   end module kernel
10
11   program minimal
12     use cudafor
13     use kernel
14     implicit none
15     integer, parameter :: n=32
16     real :: a(n)
17     real, device, allocatable :: a0_d(:), a1_d(:)
18     integer :: nDevices, istat
19
20     istat = cudaGetDeviceCount(nDevices)
21     if (nDevices < 2) then
22       write(*,*) 'This program requires at least two GPUs'
23       stop
24     end if
25
26     istat = cudaSetDevice(0)
27     allocate(a0_d(n))
28     call assign<<<1,n>>>(a0_d, 3.0)
29     a = a0_d
30     deallocate(a0_d)
31     write(*,*) 'Device 0: ', a(1)
32
33     istat = cudaSetDevice(1)
34     allocate(a1_d(n))
35     call assign<<<1,n>>>(a1_d, 4.0)
36     a = a1_d
37     deallocate(a1_d)
38     write(*,*) 'Device 1: ', a(1)
39   end program minimal
```

The kernel code used to assign values in lines 3–8 is no different than kernel code for single GPU use; all of the differences between single- and multi-GPU code occurs in host code. The declaration of device arrays on line 17 uses the `allocatable` variable attribute. Device arrays that are not declared with the `allocatable` attribute are implicitly allocated on the default device (device 0). To declare arrays intended to reside on other devices, the allocation must be done after the current device is set to the appropriate device; hence the variable attribute `allocatable` is needed. Lines 20–24 ensure that there are at least two CUDA-capable GPUs on the system and terminate the program if that is not the case.

The current device is set to device 0 on line 26. This is not necessary since the default device is 0, but we include it for clarity. In this code, the allocation, kernel launch, device-to-host transfer, and deallocation of device data on lines 27–30 all require that the current device be set to the device where the array a0_d resides. On lines 34–37, similar operations are performed with a device array allocated on device 1.

To compile this code we must use the CUDA 4.0 or newer libraries, which is the case for recent compiler versions, so compilation and execution of this code are as simple as:

```
% pgf90   minimal.cuf  -o minimal
% ./minimal
Device  0:      3.000000
Device  1:      4.000000
```

4.1.1 Peer-to-peer communication

Up to this point we have discussed multi-GPU programming whereby the GPUs operate independently using local data. If data from one GPU is needed by another, one would have to stage the transfer through the host using two transfers, one device-to-host transfer from the GPU where the data resides, followed by a host-to-device transfer to the destination GPU.

CUDA permits peer-to-peer access under certain conditions where such transfers are not staged through the CPU. With peer-to-peer access enabled between two devices, we can transfer data between GPUs as simply as we can transfer data between host and device:

```
a1_d = a0_d
```

Not only is the coding easier in this case, but there can be significant performance gains as such *direct transfers* occur across the PCIe bus without any interaction from the host (aside from initiating the transfer), as depicted on the left of Figure 4.1. In addition to *direct transfers*, it is possible for a kernel executing on one GPU to access data from another GPU, a feature called *direct access*. All of this is made possible by a feature introduced in CUDA 4.0 called *Unified Virtual Addressing*, or *UVA*. In UVA, the host and all GPU memories are combined into a single virtual address space, where each device's memory occupies a contiguous set of addresses in this virtual space. Based on the value of the virtual address for a given variable, the runtime is able to determine where the data resides.

4.1.1.1 *Requirements for peer-to-peer communication*

There are several requirements that must be met to use peer-to-peer features. Aside from using a CUDA Toolkit of version 4.0 or newer, the generated code must target a compute capability of 2.0 or higher. Additionally, the operating system must be 64-bit, and the pair or pairs of GPUs to perform peer-to-peer

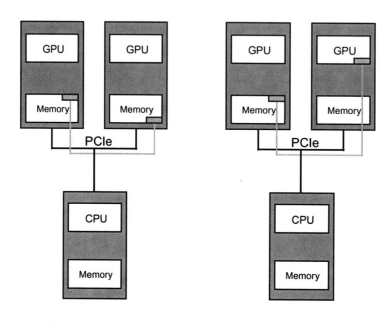

FIGURE 4.1

Depiction of *direct transfer*, left, and *direct access*, right, via peer-to-peer communication.

transfers must be of the same generation and located on the same I/O Hub (IOH) chipset. This last requirement might not be as readily verified as the others, but we can use the peer-to-peer API to determine which GPUs are capable of peer access with each other, as is done in the following code:

```
1  program checkP2pAccess
2    use cudafor
3    implicit none
4    integer, allocatable :: p2pOK(:,:)
5    integer :: nDevices, i, j, istat
6    type (cudaDeviceProp) :: prop
7
8    istat = cudaGetDeviceCount(nDevices)
9    write(*,"('Number of CUDA-capable devices: ', i0,/)") &
10        nDevices
11
12   do i = 0, nDevices-1
13      istat = cudaGetDeviceProperties(prop, i)
14      write(*,"('Device ', i0, ': ', a)") i, trim(prop%name)
15   enddo
16   write(*,*)
17
18   allocate(p2pOK(0:nDevices-1, 0:nDevices-1))
```

```
19   p2pOK = 0
20
21   do j = 0, nDevices -1
22      do i = j+1, nDevices -1
23         istat = cudaDeviceCanAccessPeer(p2pOK(i,j), i, j)
24         p2pOK(j,i) = p2pOK(i,j)
25      end do
26   end do
27
28   do i = 0, nDevices -1
29      write(*,"(3x,i3)", advance='no') i
30   enddo
31   write(*,*)
32
33   do j = 0, nDevices -1
34      write(*,"(i3)", advance='no') j
35      do i = 0, nDevices -1
36         if (i == j) then
37            write(*,"(2x,'-',3x)", advance='no')
38         else if (p2pOK(i,j) == 1) then
39            write(*,"(2x, 'Y',3x)",advance='no')
40         else
41            write(*,"(6x)",advance='no')
42         end if
43      end do
44      write(*,*)
45   end do
46   end program checkP2pAccess
```

In this code, after listing all the CUDA-capable devices in the loop from lines 12–15, the code performs a double-nested loop in lines 21–26 that evaluates whether GPUs can access each others' memories.

```
21   do j = 0, nDevices -1
22      do i = j+1, nDevices -1
23         istat = cudaDeviceCanAccessPeer(p2pOK(i,j), i, j)
24         p2pOK(j,i) = p2pOK(i,j)
25      end do
26   end do
```

The function cudaDeviceCanAccessPeer() on line 23 determines if device i is capable of accessing the memory of device j and sets p2pOK(i,j) to either 1 or 0 if this is possible or not, respectively. Although there is a directionality of transfer implied by this function, any of the restrictions that would prevent peer access do not relate to the direction of transfer. In essence, the cudaDeviceCanAccessPeer() call can be interpreted as generally determining whether or not peer access is possible between the devices specified in the last two arguments. It is for this reason that the loop for i on line 22 is set up to determine accessibility when i>j, and line 24 applies the result to the cases where j>i.

The remainder of the code prints out a matrix reflecting peer-to-peer accessibility. On a node with two Tesla S2050 systems (each Tesla S2050 contains four GPUs) connected to the same IOH chipset, we have:

```
% pgf90 p2pAccess.cuf -o p2pAccess
%   ./p2pAccess
Number of CUDA-capable devices: 8

Device 0:  Tesla  S2050
Device 1:  Tesla  S2050
Device 2:  Tesla  S2050
Device 3:  Tesla  S2050
Device 4:  Tesla  S2050
Device 5:  Tesla  S2050
Device 6:  Tesla  S2050
Device 7:  Tesla  S2050


      0     1     2     3     4     5     6     7
 0    -     Y     Y     Y     Y     Y     Y     Y
 1    Y     -     Y     Y     Y     Y     Y     Y
 2    Y     Y     -     Y     Y     Y     Y     Y
 3    Y     Y     Y     -     Y     Y     Y     Y
 4    Y     Y     Y     Y     -     Y     Y     Y
 5    Y     Y     Y     Y     Y     -     Y     Y
 6    Y     Y     Y     Y     Y     Y     -     Y
 7    Y     Y     Y     Y     Y     Y     Y     -
```

which shows that each GPU is capable of accessing the other's memory. It is important to remember that device ordering is zero-based to be compatible with the underlying CUDA C runtime.

If we have a code that requires peer access between all GPUs, we can use the environment variable CUDA_VISIBLE_DEVICES to enumerate which devices are available to CUDA programs and in what order. For example, if we continue in the previous shell:

```
% export CUDA_VISIBLE_DEVICES=2,4,1,3
% ./p2pAccess
Number of CUDA-capable devices: 4

Device 0:  Tesla  S2050
Device 1:  Tesla  S2050
Device 2:  Tesla  S2050
Device 3:  Tesla  S2050
```

	0	1	2	3
0	–	Y	Y	Y
1	Y	–	Y	Y
2	Y	Y	–	Y
3	Y	Y	Y	–

Recall that the Tesla K10 is essentially two devices in a single form factor. If we run this code on a system with two Tesla K10s in it, we obtain:

```
% pgf90 p2pAccess.cuf -o p2pAccess
% ./p2pAccess
Number of CUDA-capable devices: 4

Device 0: Tesla K10.G1.8GB
Device 1: Tesla K10.G1.8GB
Device 2: Tesla K10.G2.8GB
Device 3: Tesla K10.G2.8GB

        0     1     2     3
   0    -     Y
   1    Y     -
   2                -     Y
   3                Y     -
```

Devices 0 and 1 belong to one K10, and devices 2 and 3 belong to the other. Whereas the two devices within a K10 are peer-to-peer accessible with each other, on this particular system the two K10s reside on different IOH chipsets and do not have peer access with each other.

In addition to using the CUDA API to determine which pairs of cards in a system are capable of peer-to-peer communication, the Linux command /sbin/lspci -tv can be used to print the PCIe tree.

4.1.2 Peer-to-peer direct transfers

We begin our discussion of peer-to-peer direct transfers using the following code that copies data from an array from one device to another using three different methods: transfer via assignment, which implicitly uses cudaMemcpy(); transfer via cudaMemcpyPeer() with peer access enabled, and transfer via cudaMemcpyPeer() with peer access disabled. The code also times the transfers twice, using events on each device. The code is listed here, followed by a discussion:

```
1  program directTransfer
2    use cudafor
3    implicit none
```

```fortran
 4    integer, parameter :: N = 4*1024*1024
 5    real, pinned, allocatable :: a(:), b(:)
 6    real, device, allocatable :: a_d(:), b_d(:)
 7
 8    ! these hold free and total memory before and after
 9    ! allocation, used to verify allocation is happening
10    ! on proper devices
11    integer(int_ptr_kind()), allocatable :: &
12        freeBefore(:), totalBefore(:), &
13        freeAfter(:), totalAfter(:)
14
15    integer :: istat, nDevices, i, accessPeer, timingDev
16    type (cudaDeviceProp) :: prop
17    type (cudaEvent) :: startEvent, stopEvent
18    real :: time
19
20    ! allocate host arrays
21    allocate(a(N), b(N))
22    allocate(freeBefore(0:nDevices-1), &
23        totalBefore(0:nDevices-1))
24    allocate(freeAfter(0:nDevices-1), &
25        totalAfter(0:nDevices-1))
26
27    ! get device info (including total and free memory)
28    ! before allocating a_d and b_d on devices 0 and 1
29    istat = cudaGetDeviceCount(nDevices)
30    if (nDevices < 2) then
31      write(*,*) 'Need at least two CUDA capable devices'
32      stop
33    endif
34    write(*,"('Number of CUDA-capable devices: ', i0,/)") &
35        nDevices
36    do i = 0, nDevices-1
37        istat = cudaGetDeviceProperties(prop, i)
38        istat = cudaSetDevice(i)
39        istat = cudaMemGetInfo(freeBefore(i), totalBefore(i))
40    enddo
41    istat = cudaSetDevice(0)
42    allocate(a_d(N))
43    istat = cudaSetDevice(1)
44    allocate(b_d(N))
45
46    ! print out free memory before and after allocation
47    write(*,"('Allocation summary')")
48    do i = 0, nDevices-1
49        istat = cudaGetDeviceProperties(prop, i)
50        write(*,"('  Device ', i0, ': ', a)") &
```

```
51          i, trim(prop%name)
52       istat = cudaSetDevice(i)
53       istat = cudaMemGetInfo(freeAfter(i), totalAfter(i))
54       write(*,"('     Free memory before: ', i0, &
55            ', after: ', i0, ', difference: ',i0,/)") &
56            freeBefore(i), freeAfter(i), &
57            freeBefore(i)-freeAfter(i)
58    enddo
59
60    ! check whether devices 0 and 1 can use P2P
61    if (nDevices > 1) then
62       istat = cudaDeviceCanAccessPeer(accessPeer, 0, 1)
63       if (accessPeer == 1) then
64          write(*,*) 'Peer access available between 0 and 1'
65       else
66          write(*,*) 'Peer access not available between 0 and 1'
67       endif
68    endif
69
70    ! initialize
71    a = 1.0
72    istat = cudaSetDevice(0)
73    a_d = a
74
75    ! perform test twice, timing on both sending GPU
76    ! and receiving GPU
77    do timingDev = 0, 1
78       write(*,"(/,'Timing on device ', i0, /)") timingDev
79
80       ! create events on the timing device
81       istat = cudaSetDevice(timingDev)
82       istat = cudaEventCreate(startEvent)
83       istat = cudaEventCreate(stopEvent)
84
85       if (accessPeer == 1) then
86          ! enable P2P communication
87          istat = cudaSetDevice(0)
88          istat = cudaDeviceEnablePeerAccess(1, 0)
89          istat = cudaSetDevice(1)
90          istat = cudaDeviceEnablePeerAccess(0, 0)
91
92          ! transfer (implicitly) across devices
93          b_d = -1.0
94          istat = cudaSetDevice(timingDev)
95          istat = cudaEventRecord(startEvent,0)
96          b_d = a_d
97          istat = cudaEventRecord(stopEvent,0)
```

```
98          istat = cudaEventSynchronize(stopEvent)
99          istat = cudaEventElapsedTime(time, &
100             startEvent, stopEvent)
101         b = b_d
102         if (any(b /= a)) then
103             write(*,"('Transfer failed')")
104         else
105             write(*,"('b_d=a_d transfer (GB/s): ', f)") &
106                 N*4/time/1.0E+6
107         endif
108      end if
109
110      ! transfer via cudaMemcpyPeer()
111      if (accessPeer == 0) istat = cudaSetDevice(1)
112      b_d = -1.0
113
114      istat = cudaSetDevice(timingDev)
115      istat = cudaEventRecord(startEvent,0)
116      istat = cudaMemcpyPeer(b_d, 1, a_d, 0, N)
117      istat = cudaEventRecord(stopEvent,0)
118      istat = cudaEventSynchronize(stopEvent)
119      istat = cudaEventElapsedTime(time, startEvent, &
120          stopEvent)
121      if (accessPeer == 0) istat = cudaSetDevice(1)
122      b = b_d
123      if (any(b /= a)) then
124          write(*,"('Transfer failed')")
125      else
126          write(*,"('cudaMemcpyPeer transfer (GB/s): ', f)") &
127              N*4/time/1.0E+6
128      endif
129
130      ! cudaMemcpyPeer with P2P disabled
131      if (accessPeer == 1) then
132          istat = cudaSetDevice(0)
133          istat = cudaDeviceDisablePeerAccess(1)
134          istat = cudaSetDevice(1)
135          istat = cudaDeviceDisablePeerAccess(0)
136          b_d = -1.0
137
138          istat = cudaSetDevice(timingDev)
139          istat = cudaEventRecord(startEvent,0)
140          istat = cudaMemcpyPeer(b_d, 1, a_d, 0, N)
141          istat = cudaEventRecord(stopEvent,0)
142          istat = cudaEventSynchronize(stopEvent)
143          istat = cudaEventElapsedTime(time, startEvent, &
144              stopEvent)
```

```
145
146            istat = cudaSetDevice(1)
147            b = b_d
148            if (any(b /= a)) then
149               write(*,"('Transfer failed')")
150            else
151               write(*,"('cudaMemcpyPeer transfer w/ P2P', &
152                     ' disabled (GB/s): ', f)") N*4/time/1.0E+6
153            endif
154         end if
155
156         ! destroy events associated with timingDev
157         istat = cudaEventDestroy(startEvent)
158         istat = cudaEventDestroy(stopEvent)
159      end do
160
161      ! clean up
162      deallocate(freeBefore, totalBefore, freeAfter, totalAfter)
163      deallocate(a, b, a_d, b_d)
164   end program directTransfer
```

After declaring and allocating host data, the device management API is used to determine the number and types of GPUs on the system from lines 29–40. Of special note here is:

```
39         istat = cudaMemGetInfo(freeBefore(i), totalBefore(i))
```

which is used to determine the available memory on each device before array allocations. The device arrays are allocated on lines 42 and 44. After the device allocations, `cudaMemGetInfo()` is used again on line 53 to determine the available memory on all devices after allocations, and the difference in available memory before and after is printed out. We do this to verify that arrays are being allocated on the intended devices.

Whether peer access is possible between devices 0 and 1 is determined on lines 61–68, which is followed by initialization of host data and a loop that performs and times the data transfers between devices. To enable bidirectional peer access between two devices, we must use `cudaDeviceEnablePeerAccess()` twice, but to determine whether peer access is possible between two devices, only a single call to `cudaDeviceCanAccessPeer()` is needed.

The main loop starting at line 77 is over the timing device, `timingDev`, since both device 0 and 1 are used to time execution. We time on each device not because we expect different answers; rather, we do this to demonstrate some features of using events in multi-GPU code. CUDA events use the GPU clock and are therefore associated with the current device at the time the events are created. It is for this reason that the events are created within the timing device loop on lines 82–83 after the current device is set to the timing device on line 81. After this, if peer access between devices 0 and 1 is possible, it is enabled on lines 87–90 and the direct transfer of data via assignment statement is performed on line 96. Before any call to the CUDA event API, the current device must be set to `timingDev`.

Note that before the transfer of b_d from device 1 to the host on line 101, we do not need to set the current device, which is timingDevice, to device 1. The current device does not need to be on the sending or receiving end of a data transfer; it only needs to have peer access to the device or devices involved in such a transfer. It is for this reason that we enable bidirectional access between devices 0 and 1 on lines 88 and 90: to accommodate device-to-host transfers when the current device is not sending or receiving data. The same logic applies to data transfers between two devices. The transfer is a valid operation as long as the current device has peer access to the memory of both devices involved in a data transfer.

Data transfer by explicitly calling cudaMemcpyPeer() can be done whether peer access is enabled or not. If peer access is enabled, the transfer is done without being staged through the CPU, and we should obtain a similar transfer rate as the above implicit transfer via assignment. When peer access is not enabled, cudaMemcpyPeer() issues a device-to-host transfer from the device on which the source array resides, followed by a host-to-device transfer to the device on which the destination array resides. In addition, when peer access is not enabled, we must be careful that the current device is set properly when we are initializing device data, as on line 112:

```
111    if (accessPeer == 0) istat = cudaSetDevice(1)
112    b_d = -1.0
```

and when retrieving the results on line 122. When peer access is enabled, we do not need to set the current device as long as the current device has access to devices involved in the transfer.

Finally, we time the transfer after explicitly disabling peer-to-peer communication on lines 133 and 135. Once again, here we use cudaMemcpyPeer() on line 140. The result of running this program on a system with two peer-to-peer capable cards is:

```
Number of CUDA-capable devices: 2

Allocation summary
  Device 0: Tesla M2050
    Free memory before: 2748571648, after: 2731794432, difference: 16777216

  Device 1: Tesla M2050
    Free memory before: 2748571648, after: 2731794432, difference: 16777216

  Peer access available between 0 and 1

Timing on device 0

b_d=a_d transfer (GB/s):        5.0965576
cudaMemcpyPeer transfer (GB/s):        5.3010325
cudaMemcpyPeer transfer w/ P2P disabled (GB/s):        3.4764111

Timing on device 1

b_d=a_d transfer (GB/s):        5.2460275
cudaMemcpyPeer transfer (GB/s):        5.2518082
cudaMemcpyPeer transfer w/ P2P disabled (GB/s):        3.5856843
```

As we expect, the transfer rates for transfers with peer-to-peer disabled are substantially slower than those where it is enabled.

On the system with two Tesla K10 GPUs, we obtain the following:

```
Number of CUDA-capable devices: 4

Allocation summary
  Device 0: Tesla K10.G1.8GB
    Free memory before: 4240695296, after: 4223918080, difference: 16777216

  Device 1: Tesla K10.G1.8GB
    Free memory before: 4240695296, after: 4223918080, difference: 16777216

  Device 2: Tesla K10.G2.8GB
    Free memory before: 4240695296, after: 4240695296, difference: 0

  Device 3: Tesla K10.G2.8GB
    Free memory before: 4240695296, after: 4240695296, difference: 0

 Peer access available between 0 and 1

Timing on device 0

b_d=a_d transfer (GB/s):         10.8029337
cudaMemcpyPeer transfer (GB/s):        11.6984177
cudaMemcpyPeer transfer w/ P2P disabled (GB/s):       8.2490988

Timing on device 1

b_d=a_d transfer (GB/s):         11.3913746
cudaMemcpyPeer transfer (GB/s):        11.6451511
cudaMemcpyPeer transfer w/ P2P disabled (GB/s):       8.9019289
```

Here we observe higher bandwidth because the two devices within a single K10 are connected by a PCIe Gen 3 switch. We can use the environment variable CUDA_VISIBLE_DEVICES to perform the transfer between two devices on different K10s. On this particular system, each K10 is in a PCIe Gen 3 slot:

```
% export CUDA_VISIBLE_DEVICES=0,2
% ./directTransfer
Number of CUDA-capable devices: 2

Allocation summary
  Device 0: Tesla K10.G1.8GB
    Free memory before: 4240695296, after: 4223918080, difference: 16777216

  Device 1: Tesla K10.G2.8GB
    Free memory before: 4240695296, after: 4223918080, difference: 16777216

 Peer access not available between 0 and 1
```

```
Timing on device 0

cudaMemcpyPeer transfer (GB/s):        8.3558540

Timing on device 1

cudaMemcpyPeer transfer (GB/s):        8.8945284
```

In the beginning of this chapter we discussed a code used to print a matrix of which pairs of devices are capable of using peer-to-peer communication. The code just above printed out the bandwidth of data transfers between two devices. We can combine these features in one code to print a matrix of bandwidth between two devices:

```
1  program p2pBandwidth
2    use cudafor
3    implicit none
4    integer, parameter :: N = 4*1024*1024
5    type distributedArray
6       real, device, allocatable :: a_d(:)
7    end type distributedArray
8    type (distributedArray), allocatable :: distArray(:)
9
10   real, allocatable :: bandwidth(:,:)
11   real :: array(N), time
12   integer :: nDevices, access, i, j, istat
13   type (cudaDeviceProp) :: prop
14   type (cudaEvent) :: startEvent, stopEvent
15
16   istat = cudaGetDeviceCount(nDevices)
17   write(*,"('Number of CUDA-capable devices: ', i0,/)") &
18        nDevices
19
20   do i = 0, nDevices-1
21      istat = cudaGetDeviceProperties(prop, i)
22      write(*,"('Device ', i0, ': ', a)") i, trim(prop%name)
23   enddo
24   write(*,*)
25
26   allocate(distArray(0:nDevices-1))
27
28   do j = 0, nDevices-1
29      istat = cudaSetDevice(j)
30      allocate(distArray(j)%a_d(N))
31      distArray(j)%a_d = j
32      do i = j+1, nDevices-1
```

```
33          istat = cudaDeviceCanAccessPeer(access, j, i)
34          if (access == 1) then
35             istat = cudaSetDevice(j)
36             istat = cudaDeviceEnablePeerAccess(i, 0)
37             istat = cudaSetDevice(i)
38             istat = cudaDeviceEnablePeerAccess(j, 0)
39          endif
40       enddo
41    end do
42
43    allocate(bandwidth(0:nDevices-1, 0:nDevices-1))
44    bandwidth = 0.0
45
46    do j = 0, nDevices-1
47       istat = cudaSetDevice(j)
48       istat = cudaEventCreate(startEvent)
49       istat = cudaEventCreate(stopEvent)
50       do i = 0, nDevices-1
51          if (i == j) cycle
52          istat = cudaMemcpyPeer(distArray(j)%a_d, j, &
53                distArray(i)%a_d, i, N)
54          istat = cudaEventRecord(startEvent,0)
55          istat = cudaMemcpyPeer(distArray(j)%a_d, j, &
56                distArray(i)%a_d, i, N)
57          istat = cudaEventRecord(stopEvent,0)
58          istat = cudaEventSynchronize(stopEvent)
59          istat = cudaEventElapsedTime(time, &
60                startEvent, stopEvent)
61
62          array = distArray(j)%a_d
63          if (all(array == i)) bandwidth(j,i) = N*4/time/1.0E+6
64       end do
65       distArray(j)%a_d = j
66       istat = cudaEventDestroy(startEvent)
67       istat = cudaEventDestroy(stopEvent)
68    enddo
69
70    write(*,"('Bandwidth (GB/s) for transfer size (MB): ', &
71          f9.3,/)") N*4.0/1024**2
72    write(*,"(' S\\R    0')", advance='no')
73    do i = 1, nDevices-1
74       write(*,"(5x,i3)", advance='no') i
75    enddo
76    write(*,*)
77
78    do j = 0, nDevices-1
79       write(*,"(i3)", advance='no') j
```

```
80      do i = 0, nDevices -1
81         if (i == j) then
82            write(*,"(4x,'-',3x)", advance='no')
83         else
84            write(*,"(f8.2)",advance='no') bandwidth(j,i)
85         end if
86      end do
87      write(*,*)
88   end do
89
90   ! cleanup
91   do j = 0, nDevices -1
92      deallocate(distArray(j)%a_d)
93   end do
94   deallocate(distArray,bandwidth)
95
96 end program p2pBandwidth
```

where we use `cudaMemcpyPeer()` for all transfers, with peer access enabled if possible. Most of the content of this code appeared in one of the two aforementioned codes, the exception being how the device arrays are organized in this code. We define a derived type `distributedArray` on lines 5–7 that contains an allocatable device array a_d. On line 8 we declare an allocatable host array of this type as `distArray`. After determining the number of devices on the system, the host array `distArray` is allocated on line 26 using zero offset to correspond to the way CUDA enumerates devices. We then loop over devices and allocate `distArray(j)%a_d` on device j on line 30. Using derived types in this manner is a convenient and general way to deal with data that are distributed across multiple devices. Peer access is enabled if possible in the loop from 36–40, the transfers are performed and timed on lines 46–68, and the bandwidth matrix is printed out on lines 70–88. Running this code on the dual Tesla K10 system, we obtain:

```
Number of CUDA-capable devices: 4

Device 0: Tesla K10.G1.8GB
Device 1: Tesla K10.G1.8GB
Device 2: Tesla K10.G2.8GB
Device 3: Tesla K10.G2.8GB


Bandwidth (GB/s) for transfer size (MB):    16.000

  S\R    0        1        2        3
   0     -      11.64     9.60     9.74
   1    11.57     -       9.83     9.67
   2     9.53    9.61      -      11.70
   3     9.95    9.71    11.64     -
```

The rows in the output correspond to the sending devices, and the columns are the receiving devices for the transfers. As shown before, we observe better bandwidth between the two devices of a single K10. On a node with two Tesla S2050 systems, we get:

```
Number of CUDA-capable devices: 8

Device 0: Tesla S2050
Device 1: Tesla S2050
Device 2: Tesla S2050
Device 3: Tesla S2050
Device 4: Tesla S2050
Device 5: Tesla S2050
Device 6: Tesla S2050
Device 7: Tesla S2050

Bandwidth (GB/s) for transfer size (MB):    16.000

  S\R    0       1       2       3       4       5       6       7
   0     -      6.61    6.61    6.61    5.25    5.25    5.25    5.25
   1    6.61     -      6.61    6.61    5.25    5.25    5.25    5.25
   2    6.61    6.61     -      6.61    5.24    5.25    5.25    5.25
   3    6.61    6.61    6.61     -      5.25    5.25    5.25    5.25
   4    5.25    5.25    5.25    5.25     -      6.61    6.61    6.61
   5    5.25    5.25    5.25    5.25    6.61     -      6.61    6.61
   6    5.25    5.25    5.25    5.25    6.61    6.61     -      6.61
   7    5.25    5.25    5.25    5.23    6.61    6.61    6.61     -
```

where we observe slightly better performance when the transfers occur within a single S2050.

4.1.3 Peer-to-peer transpose

In this section we extend the matrix transpose example of Section 3.4 to operate on a matrix that is distributed across multiple GPUs. The data layout is shown in Figure 4.2 for an $nx \times ny = 1024 \times 768$ element matrix that is distributed among four devices. Each device contains a horizontal slice of the input matrix shown in the figure as well as a horizontal slice of the output matrix. These input matrix slices of 1024×192 elements are divided into four tiles containing 256×192 elements each, which are referred to as p2pTile in the code. As the name indicates, the p2pTiles are used for peer-to-peer transfers. After a p2pTile has been transferred to the appropriate device if necessary (tiles on the block diagonal do not need to be transferred since the input and output tiles are on the same device), a CUDA transpose kernel launch transposes the elements within the p2pTile using thread blocks that process smaller tiles of 32×32 elements.

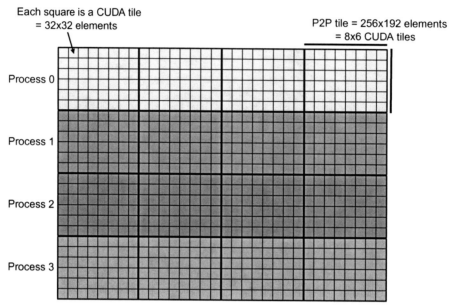

FIGURE 4.2

Device data layout for peer-to-peer transpose with a nx × ny = 1024 × 768 matrix on four devices. Each device holds a 1024 × 192 horizontal slice of input matrix (as well as a 768 × 256 horizontal slice of the output matrix). Each slice of the input matrix is broken into four tiles of 256 × 192 elements, which are used for peer-to-peer transfers. The CUDA kernel transposes this tile using 48 thread blocks, each of which processes a 32 × 32 tile.

The full code is contained in Appendix D.4.1. In this section we pull in only the relevant parts for our discussion. We start the discussion of the code with the transpose kernel:

```
14    attributes(global) subroutine cudaTranspose( &
15        odata, ldo, idata, ldi)
16      implicit none
17      real, intent(out) :: odata(ldo,*)
18      real, intent(in) :: idata(ldi,*)
19      integer, value, intent(in) :: ldo, ldi
20      real, shared :: tile(cudaTileDim+1, cudaTileDim)
21      integer :: x, y, j
22
23      x = (blockIdx%x-1) * cudaTileDim + threadIdx%x
24      y = (blockIdx%y-1) * cudaTileDim + threadIdx%y
25
26      do j = 0, cudaTileDim-1, blockRows
27        tile(threadIdx%x, threadIdx%y+j) = idata(x,y+j)
28      end do
```

```
29
30        call syncthreads()
31
32        x = (blockIdx%y-1) * cudaTileDim + threadIdx%x
33        y = (blockIdx%x-1) * cudaTileDim + threadIdx%y
34
35        do j = 0, cudaTileDim-1, blockRows
36           odata(x,y+j) = tile(threadIdx%y+j, threadIdx%x)
37        end do
38     end subroutine cudaTranspose
```

This transpose is basically the same kernel we developed in Section 3.4 for the single-GPU transpose, with the exception that two additional parameters are passed to the kernel, ldi and ldo, the leading dimensions of the input and output matrices. These parameters are needed because each kernel call transposes a submatrix of each device's slice of the matrix. We could do without modifying the kernel at all by copying data to and from a temporary array, but such intermediate data transfers would greatly affect performance. Note that the leading dimension parameters are only used in the declaration of the input and output matrices on lines 17 and 18; the rest of the code is identical to the single-GPU code.

Most of the host code performs mundane tasks such as getting the number and types of devices (lines 85–94), checking that all devices are peer-to-peer capable and enabling peer-to-peer communication (lines 96–119), verifying that the matrix divides evenly into the various tile sizes (121–140), printing out the various sizes (lines 146–165), and initializing host data and transposing on the host (lines 169–170).

Because we want to overlap the execution of the transpose kernel with the data transfer between GPUs, we want to avoid using the default stream for peer-to-peer communication as well as kernel execution. We want each device to have nDevices streams, one for each transpose call. Since there are nDevices devices, each requiring nDevices streams, we use a two-dimensional variable to hold the stream IDs:

```
180    allocate(streamID(0:nDevices-1,0:nDevices-1))
181    do p = 0, nDevices-1
182       istat = cudaSetDevice(p)
183       do stage = 0, nDevices-1
184          istat = cudaStreamCreate(streamID(p,stage))
185       enddo
186    enddo
```

where the first index to streamID corresponds to the particular device the stream is associated with, and the second index refers to the stages of the calculation.

The stages of the transpose, enumerated zero to nDevices-1, are organized as follows: In the zeroth stage, each device transposes the submatrix that lies along the block diagonal of the global matrix, which is depicted in the top diagram of Figure 4.3. This is done first because no peer-to-peer communication is involved, and the kernel execution can overlap data transfers in the first stage.

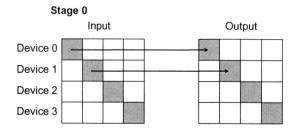

Stage 0

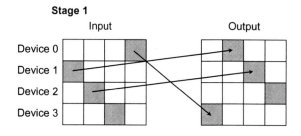

Stage 1

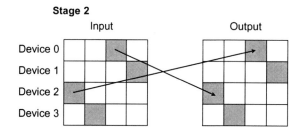

Stage 2

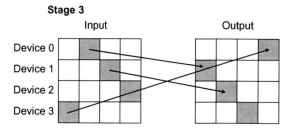

Stage 3

FIGURE 4.3

Stages of the matrix transpose. In stage zero, each device transposes the block along the global matrix diagonal, which requires no peer-to-peer communication. In stage one, blocks from the first subdiagonal of the input matrix are transferred to the device holding the respective block superdiagonal, after which the transpose is performed on the receiving device. Subsequent stages (such as stage 2) do the same for subsequent sub- and superdiagonals. The wrapping of the diagonals becomes more pronounced for subsequent stages, culminating in the last stage's communication pattern being the reverse of the first stage.

In stage one, data from what is primarily the first block-subdiagonal of the input matrix is sent to the devices that hold the corresponding first block-superdiagonal, as depicted in Figure 4.3. After the transfer completes, the receiving device performs the transpose. Note that one of the blocks transferred during stage one is not on the subdiagonal, since we wrap the pattern so that all devices both send and receive data during each stage. The following stages do similar operations on additional block sub- and super diagonals until all of the blocks have been transposed. The wrapping during these stages becomes more pronounced, so that in the final stage the communication pattern is the reverse of the first stage. In using this arrangement, during each stage other than the zeroth, each device sends and receives a block of data, and both of these transfers can overlap if transferred asynchronously, since the devices have separate send and receive copy engines.

The distributed global matrices are stored using the derived type `deviceArray`:

```
68      ! distributed arrays
69      type deviceArray
70         real, device, allocatable :: v(:,:)
71      end type deviceArray
72
73      type (deviceArray), allocatable :: &
74          d_idata(:), d_tdata(:), d_rdata(:)    ! (0:nDevices-1)
```

This same technique was used in the `p2pBandwidth` code in the previous section. Instances of this derived type will be host data, but the member `v` is device data. There are three allocatable array declarations of this drived type on line 74: `d_idata` for the input data; `d_rdata`, which is a receive buffer used in the transfers; and `d_tdata`, which holds the final transposed data. These variables are allocated by:

```
190     allocate(d_idata(0:nDevices-1),&
191         d_tdata(0:nDevices-1), d_rdata(0:nDevices-1))
```

which represents decomposition of the global array into the horizontal slices depicted in Figure 4.2. The members of the derived type hold the horizontal slices, which are allocated and initialized by:

```
193     do p = 0, nDevices-1
194        istat = cudaSetDevice(p)
195        allocate(d_idata(p)%v(nx,p2pTileDimY), &
196            d_rdata(p)%v(nx,p2pTileDimY), &
197            d_tdata(p)%v(ny,p2pTileDimX))
198
199        yOffset = p*p2pTileDimY
200        d_idata(p)%v(:,:) = h_idata(:, &
201            yOffset+1:yOffset+p2pTileDimY)
202        d_rdata(p)%v(:,:) = -1.0
```

```
203        d_tdata(p)%v(:,:) = -1.0
204     enddo
```

where nx and ny are the global matrix sizes, and p2pTileDimY and p2pTileDimX are the sizes
of the horizontal slices of the input and transposed matrices, respectively. Note that the device is set
on line 194 to the appropriate device before each member v is allocated. Also, since the matrix on the
host is stored in h_idata(nx,ny), the offset yOffset is used in initializing d_idata on lines
200–201.

The code that performs the various transpose stages is:

```
216     ! Stage 0:
217     ! transpose diagonal blocks (local data) before kicking off
218     ! transfers and transposes of other blocks
219
220     do p = 0, nDevices-1
221        istat = cudaSetDevice(p)
222        if (asyncVersion) then
223           call cudaTranspose &
224                <<<dimGrid, dimBlock, 0, streamID(p,0)>>> &
225                (d_tdata(p)%v(p*p2pTileDimY+1,1), ny, &
226                d_idata(p)%v(p*p2pTileDimX+1,1), nx)
227        else
228           call cudaTranspose<<<dimGrid, dimBlock>>> &
229                (d_tdata(p)%v(p*p2pTileDimY+1,1), ny, &
230                d_idata(p)%v(p*p2pTileDimX+1,1), nx)
231        endif
232     enddo
233
234     ! now send data to blocks to the right of diagonal
235     ! (using mod for wrapping) and transpose
236
237     do stage = 1, nDevices-1      ! stages = offset diagonals
238        do rDev = 0, nDevices-1   ! device that receives
239           sDev = mod(stage+rDev, nDevices)  ! dev that sends
240
241           if (asyncVersion) then
242              istat = cudaSetDevice(rDev)
243              istat = cudaMemcpy2DAsync( &
244                   d_rdata(rDev)%v(sDev*p2pTileDimX+1,1), nx, &
245                   d_idata(sDev)%v(rDev*p2pTileDimX+1,1), nx, &
246                   p2pTileDimX, p2pTileDimY, &
247                   stream=streamID(rDev,stage))
248           else
249              istat = cudaMemcpy2D( &
250                   d_rdata(rDev)%v(sDev*p2pTileDimX+1,1), nx, &
```

```
251              d_idata(sDev)%v(rDev*p2pTileDimX+1,1), nx, &
252              p2pTileDimX, p2pTileDimY)
253        end if
254
255        istat = cudaSetDevice(rDev)
256        if (asyncVersion) then
257           call cudaTranspose &
258                <<<dimGrid, dimBlock, 0, &
259                streamID(rDev,stage)>>>  &
260                (d_tdata(rDev)%v(sDev*p2pTileDimY+1,1), ny, &
261                d_rdata(rDev)%v(sDev*p2pTileDimX+1,1), nx)
262        else
263           call cudaTranspose<<<dimGrid, dimBlock>>> &
264                (d_tdata(rDev)%v(sDev*p2pTileDimY+1,1), ny, &
265                d_rdata(rDev)%v(sDev*p2pTileDimX+1,1), nx)
266        endif
267     enddo
268  enddo
```

Stage 0 occurs in the loop on lines 220–232. After the device is set on line 221, the transpose of the diagonal block is performed either using the default blocking stream on line 228 or in a non-default stream on line 223. The parameter `asyncVersion` is used to toggle between asynchronous and synchronous execution. The execution configuration used in the kernel launches is determined by:

```
142  dimGrid = dim3(p2pTileDimX/cudaTileDim, &
143       p2pTileDimY/cudaTileDim, 1)
144  dimBlock = dim3(cudaTileDim, blockRows, 1)
```

where the thread block is the same as in the single-GPU case, and each kernel launch operates on a submatrix of size p2pTileDimX×p2pTileDimY.

The other stages are performed in the loop from line 237–268. After the sending and receiving devices are determined on lines 238 and 239, the peer-to-peer transfer is performed using either cudaMemcpy2DAsync() or cudaMemcpy2D(), depending on asyncVersion. If the asynchronous version is used, then the device is set to the receiving device on line 242, and accordingly, the nondefault stream used for the transfer is the stream associated with the receiving device. We use the stream associated with the device receiving the data rather than the device sending the data because we want to block the launch of the transpose kernel on the receiving device until the transfer is complete. This is accomplished by default when the same stream is used for the transfer and transpose. For the synchronous data transfer, the device does not need to be specified via cudaSetDevice(). Note that the array receiving the data is d_rdata. The out-of-place transpose from d_rdata to d_tdata is then performed by the kernel launch on line 257 or 263. Regardless of whether the default stream is used or not, the device must be set as done on line 255.

The remainder of the code transfers the data back to the host, checks for correctness, and reports the effective bandwidth. Timing in this case is done using a wall-clock timer. This code uses the C function gettimeofday():

```
1   #include <time.h>
2   #include <sys/types.h>
3   #include <sys/times.h>
4   #include <sys/time.h>
5
6   double wallclock()
7   {
8      struct timeval tv;
9      struct timezone tz;
10     double t;
11
12     gettimeofday(&tv, &tz);
13
14     t = (double)tv.tv_sec;
15     t += ((double)tv.tv_usec)/1000000.0;
16
17     return t;
18  }
```

which is accessed in the Fortran code using the timing module:

```
1   module timing
2      interface wallclock
3         function wallclock() result(res) bind(C, name='wallclock')
4            use iso_c_binding
5            real (c_double) :: res
6         end function wallclock
7      end interface wallclock
8   end module timing
```

Whenever this routine is called, we explicitly check to make sure there is no pending or executing operations on the device:

```
271    do p = 0, nDevices-1
272       istat = cudaSetDevice(p)
273       istat = cudaDeviceSynchronize()
274    enddo
275    timeStop = wallclock()
```

Note that most of this multi-GPU code is overhead associated with declaring and initializing arrays and enabling peer-to-peer communication. The actual data transfers and kernel launches are contained in approximately 50 lines of code, which contains branches for synchronous and asynchronous execution. The transpose kernel itself is only slightly modified from the single-GPU transpose to allow for arbitrary leading dimensions of the arrays.

We use a compute node with two devices for running this transpose code. To compare to the single-GPU transpose results in Section 3.4, which used 1024×1024 matrices, we choose an overall matrix size of 2048×2048. In this case each transpose kernel processes a 1024×1024 submatrix, the same as in the single-GPU case. When we use blocking transfers, we obtain the results:

```
Number of CUDA-capable devices: 2

  Device 0: Tesla M2050
  Device 1: Tesla M2050


Array size: 2048x2048

CUDA block size: 32x8,  CUDA tile size: 32x32
dimGrid: 32x32x1,   dimBlock: 32x8x1

nDevices: 2,  Local input array size: 2048x1024
p2pTileDim: 1024x1024

async mode:  F


Bandwidth (GB/s):   16.43
```

and when we use asynchronous transfers, we have:

```
Number of CUDA-capable devices: 2

  Device 0: Tesla M2050
  Device 1: Tesla M2050


Array size: 2048x2048

CUDA block size: 32x8,  CUDA tile size: 32x32
dimGrid: 32x32x1,   dimBlock: 32x8x1

nDevices: 2,  Local input array size: 2048x1024
p2pTileDim: 1024x1024
```

```
async mode:    T


Bandwidth (GB/s):    29.73
```

While both these numbers fall short of the effective bandwidth achieved in the single-GPU case, we must take into account that half of the data is being transferred over the PCIe bus, which is over an order of magnitude slower that the global memory bandwidth within a GPU. In light of this fact, the use of asynchronous transfers that overlap kernel execution is very advantageous, as can be seen from the results. In addition, typically the transpose is used as a means to some other operation that can be done in parallel, in which case cost of the PCIe transfer is further amortized.

4.2 Multi-GPU Programming with MPI

In the preceding section we explored using multiple GPUs from a single host thread. Toggling between GPUs using `cudaSetDevice()` provides a convenient way to distribute data and processing among several GPUs. As problems scale up, however, this approach reaches a limit in how many GPUs can be attached to a single node. When this limit is reached, we need to program for multiple nodes using MPI. MPI can be used in conjunction with the multi-GPU techniques we have described, where MPI can be used to transfer data between nodes and the CUDA 4.0 multi-GPU features used to distribute and process data among the GPUs attached to that node. This is analogous to the way that OpenMP and MPI are used on CPUs in clusters. We can even combine MPI, OpenMP, and multi-GPU models in an application.

We briefly discuss the MPI library calls used in this section as they are introduced in the text. For readers who are new to MPI, a more detailed discussion of the API routines can be found in *MPI: The Complete Reference* (Snir, 1966) and *Using MPI: Portable Parallel Programming with the Message-Passing Interface* (Gropp et al., 1999). Before we jump into MPI code, we should mention some high-level aspects of the MPI programming model. Just as all device threads in a kernel execute the same device code, all host threads in a MPI application execute the same host code. In CUDA we use predefined variables to identify the individual device threads in device code. In MPI, individual MPI threads, or *ranks*, are identified through the library call `MPI_COMM_RANK()`. While the CUDA programming model benefits from fine-grained parallelism (e.g., coalescing), MPI generally benefits from coarse-grained parallelism, where each MPI rank operates on a large partition of the data.

Compilation of MPI CUDA Fortran code is performed using the MPI wrapper `mpif90` supplied with numerous MPI distributions. Execution of MPI programs is typically performed with the command `mpirun`, whereby the program executable as well as the number of MPI ranks used are provided on the command line. Because of the CUDA-aware features of the MPI implementation of MVAPICH (available at `http://mvapich.cse.ohio-state.edu`) that are discussed later in this section, we use the MVAPICH package for our examples.

There are many ways to use CUDA Fortran in conjunction with MPI in terms of the way devices are mapped to MPI ranks. In this section we opt for a simple, versatile approach whereby each MPI rank is associated with a single GPU. In this configuration we can still use multiple GPUs per node simply by using multiple MPI ranks per node, which is determined by the way the application is launched rather than from within the code. If the nature of the application merits a different mapping of GPUs to MPI ranks, we can add this later using the techniques discussed earlier in this chapter, but in general the one-GPU-per-MPI rank model is a good first approach.

4.2.1 Assigning devices to MPI ranks

One of the first issues we confront in writing multi-GPU MPI code using the configuration in which each MPI rank has a unique device is how to ensure that no device is assigned to multiple MPI ranks. The way devices are associated with CPU processes and threads depends on how the system is configured via nvidia-smi. NVIDIA's System Management Interface (nvidia-smi) is a tool distributed with the driver that allows users to display and administrators to modify settings of devices attached to the system.[1] We can use this utility to simply print the devices attached to the system:

```
% nvidia-smi -L
GPU 0: Tesla M2050 (S/N: 0322210101582)
GPU 1: Tesla M2050 (S/N: 0322210101238)
```

as well as getting detailed information about temperature, power, and various settings. The setting we are concerned with here is the compute mode. The compute mode determines if multiple processes or threads can use the same GPU. The four modes are:

default: 0 In this mode, multiple host threads can use the same device via calls to cudaSetDevice().

exclusive thread: 1 In this mode, only a single context can be created by a single process systemwide, and this context can be current to at most one thread of the process at a time.

prohibited: 2 In this mode, no contexts can be created on the device.

exclusive process: 3 In this mode, only a single context can be created by a single process systemwide, and this context can be current to all threads of that process.

One can query the compute mode as follows:

```
% nvidia-smi -q -d COMPUTE
==============NVSMI LOG===============
Timestamp                           : Wed Feb  1 17:06:23 2012
Driver Version                      : 285.05.32
Attached GPUs                       : 2
GPU 0000:02:00.0
   Compute Mode                     : Exclusive_Process
GPU 0000:03:00.0
   Compute Mode                     : Exclusive_Process
```

which indicates that both devices are in the exclusive process mode.

---

[1] nvidia-smi is discussed in more detail in Appendix B.

To illustrate the different behavior of these modes, we use the following simple program:

```
1   program mpiDevices
2     use cudafor
3     use mpi
4     implicit none
5
6     ! global array size
7     integer, parameter :: n = 1024*1024
8     ! MPI  variables
9     integer :: myrank, nprocs, ierr
10    ! device
11    type(cudaDeviceProp) :: prop
12    integer(int_ptr_kind()) :: freeB, totalB, freeA, totalA
13    real, device, allocatable :: d(:)
14    integer :: i, j, istat
15
16    ! MPI initialization
17    call MPI_init(ierr)
18    call MPI_comm_rank(MPI_COMM_WORLD, myrank, ierr)
19    call MPI_comm_size(MPI_COMM_WORLD, nProcs, ierr)
20
21    ! print compute mode for device
22    istat = cudaGetDevice(j)
23    istat = cudaGetDeviceProperties(prop, j)
24    do i = 0, nprocs-1
25       call MPI_BARRIER(MPI_COMM_WORLD, ierr)
26       if (myrank == i) write(*,"('[',i0,'] using device: ', &
27             i0, ' in compute mode: ', i0)") &
28             myrank, j, prop%computeMode
29    enddo
30
31    ! get memory use before large allocations,
32    call MPI_BARRIER(MPI_COMM_WORLD, ierr)
33    istat = cudaMemGetInfo(freeB, totalB)
34
35    ! now allocate arrays, one rank at a time
36    do j = 0, nProcs-1
37
38       ! allocate on device associated with rank j
39       call MPI_BARRIER(MPI_COMM_WORLD, ierr)
40       if (myrank == j) allocate(d(n))
41
42       ! Get free memory after allocation
43       call MPI_BARRIER(MPI_COMM_WORLD, ierr)
44       istat = cudaMemGetInfo(freeA, totalA)
```

```
45
46          write(*,"('    [',i0,'] after allocation on rank: ', i0, &
47                 ', device arrays allocated: ', i0)") &
48              myrank, j, (freeB-freeA)/n/4
49
50     end do
51
52     deallocate(d)
53     call MPI_Finalize(ierr)
54  end program mpiDevices
```

This code simply has each rank allocate a device array and reports the memory usage on each device as the allocations are performed. The module containing all of the MPI interfaces and parameters is included on line 3. The typical MPI initialization occurs on lines 17–20. The call to MPI_init() on line 17 initializes MPI, the call to MPI_comm_rank() on line 18 returns the MPI rank in the myrank variable, and the call to MPI_comm_size() returns the number of ranks launched by the application. The device number each rank uses as well its compute mode are printed in lines 22–29. The loop used for printing on line 24 is not technically needed, but it is used along with the MPI_BARRIER() call to avoid collisions in output from different ranks. The synchronization barrier MPI_BARRIER() blocks execution of all MPI processes until every MPI process has reached that point in the code, similar to CUDA's syncthreads() used in device code. After printing the device number and compute mode, the amount of free space on each device is determined on line 33. In each iteration of the loop from lines 36–50, a device array is allocated on the device associated with a particular rank (line 40), the free memory after allocation is determined (line 44), and the number of arrays allocated on each device is printed out (line 46).

When this code is run using two MPI processes on a single node with two devices in exclusive mode, we obtain:

```
[0] using device: 1 in compute mode: 3
[1] using device: 0 in compute mode: 3
   [0] after allocation on rank: 0, device arrays allocated: 1
   [1] after allocation on rank: 0, device arrays allocated: 0
   [0] after allocation on rank: 1, device arrays allocated: 1
   [1] after allocation on rank: 1, device arrays allocated: 1
```

which indicates that two separate devices are used by the two ranks from the devices listed in the first two lines, which is verified from the memory utilization in the remainder of the output.

On a node with devices in default compute mode, a two-MPI-process run results in:

```
[0] using device: 0 in compute mode: 0
[1] using device: 0 in compute mode: 0
   [0] after allocation on rank: 0, device arrays allocated: 1
```

```
[1] after allocation on rank: 0, device arrays allocated: 1
[0] after allocation on rank: 1, device arrays allocated: 2
[1] after allocation on rank: 1, device arrays allocated: 2
```

which indicates that device 0 is being used for both MPI ranks, which is verified in the allocation summary whereby after each allocation stage, the free memory on all ranks decreases.

One way to ensure that each MPI rank has a unique device regardless of the compute mode setting is to use the following module:

```fortran
1  module mpiDeviceUtil
2    interface
3      subroutine quicksort(base, nmemb, elemsize, compar) &
4           bind(C,name='qsort')
5        use iso_c_binding
6        implicit none
7        !pgi$ ignore_tkr base,nmemb,elemsize,compar
8        type(C_PTR), value :: base
9        integer(C_SIZE_T), value :: nmemb, elemsize
10       type(C_FUNPTR), value :: compar
11      end subroutine quicksort
12
13      integer function strcmp(a,b) bind(C,name='strcmp')
14        use iso_c_binding
15        implicit none
16        !pgi$ ignore_tkr a,b
17        type(C_PTR), value :: a, b
18      end function strcmp
19    end interface
20  contains
21    subroutine assignDevice(dev)
22      use mpi
23      use cudafor
24      implicit none
25      integer :: dev
26      character (len=MPI_MAX_PROCESSOR_NAME), allocatable :: hosts(:)
27      character (len=MPI_MAX_PROCESSOR_NAME) :: hostname
28      integer :: namelength, color, i
29      integer :: nProcs, myrank, newComm, newRank, ierr
30
31      call MPI_COMM_SIZE(MPI_COMM_WORLD, nProcs, ierr)
32      call MPI_COMM_RANK(MPI_COMM_WORLD, myrank, ierr)
33
34      ! allocate array of hostnames
35      allocate(hosts(0:nProcs-1))
36
37      ! Every process collects the hostname of all the nodes
38      call MPI_GET_PROCESSOR_NAME(hostname, namelength, ierr)
39      hosts(myrank)=hostname(1:namelength)
```

```
40
41       do i=0,nProcs-1
42          call MPI_BCAST(hosts(i),MPI_MAX_PROCESSOR_NAME, &
43               MPI_CHARACTER,i,MPI_COMM_WORLD,ierr)
44       end do
45
46       ! sort the list of names
47       call quicksort(hosts,nProcs,MPI_MAX_PROCESSOR_NAME,strcmp)
48
49       ! assign the same color to the same node
50       color=0
51       do i=0,nProcs-1
52          if (i > 0) then
53             if ( lne(hosts(i-1),hosts(i)) ) color=color+1
54          end if
55          if ( leq(hostname,hosts(i)) ) exit
56       end do
57
58       call MPI_COMM_SPLIT(MPI_COMM_WORLD,color,0,newComm,ierr)
59       call MPI_COMM_RANK(newComm, newRank, ierr)
60
61       dev = newRank
62       ierr = cudaSetDevice(dev)
63
64       deallocate(hosts)
65     end subroutine assignDevice
66
67     ! lexical .eq.
68     function leq(s1, s2) result(res)
69       implicit none
70       character (len=*) :: s1, s2
71       logical :: res
72       res = .false.
73       if (lle(s1,s2) .and. lge(s1,s2)) res = .true.
74     end function leq
75
76     ! lexical .ne.
77     function lne(s1, s2) result(res)
78       implicit none
79       character (len=*) :: s1, s2
80       logical :: res
81       res = .not. leq(s1, s2)
82     end function lne
83   end module mpiDeviceUtil
```

where the subroutine `assignDevice()` on lines 21–65 is responsible for finding and setting a unique device. This subroutine uses the MPI routines `MPI_GET_PROCESSOR_NAME()` (line 38) and `MPI_BCAST()` (line 42) to compile a list of hostnames used by all ranks. Once each rank has the entire list of hostnames, the C `quicksort()` function is called using the comparator `strcmp` to sort the list. (These C routines are accessed through interfaces defined on lines 3–18.) A color is associated with each node in the loop on lines 51–56, which is used by the call to MPI_COMM_SPLIT() to determine a set of new MPI *communicators*. An MPI *communicator* is simply a group of MPI processes. Each new communicator contains only the MPI ranks on the associated node, and a call to MPI_COMM_RANK() returns the new rank with respect to the new communicator. This new rank is used to enumerate CUDA devices on the node (line 61) and to set the current device (line 62). Once again, we emphasize that this routine can be used regardless of the compute mode setting. The code can be modified to select only GPUs with certain characteristics, such as double-precision capable devices or devices with a certain amount of memory, by adding more logic before the cudaSetDevice() call on line 62.

The following code shows how this module is used:

```fortran
1   program main
2     use mpi
3     use mpiDeviceUtil
4     use cudafor
5     implicit none
6
7     ! global array size
8     integer, parameter :: n = 1024*1024
9     ! mpi
10    character (len=MPI_MAX_PROCESSOR_NAME) :: hostname
11    integer :: myrank, nprocs, ierr, namelength
12    ! device
13    type(cudaDeviceProp) :: prop
14    integer(int_ptr_kind()) :: freeB, totalB, freeA, totalA
15    real, device, allocatable :: d(:)
16    integer :: deviceID, i, istat
17
18    call MPI_INIT(ierr)
19    call MPI_COMM_RANK(MPI_COMM_WORLD, myrank, ierr)
20    call MPI_COMM_SIZE(MPI_COMM_WORLD, nProcs, ierr)
21
22    ! get and set unique device
23    call assignDevice(deviceID)
24
25    ! print hostname and device ID for each rank
26    call MPI_GET_PROCESSOR_NAME(hostname, namelength, ierr)
27    do i = 0, nProcs-1
28       call MPI_BARRIER(MPI_COMM_WORLD, ierr)
29       if (i == myrank) &
30            write(*,"('[',i0,'] host: ', a, ',  device: ', i0)") &
31            myrank, trim(hostname), deviceID
32    enddo
33
34    ! get memory use before large allocations,
35    call MPI_BARRIER(MPI_COMM_WORLD, ierr)
36    istat = cudaMemGetInfo(freeB, totalB)
```

```
37
38    ! allocate memory on each device
39    call MPI_BARRIER(MPI_COMM_WORLD, ierr)
40    allocate(d(n))
41
42    ! Get free memory after allocation
43    call MPI_BARRIER(MPI_COMM_WORLD, ierr)
44    istat = cudaMemGetInfo(freeA, totalA)
45
46    do i = 0, nProcs-1
47        call MPI_BARRIER(MPI_COMM_WORLD, ierr)
48        if (i == myrank) &
49            write(*,"('  [', i0, ']  ', &
50            'device arrays allocated: ', i0)") &
51            myrank, (freeB-freeA)/n/4
52    end do
53
54    deallocate(d)
55    call MPI_FINALIZE(ierr)
56 end program main
```

One simply needs to use mpiDeviceUtil (line 3) and call assignDevice() (line 23) after MPI_INIT() (line 18) is called. When run using five MPI ranks across three nodes, the code produces:

```
% mpirun -np 5 -host c0-7,c0-2,c0-7,c0-3,c0-7 assignDevice
[0] host: compute-0-7.local,  device: 0
[1] host: compute-0-7.local,  device: 1
[2] host: compute-0-7.local,  device: 2
[3] host: compute-0-2.local,  device: 0
[4] host: compute-0-3.local,  device: 0
  [0] device arrays allocated: 1
  [1] device arrays allocated: 1
  [2] device arrays allocated: 1
  [3] device arrays allocated: 1
  [4] device arrays allocated: 1
```

where, to save space in the output, the code prints the arrays allocated on each device only after all allocations are made. The code is successful at assigning different devices to the MPI ranks.

4.2.2 MPI transpose

The MPI transpose code, listed in its entirety in Appendix D.4.2, shares much in common with the peer-to-peer transpose code discussed previously in this chapter: The domain decomposition, the transpose kernel, the execution configuration, and the communication pattern and stages are the same. One small difference is the code needed to initialize MPI and assign the device to the MPI rank, as shown in the previous section:

```
73    call MPI_init(ierr)
74    call MPI_comm_rank(MPI_COMM_WORLD, myrank, ierr)
75    call MPI_comm_size(MPI_COMM_WORLD, nProcs, ierr)
76
77    ! get and set device
78
79    call assignDevice(deviceID)
```

where we use the mpiDeviceUtil module introduced in the previous section to assign a unique device to the MPI rank. Parameter checking and initialization are the same in both codes. Timing in the MPI code is done using the MPI function MPI_Wtime() after a call to MPI_BARRIER().

The main difference between the peer-to-peer and MPI codes occurs within the loop over communication stages:

```
176   do stage = 1, nProcs-1
177      ! sRank = the rank to which myrank sends data
178      ! rRank = the rank from which myrank receives data
179      sRank = modulo(myrank-stage, nProcs)
180      rRank = modulo(myrank+stage, nProcs)
181
182      call MPI_BARRIER(MPI_COMM_WORLD, ierr)
183
184      ! D2H transfer - pack into contiguous host array
185      ierr = cudaMemcpy2D(sTile, mpiTileDimX, &
186           d_idata(sRank*mpiTileDimX+1,1), nx, &
187           mpiTileDimX, mpiTileDimY)
188
189      ! MPI transfer
190      call MPI_SENDRECV(sTile, mpiTileDimX*mpiTileDimY, &
191           MPI_REAL, sRank, myrank, &
192           rTile, mpiTileDimX*mpiTileDimY, MPI_REAL, &
193           rRank, rRank, MPI_COMM_WORLD, status, ierr)
194
195      ! H2D transfer
196      d_rTile = rTile
197
198      ! do transpose from receive tile into final array
199      call cudaTranspose<<<dimGrid, dimBlock>>> &
200           (d_tdata(rRank*mpiTileDimY+1,1), ny, &
201           d_rTile, mpiTileDimX)
202   end do
```

The `cudaMemcpy2d()` or `cudaMemcpy2dAsync()` calls that transfer data between devices in the peer-to-peer code are replaced by a device-to-host transfer (line 185), an MPI transfer between hosts (line 190), and a host-to-device transfer (line 196).

Running this code with two MPI ranks on an overall matrix of 2048×2048, we obtain:

```
Array size: 2048x2048

CUDA block size: 32x8,  CUDA tile size: 32x32
dimGrid: 32x32x1,    dimBlock: 32x8x1

nprocs: 2,  Local input array size: 2048x1024
mpiTileDim: 1024x1024

Bandwidth (GB/s):    7.37
```

which is considerably under the performance of the synchronous peer-to-peer code, even though both MPI ranks, and therefore devices, were on the same node. This is not surprising, however, given that the transfers are staged through the host. When performing a parallel transpose on devices distributed across multiple nodes, we would expect to incur the cost of transfers between host and device. However, when MPI transfers occur between device on the same node that are peer-to-peer capable, we would like to take advantage of the peer-to-peer capability in such cases. Luckily there are MPI implementations such as MVAPICH, OpenMPI, and Cray MPI that do exactly that. In the following section we show how the GPU-aware capabilities of MVAPICH can be leveraged in the transpose code.

4.2.3 GPU-aware MPI transpose

The MVAPICH implementation of MPI[2] overloads some of the MPI calls so they can take device arrays as well as host arrays. When the array arguments are device arrays from devices that exist on different nodes or that are not peer-to-peer capable, the transfers between the host and device are taken care of behind the scenes. When the array arguments are device arrays from devices on the same node that are peer-to-peer capable, then the transfer is done (in a nondefault stream) using the peer-to-peer mechanism.

To take advantage of MVAPICH, we only need to make a few modifications to the code, which is listed in Appendix D.4.3. First, we must set the device before any MPI function is called, which rules out using the `assignDevice()` as we have done previously. Luckily, MVAPICH sets a environment variable that contains the desired information, which we simply need to read as done in the following:

```
70    ! for MVAPICH set device before MPI initialization
71
72    call get_environment_variable('MV2_COMM_WORLD_LOCAL_RANK', &
```

---

[2] For the details of the GPU-aware MVAPICH implementation, we refer the reader to the MVAPICH documentation. Since we will be using CUDA Fortran, the PGI compiler must be selected as the default Fortran compiler.

```
73          localRankStr)
74    read(localRankStr,'(i10)') localRank
75    ierr = cudaSetDevice(localRank)
```

The main loop over communication stages in the MVAPICH code is:

```
178   do stage = 1, nProcs-1
179      ! sRank = the rank to which myrank sends data
180      ! rRank = the rank from which myrank receives data
181      sRank = modulo(myrank-stage, nProcs)
182      rRank = modulo(myrank+stage, nProcs)
183
184      call MPI_BARRIER(MPI_COMM_WORLD, ierr)
185
186      ! pack tile so data to be sent is contiguous
187
188      !$cuf kernel do(2) <<<*,*>>>
189      do j = 1, mpiTileDimY
190         do i = 1, mpiTileDimX
191            d_sTile(i,j) = d_idata(sRank*mpiTileDimX+i,j)
192         enddo
193      enddo
194
195      call MPI_SENDRECV(d_sTile, mpiTileDimX*mpiTileDimY, &
196           MPI_REAL, sRank, myrank, &
197           d_rTile, mpiTileDimX*mpiTileDimY, MPI_REAL, &
198           rRank, rRank, MPI_COMM_WORLD, status, ierr)
199
200      ! do transpose from receive tile into final array
201      ! (no need to unpack)
202
203      call cudaTranspose<<<dimGrid, dimBlock>>> &
204           (d_tdata(rRank*mpiTileDimY+1,1), ny, &
205           d_rTile, mpiTileDimX)
206
207   end do ! stage
```

where the MPI_SENDRECV() call on line 195 uses two device arrays, d_sTile and d_rTile. To facilitate the transfer, the sent data are packed into the contiguous array d_sTile using the CUF kernel on lines 188–193.

When the code is run on the same node and devices as the previous MPI transpose code, we obtain:

```
Array size: 2048x2048

CUDA block size: 32x8,   CUDA tile size: 32x32
dimGrid: 32x32x1,    dimBlock: 32x8x1

nprocs: 2,  Local input array size: 2048x1024
mpiTileDim: 1024x1024

Bandwidth (GB/s):    18.06
```

which shows a performance similar to the synchronous version of the peer-to-peer code.

Case Studies

Monte Carlo Method

5

A book on high-performance and parallel computing is not complete without an example that shows how to compute π. Instead of using the classic example of numerical integration of the function $\int_0^1 \frac{4}{1+x^2} dx$, we use a Monte Carlo method to compute π.

Calculating π using a Monte Carlo method is quite simple. In a unit square, we generate a sequence of N points, (x_i, y_i) with $i = 1, \ldots, N$, where each component is a random number with uniform distribution. We then count the number of points, M, that lie on or inside the unit circle (i.e., satisfy the relationship $x_i^2 + y_i^2 \leq 1$), as shown in Figure 5.1. The ratio of M to N will give us an estimate of $\pi/4$, which is the ratio of the area of a quarter of the unit circle, $\pi/4$, to the area of the unit square, 1. The method is inherently parallel, since every point can be evaluated independently, so we expect good performance and scalability on the GPU.

The accuracy of the ratio depends on the number of points used. The convergence to the real value is very slow: simple Monte Carlo methods like the one just presented have a convergence $O(1/\sqrt{N})$. There are algorithmic improvements such as importance sampling and the use of low-discrepancy sequences (quasi-Monte Carlo methods) to improve the convergence speed, but these are beyond the scope of this book.

In writing a CUDA Fortran code to solve this problem, the first issue we face is how to generate the random numbers on the GPU. Parallel random-number generation is a fascinating subject, but we take a shortcut and use CURAND, the library for random-number generation provided by CUDA. CURAND provides a high-quality, high-performance series of random and pseudo-random generators.

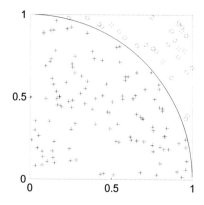

FIGURE 5.1

Monte Carlo method: π is computed as the ratio between the points inside the circle and the total number of points.

5.1 CURAND

The basic operations we need to perform in CURAND to generate a sequence of random numbers are:

- Create a generator using `curandCreateGenerator()`.
- Set a random-number seed with `curandSetPseudoRandomGeneratorSeed()`.
- Generate the data from a distribution using the functions `curandGenerateUniform()`, `curandGenerateNormal()`, or `curandGenerateLogNormal()`, depending on the distribution required.
- Destroy the generator with `curandDestroyGenerator()`.

Before applying this procedure to generate random numbers in our Monte Carlo code, we demonstrate how CURAND is used from CUDA Fortran in a simple application that generates N random numbers on the GPU, copies the results back to the CPU, and prints the first four values. There are several source code files used in this application. The main code is in the file `generate_randomnumbers.cuf`:

```
1  ! Generate N random numbers on GPU, copy them back to CPU
2  ! and print the first 4
3
4  program curand_example
5    use precision_m
6    use curand_m
7    implicit none
8    real(fp_kind), allocatable:: hostData(:)
9    real(fp_kind), allocatable, device:: deviceData(:)
10   integer(kind=int_ptr_kind()) :: gen, N, seed
11
```

```
12     ! Define how many numbers we want to generate
13     N=20
14
15     ! Allocate array on CPU
16     allocate(hostData(N))
17
18     ! Allocate array on GPU
19     allocate(deviceData(N))
20
21     if (fp_kind == singlePrecision) then
22        write(*,"('Generating random numbers in single precision')")
23     else
24        write(*,"('Generating random numbers in double precision')")
25     end if
26
27     ! Create pseudonumber generator
28     call curandCreateGenerator(gen, CURAND_RNG_PSEUDO_DEFAULT)
29
30     ! Set seed
31     seed=1234
32     call curandSetPseudoRandomGeneratorSeed( gen, seed)
33
34     ! Generate N floats or double on device
35     call curandGenerateUniform(gen, deviceData, N)
36
37     ! Copy the data back to CPU
38     hostData=deviceData
39
40     ! print the first 4 of the sequence
41     write(*,*) hostData(1:4)
42
43     ! Deallocate data on CPU and GPU
44     deallocate(hostData)
45     deallocate(deviceData)
46
47     ! Destroy the generator
48     call curandDestroyGenerator(gen)
49  end program curand_example
```

This code uses the precision_m module (line 5) to facilitate toggling between single and double precision. This module is contained in the precision_m.f90 file listed at the end of Section 1.4.1. The code also uses the curand_m module (line 6), which contains the interfaces that allow CUDA Fortran to call the CURAND library functions that are written in CUDA C. These interfaces in turn use the iso_c_binding module provided by the compiler. The curand_m module is defined in the file curand_m.cuf:

```
1  module curand_m
2    integer, public :: CURAND_RNG_PSEUDO_DEFAULT = 100
```

```fortran
3    integer, public :: CURAND_RNG_PSEUDO_XORWOW   = 101
4    integer, public :: CURAND_RNG_QUASI_DEFAULT   = 200
5    integer, public :: CURAND_RNG_QUASI_SOBOL32   = 201
6
7    interface curandCreateGenerator
8       subroutine curandCreateGenerator( &
9            generator,rng_type) &
10            bind(C,name='curandCreateGenerator')
11         use iso_c_binding
12         integer(c_size_t):: generator
13         integer(c_int),value:: rng_type
14      end subroutine curandCreateGenerator
15   end interface curandCreateGenerator
16
17   interface curandSetPseudoRandomGeneratorSeed
18       subroutine curandSetPseudoRandomGeneratorSeed( &
19            generator,seed) &
20            bind(C,name='curandSetPseudoRandomGeneratorSeed')
21         use iso_c_binding
22         integer(c_size_t), value:: generator
23         integer(c_long_long),value:: seed
24      end subroutine curandSetPseudoRandomGeneratorSeed
25   end interface curandSetPseudoRandomGeneratorSeed
26
27   interface curandGenerateUniform
28       subroutine curandGenerateUniform( &
29            generator, odata, numele) &
30            bind(C,name='curandGenerateUniform')
31         use iso_c_binding
32         integer(c_size_t),value:: generator
33         !pgi$ ignore_tr odata
34         real(c_float), device:: odata(*)
35         integer(c_size_t),value:: numele
36      end subroutine curandGenerateUniform
37
38       subroutine curandGenerateUniformDouble(&
39            generator, odata, numele) &
40            bind(C,name='curandGenerateUniformDouble')
41         use iso_c_binding
42         integer(c_size_t),value:: generator
43         !pgi$ ignore_tr odata
44         real(c_double), device:: odata(*)
45         integer(c_size_t),value:: numele
46      end subroutine curandGenerateUniformDouble
47   end interface curandGenerateUniform
48
49   interface curandGenerateNormal
```

```
50        subroutine curandGenerateNormal ( &
51            generator, odata, numele, mean,stddev) &
52            bind(C,name='curandGenerateNormal')
53          use iso_c_binding
54          integer(c_size_t),value:: generator
55          !pgi$ ignore_tr odata
56          real(c_float), device:: odata(*)
57          integer(c_size_t),value:: numele
58          real(c_float), value:: mean,stddev
59        end subroutine curandGenerateNormal
60
61        subroutine curandGenerateNormalDouble ( &
62            generator, odata, numele,mean, stddev) &
63            bind(C,name='curandGenerateNormalDouble')
64          use iso_c_binding
65          integer(c_size_t),value:: generator
66          !pgi$ ignore_tr odata
67          real(c_double), device:: odata(*)
68          integer(c_size_t),value:: numele
69          real(c_double), value:: mean,stddev
70        end subroutine curandGenerateNormalDouble
71      end interface curandGenerateNormal
72
73      interface curandDestroyGenerator
74        subroutine curandDestroyGenerator(generator) &
75            bind(C,name='curandDestroyGenerator')
76          use iso_c_binding
77          integer(c_size_t),value:: generator
78        end subroutine curandDestroyGenerator
79      end interface curandDestroyGenerator
80
81 end module curand_m
```

The use of the iso_c_binding module to interface with C functions and libraries is described in detail in Appendix C, but we should mention a few aspects of writing these interfaces here. First, CURAND contains different routines for single and double precision. Though we can use the precision_m module to toggle between single- and double-precision variables in our code, we need to use generic interfaces in curand_m to effectively toggle between functions. For example, the interface curandGenerateUniform() defined on line 27 contains the two subroutines curandGenerateUniform() and curandGenerateUniformDouble(). The correct version will be called depending on whether curandGenerateUniform() is called with single- or double-precision arguments.

Another issue encountered when we call C from Fortran is how C and Fortran pass arguments to functions: C passes arguments by value and Fortran passes arguments by address. This difference can be accommodated by using the variable qualifier `value` in the interface when declaring a dummy argument that is not a pointer. Each interface in `curand_m` uses at least one such `value` argument.

Finally, on some occasions generic C buffers are used in library functions. Because Fortran is strongly typed, to write an interface the `!pgi$ ignore_tkr` directive must be used, which effectively tells the compiler to ignore any combination of the type, kind, rank, and presence of the `device` attribute of the specified dummy arguments. For example, on lines 33 and 43 the directive is used to ignore the type and rank of `odata`.

The three source files code can be compiled with:

```
pgf90 -O3 -o rng_gpu_sp precision_m.F90 curand_m.cuf \
   generate_randomnumbers.cuf -lcurand
```

Here we need to add the CURAND library (`-lcurand`), located in the cuda subdirectory of the PGI installation, to link the proper functions. We also renamed the precision module file `precision_m.F90` so that the `-Mpreprocess` compiler option is not needed. If we execute `rng_gpu_sp`, we will see the following output:

```
./rng_gpu_sp
Generating random numbers in single precision
   0.1454676         0.8201809         0.5503992         0.2948303
```

To create a double-precision executable, we compile the code using:

```
pgf90 -DDOUBLE -O3 -o rng_gpu_dp precision_m.F90 \
   curand_m.cuf generate_randomnumbers.cuf -lcurand
```

where the option `-DDOUBLE` was added. If we execute `rng_gpu_dp`, we will see that the code is now using double precision:

```
./rng_gpu_dp
Generating random numbers in double precision
0.4348988043884129      0.9264169202024377
0.8118452111300192      0.3085554246353980
```

The two sequences are different; they are not just the same sequence with different precision.

5.2 Computing π with CUF kernels

Having established how to generate the random numbers in parallel on the GPU, we turn our attention to writing the Monte Carlo code to test whether points are inside the circle and count the number of points that satisfy this criterion. To accomplish this task, we first use a feature of CUDA Fortran called *CUF kernels*, also known as *kernel loop directives*, which were introduced in the 2011 version of the PGI compiler. CUF kernels are a set of directives that tell the compiler to generate a kernel from a loop or tightly nested loops when the data in the loop reside on the GPU (see Section 3.7 for more information on CUF kernels). These directives can greatly simplify the job of writing many trivial kernels; in addition, they are able to recognize reduction operations, such as counting the number of points that lie within the unit circle in our example.

If the random numbers are stored in two arrays X(N) and Y(N), the CPU code to determine the number of points that lie inside the unit circle is:

```
inside=0
do i=1,N
  if (  (X(i)**2 + Y(i)**2 ) <= 1._fpkind ) inside=inside+1
end do
```

If we denote X_d and Y_d as the two corresponding arrays on the GPU, the PGI compiler is able to generate a kernel that performs the same operations on the GPU simply by adding a directive:

```
inside=0
!$cuf kernel do <<< *, * >>>
do i=1,N
  if (  (X_d(i)**2 + Y_d(i)**2 ) <= 1._fpkind ) inside=inside+1
end do
```

This directive instructs the compiler to generate a kernel for the do loop that follows. Moreover, the compiler is able to detect that the variable inside is the result of a reduction operation. Without the use of CUF kernels, reductions in CUDA need to be expressed using either atomic operations or a sequence of two kernels: the first kernel generates partial sums, and the second kernel uses a single block to compute the final sum. We present these methods of performing the reduction later in this chapter. Though not difficult, getting all the details right can be time consuming.

Putting together the random-number generation with the CUF kernel that counts the number of points that lie in the unit circle, we have a fully functional Monte Carlo code. We also perform the same operation on the CPU to check the results. When the counting variable is an integer, we should get the exact same result on both platforms, since integer addition is commutative. We will see later on that when the accumulation is done on floating-point variables, there may be differences due to the different order of accumulation.

```fortran
1   ! Compute pi using a Monte Carlo method
2
3   program compute_pi
4     use precision_m
5     use curand_m
6     implicit none
7     real(fp_kind), allocatable:: hostData(:)
8     real(fp_kind), allocatable, device:: deviceData(:)
9     real(fp_kind) :: pival
10    integer :: inside_gpu, inside_cpu, N, i
11    integer(kind=int_ptr_kind()) :: gen, twoN, seed
12
13    ! Define how many numbers we want to generate
14    N=100000
15    twoN=N*2
16
17    ! Allocate array on CPU
18    allocate(hostData(twoN))
19
20    ! Allocate array on GPU
21    allocate(deviceData(twoN))
22
23    if (fp_kind == singlePrecision) then
24       write(*,"('Compute pi in single precision')")
25    else
26       write(*,"('Compute pi in double precision')")
27    end if
28
29    ! Create pseudonumber generator
30    call curandCreateGenerator(gen, CURAND_RNG_PSEUDO_DEFAULT)
31
32    ! Set seed
33    seed=1234
34    call curandSetPseudoRandomGeneratorSeed( gen, seed)
35
36    ! Generate N floats or double on device
37    call curandGenerateUniform(gen, deviceData, twoN)
38
39    ! Copy the data back to CPU to check result later
40    hostData=deviceData
41
42    ! Perform the test on GPU using CUF kernel
43    inside_gpu=0
44    !$cuf kernel do <<<*,*>>>
45    do i=1,N
46       if( (deviceData(i)**2+deviceData(i+N)**2) <= 1._fp_kind ) &
47             inside_gpu=inside_gpu+1
48    end do
49
50    ! Perform the test on CPU
```

```
51   inside_cpu=0
52   do i=1,N
53      if( (hostData(i)**2+hostData(i+N)**2) <= 1._fp_kind ) &
54          inside_cpu=inside_cpu+1
55   end do
56
57   ! Check the results
58   if (inside_cpu .ne. inside_gpu) &
59       write(*,*) "Mismatch between CPU/GPU"
60
61   ! Print the value of pi and the error
62   pival= 4._fp_kind*real(inside_gpu,fp_kind)/real(N,fp_kind)
63   write(*,"(t3,a,i10,a,f10.8,a,e11.4)") "Samples=", N, &
64        " Pi=", pival, &
65        " Error=", abs(pival-2.0_fp_kind*asin(1.0_fp_kind))
66
67   ! Deallocate data on CPU and GPU
68   deallocate(hostData)
69   deallocate(deviceData)
70
71   ! Destroy the generator
72   call curandDestroyGenerator(gen)
73  end program compute_pi
```

In this code, rather than generate two sequences of N random numbers for the *x* and *y* coordinates, we generate only one set of twoN random numbers that can be interpreted as containing all the *x* coordinates first, followed by all the *y* coordinates. Compiling the code similarly to rng_gpu_sp, for single precision, typical output will be:

```
./pi_sp
  Compute pi  in single precision
  Samples=    100000  Pi=3.13631988  Error= 0.5273E-02
```

which gives a reasonable result for the number of samples. We can add a simple do loop to study the convergence of the solution:

```
Compute pi  in single precision
  Samples=       10000  Pi=3.11120009  Error= 0.3039E-01
  Samples=      100000  Pi=3.13632011  Error= 0.5273E-02
  Samples=     1000000  Pi=3.14056396  Error= 0.1029E-02
  Samples=    10000000  Pi=3.14092445  Error= 0.6683E-03
  Samples=   100000000  Pi=3.14158082  Error= 0.1192E-04
```

From these results, which span several orders of magnitude of sample size, we observe $O(N^{-1/2})$ convergence of the method. We need to increase the sample size by two orders of magnitude to lower the error by an order of magnitude. Using double precision would not alter the convergence rate, since the rate is determined solely by the number of points; the test of whether a point it is inside or outside the unit circle is not affected by precision. A typical result in double precision is:

```
Compute pi  in double precision (seed = 1234)
   Samples =      10000  Pi=3.13440000  Error= 0.7193E-02
   Samples =     100000  Pi=3.13716000  Error= 0.4433E-02
   Samples =    1000000  Pi=3.14028800  Error= 0.1305E-02
   Samples =   10000000  Pi=3.14155360  Error= 0.3905E-04
   Samples =  100000000  Pi=3.14141980  Error= 0.1729E-03
```

where the apparent better precision of the double sequence is a consequence of a lucky seed. Changing the seed will produce a new series that will generate different results. For example, doing a simulation in double precision with a seed=1234567 will give lower accuracy than the simulation with single precision with seed=1234:

```
Compute pi  in double precision (seed=1234567)
   Samples =      10000  Pi=3.12880000  Error= 0.1279E-01
   Samples =     100000  Pi=3.14676000  Error= 0.5167E-02
   Samples =    1000000  Pi=3.14274000  Error= 0.1147E-02
   Samples =   10000000  Pi=3.14062480  Error= 0.9679E-03
   Samples =  100000000  Pi=3.14148248  Error= 0.1102E-03
```

5.2.1 IEEE-754 precision *(advanced topic)*

CPUs have been following the IEEE Standard for Floating-Point Arithmetic, also known as IEEE 754 standard, for quite some time: The original standard was published in 1985 and was updated in 2008 to IEEE 754-2008. This standard made it possible to write algorithms using floating-point arithmetic that could be executed on a variety of platforms with identical results. A detailed description is outside the scope of this book, but one of the main additions to the updated standard was the introduction of a Fused Multiply-Add (FMA) instruction. FMA computes $a \times b + c$ with only one rounding operation and has been available on several computer architectures, including IBM Power architecture and Intel Itanium. When implemented in hardware, the equivalent instruction takes about the same time as a multiply, resulting in a performance advantage for many applications.

Whereas an unfused multiply-add would compute the product $a \times b$, round it to P significant bits, add the result to c, and round back to P significant bits, a fused multiply-add would compute the entire sum $a \times b + c$ to its full precision before rounding the final result down to P significant bits.

Several generations of NVIDIA GPUs, like the Tesla C2050 (Fermi architecture) or the Tesla K20 (Kepler architecture), have support for the IEEE 754-2008 FMA in both single and double precision. In CUDA Fortran it is possible to disable generating this instruction using the compiler option `-Mcuda=nofma`.

If we revisit our calculation of π, we realize that the result of the test to see if the points are inside the unit circle is dependent on whether FMA is used or not. The test is summing the square of the coordinates of each point and comparing this value to the unity. If the value computed by the CPU and GPU is off by only one bit, the test will give different results if the point is exactly on the unit circle. The probability of finding points exactly on the unit circle is small but nonzero. If we rerun the previous code with `seed=1234567`, we observe a discrepancy between the number of interior points detected by the CPU and the one detected by the GPU when the number of samples is equal to 100 million.

```
Compute pi  in single  precision  (seed=1234567  FMA  enabled)
   Samples=      10000   Pi=3.16720009   Error=  0.2561E-01
   Samples=     100000   Pi=3.13919997   Error=  0.2393E-02
   Samples=    1000000   Pi=3.14109206   Error=  0.5007E-03
   Samples=   10000000   Pi=3.14106607   Error=  0.5267E-03
 Mismatch  between  CPU/GPU       78534862        78534859
   Samples= 100000000   Pi=3.14139414   Error=  0.1986E-03
```

There are 3 out of 100 million points for which the test is giving different results, listed in Table 5.1:

We will analyze the error in detail for the first point; however, the same analysis applies to the other points. To analyze the error, we look at results obtained by rearranging the order of the multiplications and additions. Using the notation $FMA(a, b, c) = a \times b + c$, we could compute $x^2 + y^2$ in one of three ways (the results on the left are in floating-point notation, the ones on the right in hexadecimal notation):

Table 5.1 Coordinates of the points and distance from the origin with results different between CPU and GPU. Values are in floating-point (top) and hexadecimal (bottom) representations.

N	x	y	$x^2 + y^2$ CPU	$x^2 + y^2$ GPU with FMA
2377069	6.162945032e-01	7.875158191e-01	1.000000000	1.000000119
	3F1DC57A	3F499AA3	3F800000	3F800001
33027844	2.018149495e-01	9.794237018e-01	1.000000000	1.000000119
	3E4EA894	3F7ABB83	3F800000	3F800001
81541078	6.925099492e-01	7.214083672e-01	1.000000000	1.000000119
	3F314855	3F38AE38	3F800000	3F800001

1. Compute $x*x$, compute $y*y$, and then add the two squares:
$(x*x + y*y) = 1.000000000e+00$ 3f800000
2. Compute $y*y$, use FMA $(x,x,y*y)$:
fmaf(x,x,y*y)= 1.000000000e+00 3f800000
3. Compute $x*x$, use FMA $(y,y,x*x)$:
fmaf(y,y,x*x)= 1.000000119e+00 3f800001

In theory, the last way should be the most accurate, since in this case $y > x$ and therefore we are using the full precision for the bigger term. To confirm this, we could try the following experiment: What would it happen if we recompute the distance on the CPU in double precision?

The following code performs this experiment. It loads the hex value of x and y, computes the distance with the single-precision values, casts the values of x and y to double precision and recomputes the distance in double, and finally recasts the double-precision value of the distance to single precision.

```
1   program test_accuracy
2     real :: x, y, dist
3     double precision:: x_dp, y_dp, dist_dp
4
5     x=Z'3F1DC57A'
6     y=Z'3F499AA3'
7     dist= x**2 +y**2
8
9     x_dp=real(x,8)
10    y_dp=real(y,8)
11    dist_dp= x_dp**2 +y_dp**2
12
13    print *, 'Result with operands in single precision:'
14    print '((2x,z8)) ', dist
15
16    print *, 'Result in double precision with operands'
17    print *, 'promoted to double precision:'
18    print '((2x,z16))', dist_dp
19
20    print *, 'Result in single precision with operands'
21    print *, 'promoted to double precision:'
22    print '((2x,z8))', real(dist_dp,4)
23
24  end program test_accuracy
```

```
Result with operands in single precision:
 3F800000
Result in double precision with operands
```

```
promoted to double precision:
 3FF0000015781ED0
Result in single precision with operands
promoted to double precision:
 3F800001
```

The result from `fmaf(y,y,x*x)` in single precision on the GPU matches the result on the CPU when the operands are promoted to double precision. All the operations are performed in double precision, and the final result is cast back to single.

The following detailed analysis shows why the third result differs by one *ULP* (unit in the last place or unit of least precision, the spacing between floating-point numbers) from the other two results:

```
  x   = 3f1dc57a
  y   = 3f499aa3
  x*x = 3ec277a0
  fma(y,y,x*x) =
        3f1ec431_5e83c90
      + 3ec277a0_0000000
      -----------------
        9ec431_5e83c90    // align mantissas for add
        613bd0_0000000
      -----------------
        1000001_5e83c90   // sum
        800000_af41e48    // normalized mantissa
      -----------------
      = 3f800000_af41e48  // result before rounding
      = 3f800001          // rounded result
```

As Einstein said: "A man with a watch knows what time it is. A man with two watches is never sure." Now that we have two outputs, we may get different results and need to understand the source of the possible difference. In the context of finite precision math, the difference is extremely slight. FMA instructions are being introduced in x86 processors too, so this kind of behavior can be observed on mainstream CPUs as well. Recompiling the code disabling the FMA instruction (`-Mcuda=nofma`) will generate the same value on the GPU as on the CPU, as we expected from our analysis:

```
Compute pi  in single precision (seed=1234567 FMA disabled)
   Samples=       10000  Pi=3.16720009  Error= 0.2561E-01
   Samples=      100000  Pi=3.13919997  Error= 0.2393E-02
   Samples=     1000000  Pi=3.14109206  Error= 0.5007E-03
   Samples=    10000000  Pi=3.14106607  Error= 0.5267E-03
   Samples=   100000000  Pi=3.14139462  Error= 0.1981E-03
```

5.3 Computing π with reduction kernels

The use of CUF kernels to calculate π was advantageous in that we did not need to write explicit code for a reduction; the compiler performed the reduction on our behalf. However, circumstances may arise where we need to write a reduction in CUDA Fortran, so in this section we explore how this is done in the context of our Monte Carlo code.

The most common reduction operation is computing the sum of a large array of values. Other reduction operations that are often encountered are the computation of the minimum or maximum value of an array. Before describing the approach, we should remember that the properties of a reduction operator $\otimes$ are:

- The operator is *commutative*: $a \otimes b = b \otimes a$
- The operator is *associative*: $a \otimes (b \otimes c) = (a \otimes b) \otimes c$

With these two properties, we can rearrange and combine the elements in any order. We should point out that the second property is not always true when performed on a computer: Although integer addition is always associative, floating-point addition is not. If we change the order of the partial sums and the operands are expressed as floating-point numbers, we may get different results.

We have seen that the fundamental programming paradigms of CUDA are that each block is independent and that the same shared memory is visible only to threads within a thread block. How could we perform a global operation like a reduction using multiple blocks with these two constraints? There are several ways of doing so, which we discuss in this and the following section. The approach we use in this section is to use two different kernels to perform the reduction. In the first kernel, each block will compute its partial sum and will write the result back to global memory. After the first kernel is completed, a second kernel consisting of a single block is launched, reading the partial sums and performing the final reduction. The code used for these two stages is quite similar, since the operations performed by a block in both stages are almost identical: (see Figure 5.2).

If each block would calculate a partial sum with a single accumulator (as we would do on the CPU), there will only be a single thread out of the entire thread block working and the rest would be idle. Though this is still legal CUDA code, it will give very poor performance, since the hardware utilization would be suboptimal. Luckily, there is a very well-known workaround to perform a parallel summation: a tree reduction. Figures 5.2 and 5.3 depict tree reductions. To sum N values using a tree reduction, we first sum them in pairs, ending up with $N/2$ values, and we keep repeating the procedure until there is a single value left. The level of parallelism decreases for each iteration, but it is still better than the sequential alternative.

Now let's analyze a case in which $N = 16$, assuming a block with 16 threads for illustrative purposes. (In reality we want to use many more threads in a block to hide latencies.) After we load the values in shared memory, each active thread at step M ($M = 1, \ldots, log N$) will sum its value to the one with stride 2^{M-1}, as in Figure 5.4. If we look carefully at Figure 5.4, we notice that there is room for improvement. The issue here is thread divergence. For cases where a large number of threads per block are used, a warp of threads in the latter stages of the reduction may have only one active thread. We would like to have all the active threads in as few warps as possible in order to minimize divergence. This can be achieved by storing the result of one stage of the reduction so that all the active threads for the next stage are contiguous. This is accomplished by the scenario in Figure 5.5.

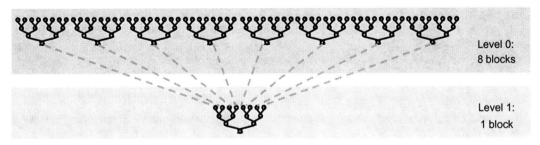

FIGURE 5.2

Two-stage reduction: Multiple blocks perform a local reduction in a first stage. A single block performs the final reduction in a second stage.

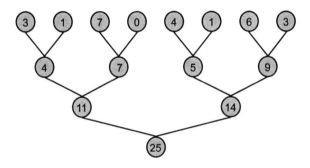

FIGURE 5.3

Tree reduction in a single block.

With this in mind we are now ready to write the kernel to perform the final reduction, where a single thread block is launched. The code to calculate the final sum is:

```
5    attributes(global) subroutine final_sum(partial,total)
6       integer :: partial(256)
7       integer, shared :: psum(*)
8       integer :: total
9       integer :: index, inext
10
11      index=threadIdx%x
12
13      psum(index)=partial(index)
14      call syncthreads()
15
16      inext=blockDim%x/2
17      do while ( inext >=1 )
```

```
18        if (index <=inext) &
19            psum(index)=psum(index)+psum(index+inext)
20        inext = inext/2
21        call syncthreads()
22    end do
23    if (index == 1) total=psum(1)
24  end subroutine final_sum
```

On line 13, each thread loads a value of the partial sum array from global memory into the shared memory array psum. To be sure that all the threads have completed this task, a call to syncthreads() forces a barrier (the control flow will resume when all the threads in a thread block have reached this point). This will ensure a consistent view of the shared memory array for all the threads. We are now ready to start the reduction. For the first stage of reduction, a thread pool composed of half the threads (inext) will sum the value at index with value at index+inext and store the result at index. For each subsequent stage, inext is halved and the procedure repeated until there is only one thread left in the pool.

When the while loop beginning on line 17 is completed, the thread with index 1 has the final value, which we will store back in global memory (line 23). The only limitation in the kernel is the requirement for the total number of threads used to be a power of 2. It will be easy to pad the array in shared memory to the next suitable number with values that are neutral to the reduction operation (for the sum, the neutral value is 0).

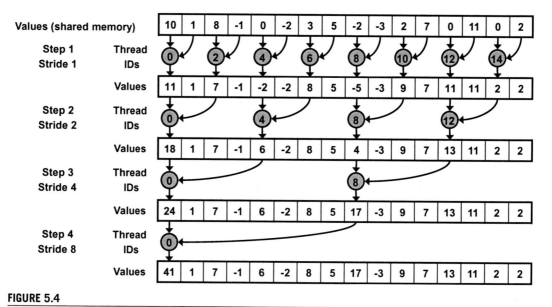

FIGURE 5.4

Tree reduction in a single block with divergence.

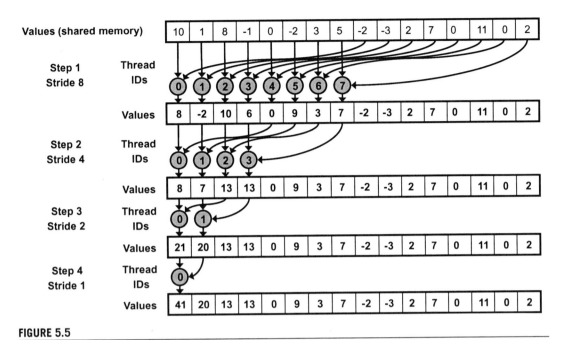

FIGURE 5.5

Tree reduction in a single block without divergence.

Having written the kernel for the final reduction, we now turn to writing the kernel to calculate the partial reduction that generates the input to the final reduction kernel. In the Monte Carlo code, to compute π the number of points used was quite large (up to 100 million). If we are going to use a 1D grid of blocks and a 1:1 mapping between threads and elements of the array, we will be limited to $65535 \times 512 \approx 33M$ (or, in the case of a GPU with compute capability greater than 2.0, $65535 \times 1024 \approx 66M$). We could use a 2D grid of blocks to increase the total number of available threads, but there is another strategy that is simpler. We could have a single thread adding up multiple elements of the array in serial fashion and start the tree reduction when each thread has exhausted the work. This will be beneficial for performance, since all the threads will be active for a long time, instead of losing half of the active threads at each step of the reduction. The code for this is as follows:

```
26    attributes(global) subroutine partial_sum(input,partial,N)
27       real(fp_kind) :: input(N)
28       integer :: partial(256)
29       integer, shared :: psum(*)
30       integer :: total
31       integer(kind=8),value :: N
32       integer :: i,index, inext,interior
33
34       index=threadIdx%x+(BlockIdx%x-1)*BlockDim%x
```

```
35
36        interior=0
37        do i=index,N/2,BlockDim%x*GridDim%x
38           if ( (input(i)**2+input(i+N/2)**2) <= 1._fp_kind ) &
39                 interior=interior+1
40        end do
41
42        ! Local reduction per block
43        index=threadIdx%x
44
45        psum(index)=interior
46        call syncthreads()
47
48        inext=blockDim%x/2
49        do while ( inext >=1 )
50           if (index <=inext) &
51                 psum(index)=psum(index)+psum(index+inext)
52           inext = inext /2
53           call syncthreads()
54        end do
55        if (index == 1) partial(BlockIdx%x)=psum(1)
56     end subroutine partial_sum
```

The listing for the partial reduction is very similar to the one for the final reduction. This time, instead of reading the partial sum from global memory, we will compute the partial sums starting from the input data. The variable `interior` will store the number of interior points that each thread will detect inside the circle. The rest of the code follows exactly the same logic of the code to compute the final sum, with the only difference that thread 1 will write the partial sum to a different global array `partial` in the position corresponding to the block number.

Now that we have the two custom kernels, the only missing piece is their invocation. In the following code we call the first kernel that computes the partial sums (using, for example, 256 blocks of 512 threads), followed by the kernel that computes the final result (using 1 block with 256 threads):

```
! Compute the partial sums with 256 blocks of 512 threads
  call partial_sum<<<256,512,512*4>>>(deviceData,partial,N)
! Compute the final sum with 1 block of 256 threads
  call final_sum<<<1,256,256*4>>>(partial,inside_gpu)
```

Once again, the sizes of the grid and thread block are independent of the number of points we process, since the loop on line 11 of the partial reduction accommodates any amount of data. We can use different block and grid sizes; the only requirement is that number of blocks in the partial reduction must correspond to the number of threads in the one block of the final reduction. To accommodate different block sizes, dynamic shared memory is used, as indicated by the third configuration parameter argument.

5.3.1 Reductions with atomic locks *(advanced topic)*

We mentioned in the previous section that there are two ways to perform a reduction, aside from using CUF kernels. The independence of blocks was circumvented in the previous section by using two kernels. There is one way for separate blocks within a single kernel launch to share and update data safely for certain operations.[1] This requires some features to ensure global synchronization among blocks, supported only in GPUs with compute capabilities of 1.1 or higher. The entire reduction code using atomic locks will be nearly identical to the code that performs the partial reduction in the two-kernel approach. The only difference is that instead of having each block store its partial sum to global memory:

```
if (index == 1) partial(BlockIdx%x)=psum(1)
```

and then run a second kernel to add these partial sums, a single value in global memory is updated using an atomic lock to ensure that only one block at a time updates the final sum:

```
if (index == 1) then
    do while ( atomiccas(lock,0,1) == 1) !set lock
    end do
    partial(1)=partial(1)+psum(1)    ! atomic update of partial(1)
    call threadfence()         ! Wait for memory transaction to be
                               ! visible to all the other threads
    lock =0                    ! release lock
end if
```

Outside of this code, the integer variable `lock` is declared in global memory and initialized to 0. To set the lock, the code uses the `atomicCAS` (atomic Compare And Swap) instruction. `atomicCAS(mem,comp,val)` compares `mem` to `comp` and atomically stores back the value `val` in `mem` if they are equal. The function returns the value of `mem`. The logic is equivalent to the following code:

```
if (mem == comp ) then
    mem = val
end if
return mem
```

with the addition of the atomic update, i.e., only one block at a time will be able to aquire the lock. Another important routine is `threadfence()`, which ensures that the global memory access made by the calling thread prior to `threadfence()` is visible to all the threads in the device. We also need to be sure that the variable that is going to store the final sum (in this case, we are reusing the first element of the partial array from the previous kernel) is initialized to zero:

---

[1]Giles, http://people.maths.ox.ac.uk/gilesm/cuda/lecs/lec4.pdf.

```
partial(1)=0
call sum<<<64,256,256*4>>>(deviceData,partial,N)
inside=partial(1)
```

As a final note in this section, we should elaborate on the degree to which atomic functions can provide cooperation between blocks. Atomic operations can only be used when the order of the operations is not important, as in the case of reductions. This is because the order in which the blocks are scheduled cannot be determined; there is no warranty, for example, that block 1 starts before block N. If we were to assume any particular order, the code may cause deadlock. Deadlocks, along with race conditions, are the most difficult bugs to diagnose and fix, since their occurrence may be sporadic and/or may cause the computer or GPU to lock. The code for the atomic lock does not rely on a particular scheduling of the blocks; it only ensures that one block at a time updates the variable, but the order of the blocks does not matter.

5.4 Accuracy of summation

The summation we used to find the number of points inside the circle used integer variables. Reductions involving floating-point variables are very common and important for a wide variety of numerical applications. When we deal with floating-point arithmetic, several numerical accuracy issues can arise (rounding, cancellation of significant digits), and particular care should be taken in designing an algorithm that reduces these errors.

The standard way of summing a sequence of N numbers:

$$S = \sum_{i=1}^{N} x_i$$

is the use of the recursive formula (hence the term *recursive summation*):

$$S_0 = 0$$
$$S_i = S_{i-1} + x_i, \quad i = 1, 2, \dots, N$$
$$S = S_N$$

The accuracy and stability properties of the recursion have been extensively studied in literature. Without going into too many details (an excellent in-depth error analysis is given by Higham (Higham, 2002)), the main source of the error is the difference in magnitude between the running sum and the terms of the sequence. When summing two floating-point numbers with big difference in magnitude, there is a loss of precision. In the extreme case, the new term of the sequence added to the running sum could be completely lost. When both negative and positive operands are present, there is also the issue of subtractive cancellation. How could we improve the accuracy of the sum?

- Minimize the intermediate sum by sorting the sequence. To keep the error small, we want the S_i term as small as possible, i.e., the smallest terms should be added first. This is very expensive and it may be difficult or impossible to apply in general cases.

Table 5.2 Sum of the series for $N = 8192$. For the single-precision results, the upper value is the sum, the lower value is the error.

x(i)		Forward Single Precision	Backward Single Precision	Reference Result
$1/i$	Result	1.644725	1.644812	1.644812003408614
	error	8.6680685225104526E-005	1.5531721686556921E-008	
$1/i^2$	Result	9.588196	9.588188	9.588190111622680
	error	5.6891585700213909E-006	1.9402359612286091E-006	

- Use an accumulator with higher precision. In double precision, there will be 53 bits to store the mantissa, and a loss of significant digits will be reduced or completely eliminated. Note that on a GPU capable only of single precision, this is not a feasible solution.
- Use multiple intermediate sums. The extreme case, *pairwise summation*, also has the nice property of exposing parallelism. This is the preferred solution on GPUs and the approach we used in the previous examples.
- Use a compensated sum, also known as *Kahan summation*. The basic idea is to have a correction term designed to reduce the rounding errors. It achieves better accuracy at the cost of increasing the arithmetic intensity by a factor of four, and it is still a serial algorithm. The algorithm is quite old (Kahan, 1965) and was written at a time when double precision was not supported on several architectures. Kahan summation is the most popular compensated summation technique, but there are several variations of this idea.

There are other algorithms (insertion, several variants of compensated sum). Higham's book (Higham, 2002) is a good reference.

Let's explore sorting the sequence before doing the summation. To verify the effectiveness of sorting, we could sum a simple series, taking $N = 8192$ and $x(i) = 1/i$ or $x(i) = 1/i^2$. The elements in the two sequences are by construction sorted and with descending magnitude. We can do a forward sum (from $i = 1$ to N) and a backward sum (from $i = N$ to 1) and compare the accuracy to a sum where the accumulator is stored in double precision and produce Table 5.2.

As predicted by the error analysis, the sum where the smallest terms are added first, in this case from $i = N$ to 1, in order to minimize the running sum, returns the closest value to the reference sum.

To examine the other algorithms, we reuse an example from Barone (Barone et al., 2006), summing an array with 10 million elements, all equal to 7.0. Clearly, in this case, sorting the array will not reduce the error. We compare the sum computed by the intrinsic Fortran90 function sum(), the recursive sum with a single-precision accumulator, the recursive sum with a double-precision accumulator, the pairwise reduction, and the Kahan sum.

```
1  program sum_accuracy
2    implicit none
3    real, allocatable :: x(:)
4    real :: sum_intrinsic,sum_cpu, sum_kahan, sum_pairwise, &
5        comp, y, tmp
```

```fortran
 6    double precision :: sum_cpu_dp
 7    integer :: i,inext,icurrent,  N=10000000
 8
 9    allocate (x(N))
10    x=7.
11
12    ! Summation using intrinsic
13    sum_intrinsic=sum(x)
14
15    ! Recursive summation
16    sum_cpu=0.
17    sum_cpu_dp=0.d0
18    do i=1,N
19       ! accumulator in single precision
20       sum_cpu=sum_cpu+x(i)
21       ! accumulator in double precision
22       sum_cpu_dp=sum_cpu_dp+x(i)
23    end do
24
25    ! Kahan summation
26    sum_kahan=0.
27    comp=0. ! running compensation to recover lost low-order bits
28
29    do i=1,N
30       y    = comp +x(i)
31       tmp  = sum_kahan + y      ! low-order bits may be lost
32       comp = (sum_kahan-tmp)+y ! (sum-tmp) recover low-order bits
33       sum_kahan = tmp
34    end do
35    sum_kahan=sum_kahan +comp
36
37    ! Pairwise summation
38    icurrent=N
39    inext=ceiling(real(N)/2)
40    do while (inext >1)
41       do i=1,inext
42          if ( 2*i <= icurrent) x(i)=x(i)+x(i+inext)
43       end do
44       icurrent=inext
45       inext=ceiling(real(inext)/2)
46    end do
47    sum_pairwise=x(1)+x(2)
48
49    write(*, "('Summming ',i10, &
50        ' elements of magnitude ',f3.1)") N,7.
51    write(*, "('Sum with intrinsic function       =',f12.1, &
52        '   Error=', f12.1)")  &
53        sum_intrinsic, 7.*N-sum_intrinsic
54    write(*, "('Recursive sum with SP accumulator =',f12.1, &
55        '   Error=', f12.1)")  sum_cpu, 7.*N-sum_cpu
56    write(*, "('Recursive sum with DP accumulator =',f12.1, &
```

```
57           '       Error=', f12.1)") sum_cpu_dp, 7.*N-sum_cpu_dp
58     write(*, "('Pairwise sum in SP               =',f12.1, &
59           '       Error=', f12.1)") sum_pairwise, 7.*N-sum_pairwise
60     write(*, "('Compensated sum in SP            =',f12.1, &
61           '       Error=', f12.1)") sum_kahan, 7.*N-sum_kahan
62
63     deallocate(x)
64 end program sum_accuracy
```

The output from compiling and running this simple Fortran code is:

```
pgf90 -O3 -o accuracy_sum accuracy_sum.f90


./accuracy_sum
Summming   10000000 elements of magnitude 7.0
Sum with intrinsic function        = 77603248.0    Error= -7603248.0
Recursive sum with SP accumulator = 77603248.0    Error= -7603248.0
Recursive sum with DP accumulator = 70000000.0    Error=        0.0
Pairwise sum in SP                 = 70000000.0    Error=        0.0
Compensated sum in SP              = 70000000.0    Error=        0.0
```

As we can see from the output, both the intrinsic sum and the recursive sum in single precision give us a wrong answer, overestimating the sum. The recursive sum with the double-precision accumulator, the pairwise summation, and the Kahan summation are instead delivering the correct result. It should be mentioned that this is the ideal case for pairwise reduction, since all the arguments at each stage are equal.

If we increase the number of elements by a factor of two, we will see that the two methods that were giving the incorrect result are still giving the wrong answer but are now underestimating the sum.

```
pgf90 -O3 -o accuracy_sum accuracy_sum.f90

./accuracy_sum
Summming   20000000 elements of magnitude 7.0
Sum with intrinsic function        = 134217728.0    Error=  5782272.0
Recursive sum with SP accumulator = 134217728.0    Error=  5782272.0
Recursive sum with DP accumulator = 140000000.0    Error=        0.0
Pairwise sum in SP                 = 140000000.0    Error=        0.0
Compensated sum in SP              = 140000000.0    Error=        0.0
```

It is instructive to see how the error behaves when we vary the range. Figure 5.6 shows the sum computed with the recursive formula compared with the expected value and a plot of the error when the number of terms in the sequence varies over a wide range. We can observe two different regions in the error plot. The first part is where the main source of the error is coming from rounding (in this case rounding up), causing an overestimation of the sum. The second part is where the main source of the error is due to the difference in magnitude that completely neglects the additional terms in the sum.

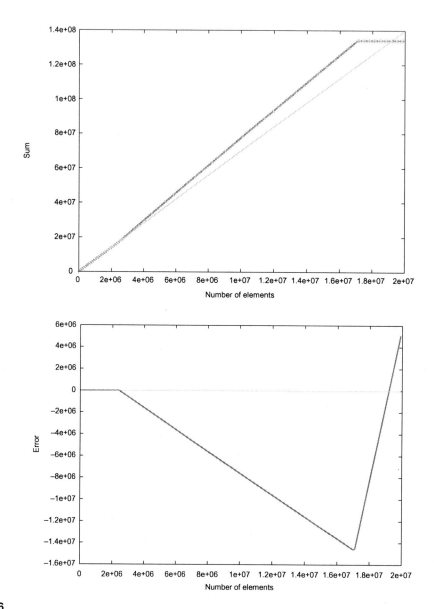

FIGURE 5.6

Top: Computed value for the recursive sum (dotted line) compared to exact result (solid line). Bottom: Difference between the two values.

The first value at which the sum is computed incorrectly is $N = 2396746$. This is easily computed since a single-precision IEEE floating-point number has 23 digits in the mantissa, plus an implicit leading digit, so the last number for which there will be no loss of precision will be $2^{24}/7 = 2396745$.

The same behavior could be observed for sums in which the elements are all different but very small. Using double-precision representation for the floating point numbers, the problem will still be present but appears when N in the order of 10^{16}.

Is there anything else we could learn from this example? Yes, there is another important aspect. Modern CPUs have vector instructions (SSE, SSE2, SSE3, SSE4, AVX) that enable the CPU to perform the same operation on multiple data (the exact number of concurrent operations will depend on the width of the vector hardware and the type of data used). After the debug phase, it is not unusual to enable aggressive optimizations with flags similar to -fast or -fastsse. If we recompile our simple example with the flag -fast, we will see a similar behavior, but the errors will be smaller in magnitude.

```
pgf90  -fast   -o accuracy_sum_sse accuracy_sum.f90

./accuracy_sum_sse
Summming   10000000 elements of magnitude 7.0
Sum with intrinsic function       = 70413008.0    Error=    413008.0
Recursive sum with SP accumulator = 70413008.0    Error=    413008.0
Recursive sum with DP accumulator = 70000000.0    Error=         0.0
Pairwise sum in SP                = 70000000.0    Error=         0.0
Compensated sum in SP             = 70000000.0    Error=         0.0
```

With the -fast option, the compiler is generating vector instructions and using multiple accumulators. The multiple accumulators have a smaller magnitude than the single one, extending the range in which the sum is correct. To find out exactly what the compiler is doing, we had to inspect the assembler code and notice the use of Horizontal Add Packed Single-FP (HADDPS), which, from two input vector registers {A0,A1,A2,A3} and {B0,B1,B2,B3}, generates the output {A0+A1,A2+A3,B0+B1,B2+B3}.

We can also recompute the same sequence we used with the forward and backward summations to compare the errors of all the methods.

```
Summming       8192 elements of magnitude 1/(i)
Sum with intrinsic function = 0.9588196E+01   Error= 0.5689159E-05
Recursive SP forward sum    = 0.9588196E+01   Error= 0.5689159E-05
Recursive DP forward sum    = 0.9588190E+01   Error= 0.0000000E+00
Pairwise sum in SP          = 0.9588190E+01   Error=-0.3288733E-07
Compensated sum in SP       = 0.9588190E+01   Error=-0.3288733E-07

Summming       8192 elements of magnitude 1/(i*i)
Sum with intrinsic function = 0.1644725E+01   Error=-0.8668069E-04
Recursive SP forward sum    = 0.1644725E+01   Error=-0.8668069E-04
Recursive DP forward sum    = 0.1644812E+01   Error= 0.0000000E+00
Pairwise sum in SP          = 0.1644812E+01   Error=-0.1347410E-06
Compensated sum in SP       = 0.1644812E+01   Error=-0.1553172E-07
```

This section reminds us that the effect of different algorithms and the proprieties of floating-point arithmetics could present unexpected results. When we perform a sum on a GPU, we are probably going to use something similar to a pairwise summation, which, as we have seen, has excellent accuracy. If we were going to compare the results with a naive implementation of the CPU, we could get quite different results. It is important to understand why this happens and which implementation is giving the more precise result.

5.5 Option pricing

Now that we have all the basic components to perform a Monte Carlo simulation, let's increase the complexity of the problem: Instead of computing the value of π, we will use the Monte Carlo method to value stock options.

Without going into technical details (see Willmott et al., 1995; Higham, 2004), an option is a derivative financial instrument where the buyer gains the right (but not the obligation) to buy or sell an underlying stock. When the right is to buy, the option is called a *call*; when the right is to sell, the option is called a *put*. The price at which the underlying asset may be traded is called the *exercise price* or the *strike price*.

We will start with a simple European option, an option that can be exercised only at expiration. For this kind of option, there is an analytical solution, the Black-Scholes formula, that computes the value of the put and the call. If we denote by CND the cumulative distribution function of the standard normal distribution and we define the Black-Scholes parameters d_1 and d_2 as:

$$d_1 = \frac{ln(S/E) + (r + \sigma^2/2)\tau}{\sigma\sqrt{\tau}}$$

$$d_2 = \frac{ln(S/E) + (r - \sigma^2/2)\tau}{\sigma\sqrt{\tau}}$$

where:

- S is the asset price at time t
- E is the exercise (strike) price at time T
- σ is the volatility, a measure for the variation of price of the asset over time
- r is the risk free annual interest rate
- τ is the time to expiration $(T - t)$

the values for a call C and for a put P will be:

$$C(S, t) = CND(d_1)S - CND(d_2)Ee^{-r\tau}$$

$$P(S, t) = -CND(-d_1)S + CND(-d_2)Ee^{-r\tau}$$

Now that we have a reference solution, we need to find a way of computing the same quantities using a Monte Carlo method. It can be shown (Higham, 2004) that pricing the option is equivalent to finding the expected value of the random variable:

$$S(T) = S(t)exp\left[(r - \sigma^2/2)\tau + \sigma\sqrt{\tau}Z\right]$$

$$V = e^{-rT}\Lambda\left(S(T)\right)$$

where Z is a normally distributed random number and the payoff function $\Lambda = max(E - S_T, 0)$ for a European put or $\Lambda = max(S_T - E, 0)$ for a European call. Once we compute the mean a and standard deviation b for a sequence of N samples, we can also compute a 95% *confidence interval*, a range in which there is a 95% probability of including the correct result, with:

$$\text{conf} = \left[a - \frac{1.96b}{\sqrt{N}}, a + \frac{1.96b}{\sqrt{N}}\right]$$

The structure of the code will be very similar to the ones we used to compute π. We will generate on the device a set of random numbers, this time with a normal distribution. For each random number, we will compute $S(T)$ and the value of the stock at time T, apply the payoff function Λ on this value, and discount the value at present time (multiplication by the factor e^{-rT}). Once we have an array of values V, we will compute the mean and standard deviation in order to compute the expected value and the confidence interval. To compute the reference value, we need to evaluate the Cumulative Normal Distribution that is not available in the standard set of functions provided by Fortran. This is done with the Hasting's appoximation, where the 5th order polynomial is evaluated using Horner's rule. The code is also accepting an additional argument on the command line, to change the number of points used in the simulation. This is done using the command_argument_count function and the get_command_argument subroutine, now standard in Fortran 2003. In this version, for the generation of the values of the call and put options at each point and for the reductions, we are still relying on CUF kernels. The first CUF kernel computes the values and means, the second CUF kernel uses these values to compute the standard deviations. The timing is measured with CUDA events.

```
1  module blackscholes_m
2    use precision_m
3  contains
4
5    real(fp_kind)  function CND( d )
6      ! Cumulative Normal Distribution function
7      ! using Hasting's formula
8      implicit none
9      real(fp_kind), parameter :: A1 =  0.31938153_fp_kind
10     real(fp_kind), parameter :: A2 = -0.356563782_fp_kind
11     real(fp_kind), parameter :: A3 =  1.781477937_fp_kind
12     real(fp_kind), parameter :: A4 = -1.821255978_fp_kind
13     real(fp_kind), parameter :: A5 =  1.330274429_fp_kind
14     real(fp_kind) :: d, K, abs, exp, RSQRT2PI
15
16     K = 1.0_fp_kind/(1.0_fp_kind + 0.2316419_fp_kind * abs(d))
17     RSQRT2PI = 1._fp_kind/sqrt(8._fp_kind*atan(1._fp_kind))
18     CND = RSQRT2PI * exp( -0.5_fp_kind * d * d) *          &
```

```fortran
19            (K * (A1 + K * (A2 + K * (A3 + K * (A4 + K * A5)))))
20       if( d .gt. 0._fp_kind ) CND = 1.0_fp_kind - CND
21       return
22    end function CND
23
24    subroutine blackscholes(callResult, putResult, &
25          S, E, R, sigma, T)
26      ! Black-Scholes formula for call and put
27      ! S = asset price at time t
28      ! E = exercise (strike) price
29      ! sigma = volatility
30      ! R = interest rate
31      ! T = time to expiration
32      implicit none
33      real(fp_kind) :: callResult, putResult
34      real(fp_kind) :: S, E, R, sigma, T
35      real(fp_kind) :: sqrtT, d1, d2, log, exp, expRT
36
37      if ( T > 0 ) then
38         sqrtT = sqrt(T)
39         d1 = (log(S/E)+(R+0.5_fp_kind*sigma*sigma)*T) &
40              /(sigma*sqrtT)
41         d2 = d1 -sigma*sqrtT
42         expRT = exp( -R * T)
43         callResult = ( S * CND(d1) - E * expRT * CND(d2))
44         putResult = callResult + E * expRT - S
45      else
46         callResult = max(S-E,0._fp_kind)
47         putResult  = max(E-S,0._fp_kind)
48      end if
49    end subroutine blackscholes
50 end module blackscholes_m
51
52 program  mc
53   use blackscholes_m
54   use curand_m
55   use cudafor
56   implicit none
57   real(fp_kind), allocatable, device :: deviceData(:), &
58         putValue(:),callValue(:)
59   real(fp_kind) :: S, E, R, sigma, T,Sfinal, &
60         call_price, put_price
61   real(fp_kind) ::  meanPut,meanCall, &
62         stddevPut, stddevCall, confidence
63   integer(kind=int_ptr_kind()) :: gen, N, seed
64   integer :: i,n2, nargs,istat
65   type(cudaEvent) :: startEvent,stopEvent
```

```
66    real :: time
67    character*12 arg
68
69    istat=cudaEventCreate(startEvent)
70    istat=cudaEventCreate(stopEvent)
71
72    ! Number of samples
73    nargs=command_argument_count()
74    if ( nargs == 0 ) then
75       N = 1000000
76    else
77       call get_command_argument(1,arg)
78       read(arg,'(i)') N
79    endif
80
81    S      = 5._fp_kind;      E = 4._fp_kind
82    sigma  = 0.3_fp_kind;     R = 0.05_fp_kind
83    T      = 1._fp_kind
84
85    istat=cudaEventRecord(startEvent,0) !start timing
86
87    !Allocate arrays on GPU
88    allocate (deviceData(N),putValue(N),callValue(N))
89
90    if (fp_kind == singlePrecision) then
91       print *, " European option with random numbers"
92       print *, " in single precisionm using ",N," samples"
93    else
94       print *, " European option with random numbers"
95       print *, " in double precision using ",N," samples"
96    end if
97
98    ! Create pseudonumber generator
99    call curandCreateGenerator(gen, CURAND_RNG_PSEUDO_DEFAULT)
100
101   ! Set seed
102   seed=1234
103   call curandSetPseudoRandomGeneratorSeed( gen, seed)
104
105   ! Generate N floats/doubles on device w/ normal distribution
106   call curandGenerateNormal(gen, deviceData, N, &
107        0._fp_kind, 1._fp_kind)
108
109   meanPut=0._fp_kind; meanCall=0._fp_kind
110   !$cuf kernel do <<<*,*>>>
111   do i=1,N
112      Sfinal= S*exp((R-0.5_fp_kind*sigma*sigma)*T &
```

```
113              +sigma*sqrt(T)*deviceData(i))
114        putValue(i) =exp (-R *T) * max (E-Sfinal,0._fp_kind)
115        callValue(i)=exp (-R *T) * max (Sfinal-E,0._fp_kind)
116        meanPut=meanPut+putValue(i)
117        meanCall=meanCall+callValue(i)
118     end do
119     meanPut=meanPut/N
120     meanCall=meanCall/N
121
122     stddevPut=0._fp_kind; stddevCall=0._fp_kind
123     !$cuf kernel do <<<*,*>>>
124     do i=1,N
125        stddevPut= stddevPut + (putValue(i)-meanPut) **2
126        stddevCall= stddevCall + (callValue(i)-meanCall) **2
127     end do
128     stddevPut=sqrt(stddevPut/(N-1) )
129     stddevCall=sqrt(stddevCall/(N-1) )
130
131     ! compute a reference solution using Black Scholes formula
132     call blackscholes(call_price,put_price,S,E,R,sigma,T)
133
134     print *, "Montecarlo  value of put option  =", meanPut
135     print *, "BlackScholes value of put option =", put_price
136     print *, "Confidence interval of put option = [", &
137          meanPut -1.96*stddevPut/sqrt(real(N)),",",&
138          meanPut +1.96*stddevPut/sqrt(real(N)),"]"
139     print *, "Montecarlo value of call option  =", meanCall
140     print *, "BlackScholes value of call option=", call_price
141     print *, "Confidence interval of call option = [", &
142          meanCall -1.96*stddevCall/sqrt(real(N)),",",&
143          meanCall +1.96*stddevCall/sqrt(real(N)),"]"
144
145     istat=cudaEventRecord(stopEvent,0)
146     istat=cudaEventSynchronize(stopEvent)
147     istat=cudaEventElapsedTime(time,startEvent,stopEvent)
148
149     print *,"Elapsed time (ms) :",time
150
151
152     deallocate (deviceData,putValue,callValue)
153
154     ! Destroy the generator
155     call curandDestroyGenerator(gen)
156
157  end program  mc
```

As we did for the code computing π, we will generate two versions, one using single precision and the other using double precision passing a preprocessor flag.

```
pgf90 -O3 -Minfo -o mc_european_single precision_m.F90 \
curand_m.cuf montecarlo_european_option.cuf -lcurand

pgf90 -O3 -Minfo -DDOUBLE -o mc_european_double precision_m.F90 \
curand_m.cuf montecarlo_european_option.cuf -lcurand
```

The output from the compilation confirms that the compiler was able to identify the reduction variables. Since we did not specify the execution configuration in the CUF directives, the choice is left to the compiler, and kernels are invoked with 128 threads.

```
    111, CUDA kernel generated
        111, !$cuf kernel do <<< (*), (128) >>>
    116, Sum reduction generated for meanput
    117, Sum reduction generated for meancall
    124, CUDA kernel generated
        124, !$cuf kernel do <<< (*), (128) >>>
    125, Sum reduction generated for stddevput
    126, Sum reduction generated for stddevcall
```

If we run the codes on a Tesla K20x with no additional arguments, it will use 1 million samples.

```
% ./mc_european_single
  European option with  random numbers in single precision
  using                 1000000   samples
Montecarlo   value of put option   =    0.1276108
BlackScholes value of put option   =    0.1280217
Confidence interval of put option  = [0.1269990, 0.1282227]
Montecarlo value of call option    =    1.322455
BlackScholes value of call option=    1.323104
Confidence interval of call option = [1.319741, 1.325168]
Elapsed time (ms) :     18.85296

% ./mc_european_double
  European option with  random numbers in double precision
  using                 1000000   samples
Montecarlo   value of put option   =    0.1280019167019667
BlackScholes value of put option   =    0.1280215707263190
Confidence interval of put option =
    [0.1273886989425723, 0.1286151344613610]
Montecarlo value of call option    =    1.32242692975769
```

```
BlackScholes value of call option=     1.323103872723463
Confidence interval of call option =
   [1.319531953505469, 1.324953432446070]
Elapsed time (ms) :     19.21347
```

We notice that the runtime for the single- and double-precision runs are very similar. To better understand the cause of this behavior, we could use `nvprof`.

```
% nvprof ./mc_european_single
======== Profiling result:
 Time(%)   Time   Calls    Avg        Min        Max     Name
 96.87   15.89ms    1    15.89ms     15.89ms    15.89ms  generate_seed_pseudo
  1.11  182.56us    1   182.56us    182.56us   182.56us  mc_111_gpu
  0.91  149.60us    1   149.60us    149.60us   149.60us  mc_122_gpu
  0.82  134.27us    1   134.27us    134.27us   134.27us  void gen_sequenced
  0.12   19.20us    1    19.20us     19.20us    19.20us  mc_116_gpu_red
  0.12   19.10us    1    19.10us     19.10us    19.10us  mc_124_gpu_red
  0.03    5.12us    2     2.56us      2.56us     2.56us  [CUDA memcpy DtoH]
  0.02    3.01us    2     1.50us      1.34us     1.66us  [CUDA memcpy HtoD]

% nvprof ./mc_european_double
======== Profiling result:
 Time(%)   Time   Calls    Avg        Min        Max     Name
 94.94   15.91ms    1    15.91ms     15.91ms    15.91ms  generate_seed_pseudo
  2.21  371.07us    1   371.07us    371.07us   371.07us  void gen_sequenced
  1.67  280.16us    1   280.16us    280.16us   280.16us  mc_111_gpu
  0.89  149.03us    1   149.03us    149.03us   149.03us  mc_122_gpu
  0.12   20.16us    1    20.16us     20.16us    20.16us  mc_116_gpu_red
  0.12   19.90us    1    19.90us     19.90us    19.90us  mc_124_gpu_red
  0.03    5.18us    2     2.59us      2.59us     2.59us  [CUDA memcpy DtoH]
  0.02    3.01us    2     1.50us      1.31us     1.70us  [CUDA memcpy HtoD]
```

The profiler output clearly shows that almost 85% of the time is spent in the random-number generation function `generate_seed_pseudo` and this time is almost constant for the two cases (the seed generation is done using integer arithmetic and is independent of the precision used). For the other kernels we can notice the expected 1:2 ratio between single- and double-precision cases. The seed generation could be sped up by adding a call to `curandSetGeneratorOrdering` after the `curandCreateGenerator` call.

```
1  ! Create pseudonumber generator
2   call curandCreateGenerator(gen, CURAND_RNG_PSEUDO_DEFAULT)
3   call curandSetGeneratorOrdering(gen, CURAND_ORDERING_PSEUDO_SEEDED)
```

If we increase the number of points to 100 million, we will see that now there is a clear difference in runtime between the two cases.

```
%  ./mc_european_single   100000000
  European option with   random numbers  in single precision
  using                  100000000   samples
Montecarlo   value of put option    =    0.1279889
BlackScholes value of put option =    0.1280217
Confidence interval of put option  = [0.1279276,  0.1280502]
Montecarlo value of call option    =    1.323060
BlackScholes value of call option=    1.323104
Confidence interval of call option  = [1.322789,  1.323332 ]
Elapsed time (ms)  :    48.94390

%  ./mc_european_double   100000000
  European option with   random numbers  in double precision
  using                  100000000   samples
Montecarlo   value of put option    =    0.1280167276013557
BlackScholes value of put option =    0.1280215707263190
Confidence interval of put option =
  [0.1279554295131442,0.1280780256895671]
Montecarlo value of call option    =    1.323177159935128
BlackScholes value of call option=    1.323103872723463
Confidence interval of call option =
  [1.322905719832569,  1.323448600037688]
Elapsed time (ms)  :    89.72614
```

The real power of the Monte Carlo method shows when we consider more sophisticated options—for example, options that depend on the path of the stock during the contract period. Instead of going directly from time t to the expiration time T, as we did for the European option, we can set up a grid of points $t_j = j\Delta t$, with $0 \leq j \leq M$ and $\Delta t = T/M$ and compute the option value on each point:

$$S(t_{j+1}) = S(t_j)exp\left[(r - \sigma^2/2)\Delta t + \sigma\sqrt{\Delta t}Z_j\right]$$

Once we have the asset price on this underlying grid, we can compute min and max and test for barrier crossing or integrals, depending on the payoff of the exotic option.

CHAPTER
6

Finite Difference Method

CHAPTER OUTLINE HEAD

In many fields of science and engineering, the governing system of equations takes the form of either ordinary or partial differential equations. One method of solving these equations is to use finite differences, where the continuous analytical derivatives are approximated at each point on a discrete grid using function values of neighboring points. In this chapter we discuss how to optimize a particular nine-point one-dimensional scheme, although the method we discuss can be applied to different finite difference approximations quite easily. A general discussion of finite difference methods and their properties can be found in Ferziger (1981) and Ferziger and Perić (2001). We also discuss how a 2D Laplace equation can be implemented in CUDA Fortran using a compact nine-point stencil.

6.1 Nine-Point 1D finite difference stencil

Our first example uses a three-dimensional grid of size 64^3. For simplicity we assume periodic boundary conditions and only consider first-order derivatives, although extending the code to calculate higher-order derivatives with other types of boundary conditions is straightforward.

    The finite difference method uses a weighted summation of function values at neighboring points to approximate the derivative at a particular point. For a $(2N + 1)$-point stencil with a uniform spacing

Δx in the x direction, a central finite difference scheme for the derivative in x can be written as:

$$\frac{\partial f(x, y, z)}{\partial x} \approx \frac{1}{\Delta x} \sum_{i=-N}^{N} C_i f(x + i\Delta x, y, z)$$

and similarly for other directions. The coefficients C_i are typically generated from Taylor series expansions and can be chosen to obtain a scheme with desired characteristics such as accuracy and, in the context of partial differential equations, dispersion and dissipation. For explicit finite difference schemes such as the type shown here, larger stencils typically have a higher order of accuracy. For this study we use a nine-point stencil that has an eighth-order accuracy. We also choose a symmetric stencil, which can be written as:

$$\frac{\partial f_{i,j,k}}{\partial x} \approx a_x \left(f_{i+1,j,k} - f_{i-1,j,k} \right) + b_x \left(f_{i+2,j,k} - f_{i-2,j,k} \right) + c_x \left(f_{i+3,j,k} - f_{i-3,j,k} \right)$$
$$+ d_x \left(f_{i+4,j,k} - f_{i-4,j,k} \right)$$

where we specify values of the function on the computational grid using the grid indices i, j, k rather than the physical coordinates x, y, z. Here the coefficients are $a_x = \frac{4}{5}\frac{1}{\Delta x}$, $b_x = -\frac{1}{5}\frac{1}{\Delta x}$, $c_x = \frac{4}{105}\frac{1}{\Delta x}$, and $d_x = -\frac{1}{280}\frac{1}{\Delta x}$, which is a typical eighth-order scheme. For derivative in the y and z directions, the index offsets in the preceding equation are simply applied to the j and k indices and the coefficients are the same except Δy and Δz are used in place of Δx.

Because we calculate an approximation to the derivative at each point on the 64^3 periodic grid, the value of f at each point is used eight times, one time for each right-side term in the previous expression. In designing a derivative kernel, we want to exploit this data reuse by fetching the values of f from global memory as few times as possible using shared memory.

6.1.1 Data reuse and shared memory

Each block of threads can bring in a tile of data to shared memory, and then each thread in the block can access all elements of the shared memory tile as needed. How does one choose the best tile shape and size? Some experimentation is required, but characteristics of the finite-difference stencil and grid size provide some direction.

In choosing a tile shape for stencil calculations, there typically is an overlap of the tiles corresponding to half of the stencil size, as depicted on the left in Figure 6.1. Here, in order to calculate the derivative in a 16×16 tile, the values of f—not only from this tile but also from two additional 4×16 sections—must be loaded by each thread block. Overall, the f values in the 4×16 sections get loaded twice—once by the thread block that calculates the derivative at that location and once by the neighboring thread block. As a result, 8×16 values out of 16×16, or half of the values, get loaded from global memory twice. In addition, coalescing on a device with a compute capability of 2.0 and higher will be suboptimal for a 16×16 tile, since perfect coalescing on such devices requires access to data within 32 contiguous elements in global memory per load.

A better choice of tile (and thread block) that calculates the derivative for the same number of points is depicted on the right side of Figure 6.1. This tile avoids overlap altogether when we calculate the x derivative for our one-dimensional stencil on a grid of 64^3 since the tile contains all points in the

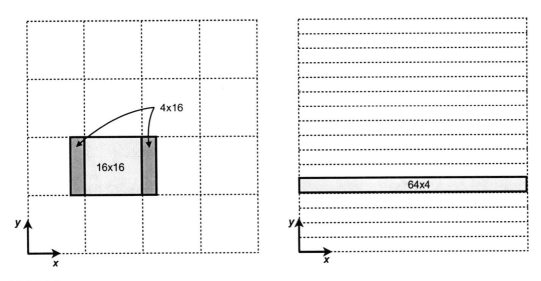

FIGURE 6.1

Possible tile configurations for the *x*-derivative calculation. On the left is a depiction of a tile needed for calculating the derivative at points in a 16 × 16 tiles. To calculate the derivative at points in this tile, data from two additional 4 × 16 sections must be loaded for each thread block. The data in these 4 × 16 sections are loaded twice—once by the thread block, which calculates the derivative at that point, and once by a neighboring thread block. As a result, half of all of the data get loaded twice. A better option is the 64 × 4 tile on the right, which, for the 64^3 mesh, loads each datum from global memory once.

direction of the derivative, as in the 64 × 4 tile shown. A minimal tile would have just one *pencil*, i.e., a one-dimensional array of all points in a direction. However, this would correspond to thread blocks of 64 threads, so, from an occupancy standpoint, it is beneficial to use multiple pencils in a tile. In our finite difference code, which is listed in its entirety in Appendix D.5, we parameterize the number of pencils to allow some experimentation. In addition to loading each value of *f* only once, every warp of threads will load contiguous data from global memory using this tile and therefore will result in perfectly coalesced accesses to global memory.

6.1.2 The *x*-derivative kernel

The first kernel we discuss is the *x*-derivative kernel:

```
129    attributes(global) subroutine deriv_x(f, df)
130      implicit none
131
132      real(fp_kind), intent(in)  :: f(mx,my,mz)
133      real(fp_kind), intent(out) :: df(mx,my,mz)
134
```

```
135    real(fp_kind), shared :: f_s(-3:mx+4,sPencils)
136
137    integer :: i,j,k,j_1
138
139    i = threadIdx%x
140    j = (blockIdx%x-1)*blockDim%y + threadIdx%y
141    ! j_1 is local variant of j for accessing shared memory
142    j_1 = threadIdx%y
143    k = blockIdx%y
144
145    f_s(i,j_1) = f(i,j,k)
146
147    call syncthreads()
148
149    ! fill in periodic images in shared memory array
150
151    if (i <= 4) then
152        f_s(i-4, j_1) = f_s(mx+i-5,j_1)
153        f_s(mx+i,j_1) = f_s(i+1,     j_1)
154    endif
155
156    call syncthreads()
157
158    df(i,j,k) = &
159        (ax_c *( f_s(i+1,j_1) - f_s(i-1,j_1) )   &
160        +bx_c *( f_s(i+2,j_1) - f_s(i-2,j_1) )   &
161        +cx_c *( f_s(i+3,j_1) - f_s(i-3,j_1) )   &
162        +dx_c *( f_s(i+4,j_1) - f_s(i-4,j_1) ))
163
164    end subroutine deriv_x
```

Here mx, my, and mz are the grid size parameters set to 64, and sPencils is 4, which is the number of pencils used to make the shared memory tile. (There are two pencil sizes used in this study. sPencils refers to a small number of pencils; we discuss use of a larger number of pencils later.) The indices i, j, and k correspond to the coordinates in the 64^3 mesh. The index i can also be used for the x coordinate in the shared memory tile, whereas the index j_1 is the local coordinate in the y direction for the shared memory tile. This kernel is launched with a block of 64 × sPencils threads, which calculated the derivatives on a $x \times y$ tile of 64 × sPencils.

The shared memory tile declared on line 135 has padding of four elements at each end of the first index to accommodate the periodic images needed to calculate the derivative at the endpoints of the x direction. On line 145, data from global memory are read into the shared memory tile for f_s(1:mx,1:sPencils). These reads from global memory are perfectly coalesced. On lines 151–154, data are copied within shared memory to fill out the periodic images[1] in the x direction. Doing

---

[1] Note that in this example, we assume that the endpoints in each direction are periodic images, so f(1,j,k) = f(mx,j,k) and similarly for the other directions.

so allows the derivative to be calculated on lines 158–162 without any index checking. Note that the threads that read the data from shared memory on lines 152 and 153 are not the same threads that write the data to shared memory on line 145, which is why the `syncthreads()` call on line 147 is required. The synchronization barrier on line 156 is required because data from `f_s(-3:0,j_l)` and `f_s(mx+1:mx+4,j_l)` are accessed in lines 158–162 by threads other than those that wrote these values on lines 152 and 153.

6.1.2.1 *Performance of the x-derivative kernel*

Compiling this kernel with the `-Mcuda=cc35,ptxinfo` option, we observe that this kernel requires only 14 registers and uses 1152 bytes of shared memory. On the Tesla K20 at full occupancy, the number of registers per thread must be 32 or less (65,536 registers/2048 threads per multiprocessor). Likewise, the 1152 bytes of shared memory used per thread block times the maximum of 16 thread blocks per multiprocessor easily fit into the 48 KB of shared memory available in each multiprocessor. With such low resource utilization, we expect the kernel to run at full occupancy. These occupancy calculations assume that we have launched enough thread blocks to realize the occupancy, which is certainly our case since 64^2/`sPencils` or 1024 blocks are launched.

The host code launches this kernel multiple times in a loop and reports the average time of execution per kernel launch. The code also compares the result to the analytical solution at the grid points. On a Tesla K20 using single precision for this kernel, we have:

```
Using shared memory tile of x-y: 64x4
  RMS error:      5.7695847E-06
  MAX error:      2.3365021E-05
  Average time (ms):     2.8503999E-02
  Average Bandwidth (GB/s):     73.57396
```

We can use the technique discussed in Section 2.2 to get a feel for what is the limiting factor in this code. If we replace lines 158–162 above with:

```
    df(i,j,k) = f_s(i,j_l)
```

we have a memory-only version of the code, which obtains:

```
x derivative mem with x-y tile: 64x4
   Average time (ms):     2.4025600E-02
   Mem Bandwidth (GB/s):     87.28822
```

Likewise, we can create a math-only version of the kernel:

```
attributes(global) subroutine derivative_math(f, df, val)
  implicit none

  real(fp_kind), intent(in)  :: f(mx,my,mz)
  real(fp_kind), intent(out) :: df(mx,my,mz)
  integer, value :: val
  real(fp_kind) :: temp

  real(fp_kind), shared :: f_s(-3:mx+4,nPencils)

  integer :: i,j,k,j_l

  i = threadIdx%x
  j = (blockIdx%x-1)*blockDim%y + threadIdx%y
  ! j_l is local variant of j for accessing shared memory
  j_l = threadIdx%y
  k = blockIdx%y

  temp = &
       (ax_c *( f_s(i+1,j_l) - f_s(i-1,j_l) )   &
       +bx_c *( f_s(i+2,j_l) - f_s(i-2,j_l) )   &
       +cx_c *( f_s(i+3,j_l) - f_s(i-3,j_l) )   &
       +dx_c *( f_s(i+4,j_l) - f_s(i-4,j_l) ))

  if (val*temp == 1) df(i,j,k) = temp

end subroutine derivative_math
```

which obtains:

```
  Average time (ms):     1.5646400E-02
```

Given this information, we know that the code is memory bound, since the memory- and math-only versions execute in approximately 85% and 55% of the time the full kernel requires, respectively. The majority of the math operations are covered by memory requests, so we do have some overlap.

To try to improve performance, we need to reassess how we utilize memory. We load data from global memory only once into shared memory in a fully coalesced fashion; we have two `syncthreads()` calls, required to safely access shared memory; and we write the output to global memory in a fully coalesced fashion. The coefficients `ax_c`, `bx_c`, `cx_c`, and `dx_c` used on lines 159–162 are in constant memory, which is cached on the chip. This is the optimal situation for constant memory, where each thread in a warp (and thread block) reads the same constant value. As operations with global and constant memories are fully optimized, we turn to see if we can do anything with the syncthreads() calls.

The derivative kernel has two calls to syncthreads(): one after data are read from global memory to shared memory and one after data are copied between shared memory locations. These barriers are needed when different threads write and then read the same shared memory values. You may have noticed that is it possible to remove the first of these synchronization barriers by modifying the indexing to shared memory. For example, in this portion of the x-derivative code:

```
145     f_s(i,j_l) = f(i,j,k)
146
147     call syncthreads()
148
149     ! fill in periodic images in shared memory array
150
151     if (i <= 4) then
152         f_s(i-4, j_l) = f_s(mx+i-5,j_l)
153         f_s(mx+i,j_l) = f_s(i+1,   j_l)
154     endif
```

we could remove this synchronization barrier on line 147 by replacing lines 151–154 with:

```
if (i>mx-5 .and. i<mx) f_s(i-(mx-1),j_l) = f_s(i,j_l)
if (i>1    .and. i<6 ) f_s(i+(mx-1),j_l) = f_s(i,j_l)
```

Using this approach, the same thread that writes to a shared memory location on line 145 reads the data from shared memory in the preceding two lines of code. Removing a synchronization barrier might seem like a sure performance win, but when we run the code we obtain:

```
Single syncthreads, using shared memory tile of x-y: 64x4
  RMS error:      5.7695847E-06
  MAX error:      2.3365021E-05
  Average time (ms):      2.8953601E-02
  Average Bandwidth (GB/s):      72.43147
```

which is slightly slower than the original code. The additional index checks in the condition of the if statement end up being slower than the syncthreads() call. Because syncthreads() acts across a block of threads that contain a small group of warps—eight warps, in our case—their cost is typically small.

At this point we decide to move on to the code for derivatives in other directions, since the x derivative is fairly optimized: The kernel is memory bound and the code uses memory very efficiently.

6.1.3 Derivatives in *y* and *z*

We can easily modify the *x*-derivative code to operate in the other directions. In the *x* derivative, each thread block calculated the derivatives in an $x \times y$ tile of $64 \times$ sPencils. For the *y* derivative, we can have a thread block calculate the derivative on a tile of sPencils $\times$ 64 in $x \times y$, as depicted on the left in Figure 6.2. Likewise, for the *z* derivative, a thread block can calculate the derivative in a $x \times z$ tile of sPencils $\times$ 64. The following kernel shows the *y*-derivative kernel using this approach:

```
255   attributes(global) subroutine deriv_y(f, df)
256      implicit none
257
258      real(fp_kind), intent(in)  :: f(mx,my,mz)
259      real(fp_kind), intent(out) :: df(mx,my,mz)
260
261      real(fp_kind), shared :: f_s(sPencils,-3:my+4)
262
263      integer :: i,i_l,j,k
264
265      i = (blockIdx%x-1)*blockDim%x + threadIdx%x
266      i_l = threadIdx%x
267      j = threadIdx%y
268      k = blockIdx%y
269
270      f_s(i_l,j) = f(i,j,k)
271
272      call syncthreads()
273
274      if (j <= 4) then
275         f_s(i_l,j-4) = f_s(i_l,my+j-5)
276         f_s(i_l,my+j) = f_s(i_l,j+1)
277      endif
278
279      call syncthreads()
280
281      df(i,j,k) = &
282            (ay_c *( f_s(i_l,j+1) - f_s(i_l,j-1) )   &
283            +by_c *( f_s(i_l,j+2) - f_s(i_l,j-2) )   &
284            +cy_c *( f_s(i_l,j+3) - f_s(i_l,j-3) )   &
285            +dy_c *( f_s(i_l,j+4) - f_s(i_l,j-4) ))
286
287   end subroutine deriv_y
```

By transposing the shared memory tile on line 261 in this manner, we can maintain the property that each element from global memory is read in only once. The disadvantage of this approach is that with

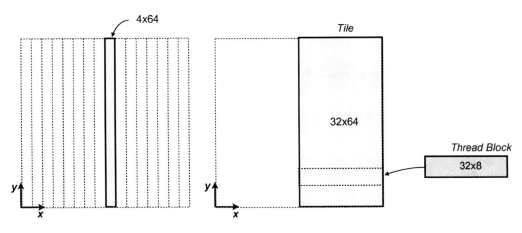

FIGURE 6.2

Possible tile configurations for the *y*-derivative calculation. Analogous to the *x* derivative, where a 64 × 4 tile is used, we can use a 4 × 64 tile as depicted on the left. This approach loads each *f* value from global memory only once; however, the coalescing characteristics are poor. A better alternative is depicted on the right, where a tile with 32 points in *x* achieves perfect coalescing, and the tile that has 64 points in *y* maintains the characteristic that *f* data get loaded only once. However, one problem with a 32 × 64 tile is that a one-to-one mapping of threads to elements cannot be used, since 2048 threads exceed the limit of threads per block. This issue can be circumvented by using a thread block of 32 × 8 where each thread calculates the derivative at 8 points.

`sPencils=4` points in *x* for these tiles, we no longer have perfect coalescing. The performance results bear this out:

```
Using shared memory tile of x-y: 4x64
 RMS error:     5.7687557E-06
 MAX error:     2.3365021E-05
 Average time (ms):     4.6841603E-02
 Average Bandwidth (GB/s):     44.77114
```

where we obtain roughly half the performance of the *x*-derivative kernel. In terms of accuracy, we obtain the same maximum error of the *x* derivative but a different RMS error for essentially the same function. This difference is due to the order in which the accumulation is done on the host. Simply swapping the order of the loops in the host code error calculation would produce the same results.

One way to improve performance is to expand the tile to contain enough pencils to facilitate perfect coalescing. For devices of compute capability of 2.0 and higher, this would require 32 pencils. Such a tile is shown on the right in Figure 6.2. Using such an approach would require a shared memory tile of 9216 bytes, which is not problematic for devices of compute capability 2.0 and higher with 48 KB of shared memory per multiprocessor. However, with a one-to-one mapping of threads to elements where the derivative is calculated, a thread block of 2048 threads would be required, whereas these devices have an upper limit of 1024 threads per thread block. The way around this limit is for each thread to calculate the derivative for multiple points. If we use a thread block of $32 \times 8 \times 1$ and have each thread calculate the derivative at eight points, as opposed to a thread block of $4 \times 64 \times 1$ and have each thread calculate the derivative at only one point, we launch a kernel with the same number of threads per block, but we regain perfect coalescing. The following code accomplishes this:

```
292    attributes(global) subroutine deriv_y_1Pencils(f, df)
293       implicit none
294
295       real(fp_kind), intent(in)  :: f(mx,my,mz)
296       real(fp_kind), intent(out) :: df(mx,my,mz)
297
298       real(fp_kind), shared :: f_s(1Pencils,-3:my+4)
299
300       integer :: i,j,k,i_l
301
302       i_l = threadIdx%x
303       i = (blockIdx%x-1)*blockDim%x + threadIdx%x
304       k = blockIdx%y
305
306       do j = threadIdx%y, my, blockDim%y
307          f_s(i_l,j) = f(i,j,k)
308       enddo
309
310       call syncthreads()
311
312       j = threadIdx%y
313       if (j <= 4) then
314          f_s(i_l,j-4) = f_s(i_l,my+j-5)
315          f_s(i_l,my+j) = f_s(i_l,j+1)
316       endif
317
318       call syncthreads()
319
320       do j = threadIdx%y, my, blockDim%y
321          df(i,j,k) = &
322             (ay_c *( f_s(i_l,j+1) - f_s(i_l,j-1) )   &
323             +by_c *( f_s(i_l,j+2) - f_s(i_l,j-2) )   &
324             +cy_c *( f_s(i_l,j+3) - f_s(i_l,j-3) )   &
325             +dy_c *( f_s(i_l,j+4) - f_s(i_l,j-4) ))
326       enddo
327
328    end subroutine deriv_y_1Pencils
```

where here lPencils is 32. Very little has changed from the previous code. The only differences are that the index j is used as a loop index on lines 306 and 320, rather than being calculated once, and is set to threadIdx%y on line 312 for copying periodic images. When compiling this code using -Mcuda=cc35,ptxinfo, we observe that each thread requires 23 registers, so register usage will not affect occupancy on the K20. However, with 9216 bytes of shared memory used per thread block, a total of five thread blocks can reside on a multiprocessor at one time. These five thread blocks contain 1280 threads, which result in an occupancy of 0.625. This should not be problematic since we are employing an eight-fold instruction-level parallelism. The results for this kernel are:

```
Using shared memory tile of x-y: 32x64
  RMS error:       5.7687557E-06
  MAX error:       2.3365021E-05
  Average time (ms):      2.6431998E-02
  Average Bandwidth (GB/s):       79.34141
```

where we have exceeded the performance of the x derivative.

We might inquire as to whether using such a larger number of pencils in the shared memory tile will improve performance of the x-derivative code presented earlier. This ends up not being the case:

```
Using shared memory tile of x-y: 64x32
  RMS error:       5.7695847E-06
  MAX error:       2.3365021E-05
  Average time (ms):      3.1697601E-02
  Average Bandwidth (GB/s):       66.16122
```

Recall that for the x derivative, we already have perfect coalescing for the case with four pencils. Since the occupancy of this kernel is high, there is no benefit from the added instruction-level parallelism. As a result, the additional code to loop over portions of the shared memory tile simply add overhead, and as a result performance decreases.

6.1.3.1 *Leveraging transpose*

An entirely different approach to handling the y and z derivatives is to leverage the transpose kernels discussed in Section 3.4. Using this approach, we would reorder our data so that the x-derivative routine can be used to calculate the derivatives in y and z. This approach has the advantage that all transactions to global memory are perfectly coalesced. It has the disadvantage, however, that it requires three roundtrips to global memory: first the transpose kernel is called to reorder the input data, then the derivative kernel is called on the reordered data, and finally the transpose kernel is called to place the results into the original order. Because of this these addition trips to global memory, this approach is not a viable solution to our problem. However, if our kernel were more complicated, such an approach may be viable, which is why we mention it here.

6.1.4 Nonuniform grids

The previous discussion dealt with obtaining derivatives on grids that are uniform, i.e., grids where the spacings Δx, Δy, and Δz are constant and do not depend on the indices i, j, and k. There are, however, many situations in which a nonuniform grid is desirable and even necessary. In the case of nonperiodic boundaries, often the function has steep gradients in the boundary region and one needs to cluster grid points in such regions, because reducing the grid spacing throughout the entire domain would be prohibitive. In addition, when we use a wide stencil, such as our nine-point stencil, in nonperiodic cases we need to use different schemes to calculate derivatives at points near the boundary. Typically we use a skewed stencil that has lower accuracy at such points. Clustering of grid points near the boundary helps minimize the effect of the reduced accuracy in such regions.

A finite difference scheme for nonuniform grids can be implemented in several ways. One way is to start from the Taylor series, used to determine the coefficients where the constant Δx of a uniform grid is replaced by the spatially dependent Δx_i in the nonuniform case. A second way, which is taken in this study, is to introduce a second (uniform) coordinate system and map the derivatives between the two systems. This method essentially boils down to applying the chain rule to the uniform derivative we have already developed.

We discuss the development of the nonuniform finite-difference scheme for the x derivative. Application of this scheme to other directions is straightforward. If x is the physical domain where our grid points are distributed nonuniformly, and s is a computational domain where the grid spacing is uniform, then the derivative can be written as:

$$\frac{df}{dx} = \frac{df}{ds}\frac{ds}{dx}$$

where the first derivative on the right-hand side is simply what has been calculated in the previous section. The remaining issue is choosing a nonuniform spacing and with it an expression for ds/dx. The two coordinate systems can be related by:

$$dx = \xi(s)ds$$

where ds is constant and $\xi(s)$ is chosen to cluster points as desired. There are many documented choices for $\xi(s)$, but in our case we choose:

$$\xi(s) = C\left(1 - \alpha \sin^2(2\pi s)\right)$$

Recalling that s is between zero and one, this function clusters points around $s = 1/4$ and $s = 3/4$ for positive α. C is chosen such that the endpoints in both coordinate systems coincide—namely, the resultant expression for $x(s)$ has $x(1) = 1$. The degree of clustering is determined by the parameter α, and when $\alpha = 0$ (and $C = 1$) we recover uniform spacing. Substituting our expression for $\xi(s)$ into the differential form and integrating, we have:

$$x = C\left[s - \alpha\left(\frac{s}{2} - \frac{\sin(4\pi s)}{8\pi}\right)\right] + D$$

We want the endpoints of our two grids to coincide, i.e., for $x(s)$ we have $x(0) = 0$ and $x(1) = 1$. The first of these conditions is satisfied by $D = 0$ and the second by $C = 2/(2 - \alpha)$. Thus we have:

$$x = \frac{2}{2 - \alpha} \left[s - \alpha \left(\frac{s}{2} - \frac{\sin(4\pi s)}{8\pi} \right) \right]$$

and

$$\frac{ds}{dx} = \frac{1 - \alpha/2}{1 - \alpha \sin^2(2\pi s)}$$

The modifications to the CUDA Fortran derivative code required to accommodate a stretched grid are relatively easy. We simply turn the scalar coefficients ax_c, bx_c, cx_c, and dx_c, along with their y and z counterparts, into arrays:

```
! stencil coefficients
! functions of index for streched grid
real(fp_kind), constant :: &
     ax_c(mx), bx_c(mx), cx_c(mx), dx_c(mx), &
     ay_c(my), by_c(my), cy_c(my), dy_c(my), &
     az_c(mz), bz_c(mz), cz_c(mz), dz_c(mz)
```

and absorb ds/dx in these coefficients:

```
dsinv = real(mx-1)
do i = 1, mx
   s = (i-1.)/(mx-1.)
   x(i) = 2./(2.-alpha)*(s - alpha*(s/2. &
        - sin(2.*twoPi*s)/(4.*twoPi)))
   scale = (1.-alpha/2.)/(1.-alpha*(sin(twoPi*s))**2)

   ax(i) =  4./  5. * dsinv * scale
   bx(i) = -1./  5. * dsinv * scale
   cx(i) =  4./105. * dsinv * scale
   dx(i) = -1./280. * dsinv * scale
enddo
ax_c = ax; bx_c = bx; cx_c = cx; dx_c = dx
```

Once again, the y and z directions are modified similarly. These coefficients are calculated once as a preprocessing step, and therefore their calculation does not affect timing of the derivative kernel. However, the conversion of these variables from scalar to array does play a role in performance in terms of the way they are accessed. For example, in the x derivative these coefficient arrays are used as follows:

```
df(i,j,k) = &
       (ax_c(i) *( f_s(i+1,j_1) - f_s(i-1,j_1) )   &
       +bx_c(i) *( f_s(i+2,j_1) - f_s(i-2,j_1) )   &
       +cx_c(i) *( f_s(i+3,j_1) - f_s(i-3,j_1) )   &
       +dx_c(i) *( f_s(i+4,j_1) - f_s(i-4,j_1) ))
```

and likewise for the other directions. Making these changes and running the code results in the following performance:

Routine	Effective Bandwidth (GB/s)	
	Uniform Grid	**Nonuniform Grid**
x derivative		
x-y tile: 64 × 4	73.6	14.2
x-y tile: 64 × 32	66.2	46.5
y derivative		
x-y tile: 4 × 64	44.8	36.4
x-y tile: 32 × 64	79.3	71.7
z derivative		
x-z tile: 4 × 64	44.7	36.2
x-z tile: 32 × 64	79.2	71.5

where we have included the performance of the uniform grid for comparison. We see roughly the same performance between nonuniform and uniform grids in the y and z directions when we use the 32×64 shared memory tile, but all other cases show a considerable performance degradation for the nonuniform case, especially the x-derivative kernels. Once again, the only difference between the uniform and nonuniform derivative kernels is that the stencil coefficients are arrays rather than scalar values. Looking at the relevant y-derivative code:

```
df(i,j,k) = &
       (ay_c(j) *( f_s(i_1,j+1) - f_s(i_1,j-1) )   &
       +by_c(j) *( f_s(i_1,j+2) - f_s(i_1,j-2) )   &
       +cy_c(j) *( f_s(i_1,j+3) - f_s(i_1,j-3) )   &
       +dy_c(j) *( f_s(i_1,j+4) - f_s(i_1,j-4) ))
```

and considering how a warp of threads accesses the coefficients, we can understand why this performs well in the 32×64 shared memory tile case. For a tile of 32×64 case, threads in a warp will have different values of i_1 but the same value of j when executing this statement.[2] Therefore, from the perspective of a warp, the stencil coefficients ay_c(j), by_c(j), cy_c(j), and dy_c(j) are essentially scalar constants. Recall that constant memory is most efficient when all threads in a warp read the same value. When threads in a warp read different values from constant memory, the requests are serialized. This is the case when the smaller shared memory tile of 4 × 64 is used. A warp of 32 threads executing the preceding code will have eight different values of j and therefore read eight values of each coefficient. These requests are serialized, which is the reason that the performance in this case drops from 45 for the uniform grid to 36 for the nonuniform case. A more drastic performance reduction is seen in the x derivative, where the 32 threads in a warp have different values of i and a warp requests 32 contiguous values for each stencil coefficient. This access pattern for constant memory is largely responsible for the 80% degradation going from uniform to nonuniform grid.

The way to avoid the performance degradation observed here is simply to use device memory rather than constant memory for the stencil coefficients. We need only change the `constant` variable qualifier to `device` in the module declaration. Note that although reading contiguous array values is a poor access pattern for constant memory, it is an ideal access pattern for global or device memory, since such a request is coalesced. Implementing the change from constant to global memory and rerunning the code, we can extend our table of results:

	Effective Bandwidth (GB/s)		
	Uniform Grid	Nonuniform Grid	Nonuniform Grid
Routine		constant	device
x derivative			
x-y tile: 64 × 4	73.6	14.2	56.3
x-y tile: 64 × 32	66.2	46.5	46.8
y derivative			
x-y tile: 4 × 64	44.8	36.4	37.4
x-y tile: 32 × 64	79.3	71.7	59.4
z derivative			
x-z tile: 4 × 64	44.7	36.2	37.4
x-z tile: 32 × 64	79.2	71.5	59.1

The conversion from constant to global memory for the stencil coefficients has greatly improved the x-derivative routines, as expected. For the y and z derivatives, using constant memory for the stencil coefficients is still preferable for the case with a 32 × 64 shared memory tile, since constant memory is optimally used.

---

[2] In the 32 × 64 tile case, each thread will take on several values of j because this statement is contained in a loop, but at any one time all threads in a warp will have the same value of j.

6.2 2D Laplace equation

In this section we solve Laplace's equation:

$$\nabla^2 \phi = 0$$

in two dimensions using a compact, nine-point, two-dimensional stencil (Ferziger, 1981). This iterative procedure calculates ϕ at iteration $n + 1$ from the values of the previous iteration (n) at the eight neighboring points:

$$\phi_{i,j}^{n+1} = \frac{1}{5} \left(\phi_{i+1,j}^{n} + \phi_{i-1,j}^{n} + \phi_{i,j+1}^{n} + \phi_{i,j-1}^{n} \right) + \frac{1}{20} \left(\phi_{i+1,j+1}^{n} + \phi_{i+1,j-1}^{n} + \phi_{i-1,j+1}^{n} + \phi_{i-1,j-1}^{n} \right)$$

where i and j are the mesh coordinates in x and y. After the update is calculated at each point, we calculate the maximum difference or residual between iterations and base a stopping criteria on this maximum residual. We also stop the calculation if a set maximum number of iterations is performed.

We implement this procedure in four ways: on the CPU, on the GPU using global memory, on the GPU using shared memory, and on the GPU using textures. The full code is listed in Appendix D.5. Here we include only sections relevant to the discussion. The CPU version of the algorithm is:

```fortran
126   ! CPU version
127
128   write(*,"(/,a,/)") 'CPU results'
129   write(*,*) 'Iteration   Max Residual'
130
131   call initialize(a, aNew)
132
133   iter=0
134   do while ( maxResidual > tol .and. iter <= iterMax )
135      maxResidual = 0.0_fp_kind
136
137      do j=2,ny-1
138         do i=2,nx-1
139            aNew(i,j) = 0.2_fp_kind * &
140                    (a(i,j-1)+a(i-1,j)+a(i+1,j)+a(i,j+1)) + &
141                    0.05_fp_kind * &
142                    (a(i-1,j-1)+a(i+1,j-1)+a(i-1,j+1)+a(i+1,j+1))
143
144            maxResidual = &
145                    max(maxResidual, abs(aNew(i,j)-a(i,j)))
146         end do
147      end do
148
149      iter = iter + 1
150      if(mod(iter,reportInterval) == 0) &
```

```
151              write(*,'(i8,3x,f10.6)'), iter, maxResidual
152        a = aNew
153     end do
```

The `do while` loop on line 134 checks our stopping criteria for each iteration, and the doubly nested loop starting on line 137 calculates aNew, equivalent to ϕ^{n+1}, at each interior point. The maximum residual is updated within the nested loops on line 144 if appropriate.

The kernel for the global memory method is:

```
30    attributes(global) subroutine jacobiGlobal(a, aNew)
31       real(fp_kind) :: a(nx,ny), aNew(nx,ny)
32       integer :: i, j
33
34       i = (blockIdx%x-1)*blockDim%x + threadIdx%x
35       j = (blockIdx%y-1)*blockDim%y + threadIdx%y
36
37       if (i>1 .and. i<nx .and. j>1 .and. j<ny) then
38          aNew(i,j) = &
39                0.2_fp_kind * ( &
40                a(i-1,j) + a(i+1,j) + &
41                a(i,j-1) + a(i,j+1)) + &
42                0.05_fp_kind * (&
43                a(i-1,j-1) + a(i+1,j-1) + &
44                a(i-1,j+1) + a(i+1,j+1))
45       endif
46    end subroutine jacobiGlobal
```

Here the global indices are calculated on lines 34 and 35, which are checked on line 37 to make sure the updated values are calculated only for interior points. This kernel is called from the host in the following code:

```
160    tBlock = dim3(BLOCK_X,BLOCK_Y,1)
161    grid = dim3(ceiling(real(nx)/tBlock%x), &
162         ceiling(real(ny)/tBlock%y), 1)
163
164    call initialize(a, aNew)
165
166    call cpu_time(start_time)
167
168    a_d = a
169    aNew_d = aNew
170
171    iter=0
```

```
172    do while ( maxResidual > tol .and. iter <= iterMax )
173       maxResidual = 0.0_fp_kind
174
175       call jacobiGlobal<<<grid, tBlock>>>(a_d, aNew_d)
176
177       !$CUF kernel do <<<*,*>>>
178       do j = 1, ny
179          do i = 1, nx
180             maxResidual = &
181                   max(maxResidual, abs(a_d(i,j)-aNew_d(i,j)))
182          enddo
183       enddo
184
185       iter = iter + 1
186       if(mod(iter,reportInterval) == 0) &
187             write(*,'(i8,3x,f10.6)'), iter, maxResidual
188       a_d = aNew_d
189    end do
190
191    a = aNew_d
192    call cpu_time(stop_time)
193    write(*,'(a,f10.3,a)')  ' Completed in ', &
194          stop_time-start_time, ' seconds'
```

In this code segment, the Fortran intrinsic `cpu_time` is used to measure elapsed time for the overall procedure, including transfers between the host and device. After the `jacobiGlobal` kernel is called, a CUF kernel on lines 177–183 is used to calculate the maximum residual. The rest of the host code is similar to the CPU version except that the elapsed time as measured by the host is reported.

The shared memory kernel is:

```
51       real(fp_kind) :: a(nx,ny), aNew(nx,ny)
52       real(fp_kind), shared :: t(0:BLOCK_X+1, 0:BLOCK_Y+1)
53       integer :: i, j, is, js
54
55       i = (blockIdx%x-1)*blockDim%x + threadIdx%x
56       j = (blockIdx%y-1)*blockDim%y + threadIdx%y
57       is = threadIdx%x
58       js = threadIdx%y
59
60       if (i > 1 .and. j > 1) &
61             t(is-1, js-1) = a(i-1, j-1)
62       if (i > 1 .and. j < ny .and. js >= BLOCK_Y-2) &
63             t(is-1, js+1) = a(i-1, j+1)
64       if (i < nx .and. j > 1 .and. is >= BLOCK_X-2) &
65             t(is+1,js-1) = a(i+1,j-1)
```

```
66      if (i < nx .and. j < ny .and. &
67           is >= BLOCK_X-2 .and. js >= BLOCK_Y-2) &
68           t(is+1,js+1) = a(i+1,j+1)
69
70      call syncthreads()
71
72      if (i > 1 .and. i < nx .and. j > 1 .and. j < ny) then
73         aNew(i,j) = 0.2_fp_kind * ( &
74              t(is,js-1) + t(is-1,js) + &
75              t(is+1,js) + t(is,js+1)) &
76              + 0.05_fp_kind * ( &
77              t(is-1,js-1) + t(is+1,js-1) + &
78              t(is-1,js+1) + t(is+1,js+1))
79      endif
80
81    end subroutine jacobiShared
```

where the shared memory tile t(0:BLOCK_X+1, 0:BLOCK_Y+1) holds values from the previous iteration. Because the kernel is launched with BLOCK_X × BLOCK_Y threads per thread block, there are not enough threads to populate the shared memory tile in one read instruction. This kernel uses four instructions to populate the shared memory tile, on lines 60–68. Following the syncthreads() call, the calculation of the updated values is performed.

The texture kernel is nearly identical to the global memory kernel except that the right-side terms are read from a texture reference pointing to the previous iteration's values rather than using the previous iteration's values themselves. This kernel has a similar memory access pattern to the texture example in Section 3.2.3. The main difference is that the values are weighted differently.

```
85    attributes(global) subroutine jacobiTexture(aNew)
86       real(fp_kind) :: aNew(nx,ny)
87       integer :: i, j
88
89       i = (blockIdx%x-1)*blockDim%x + threadIdx%x
90       j = (blockIdx%y-1)*blockDim%y + threadIdx%y
91
92       if (i > 1 .and. i < nx .and. j > 1 .and. j < ny) then
93          aNew(i,j) = 0.2_fp_kind * ( &
94               aTex(i-1,j) + aTex(i+1,j) + &
95               aTex(i,j-1) + aTex(i,j+1) ) &
96               + 0.05_fp_kind * (&
97               aTex(i-1,j-1) + aTex(i+1,j-1) + &
98               aTex(i-1,j+1) + aTex(i+1,j+1))
99       endif
100   end subroutine jacobiTexture
```

When we execute the code on a Tesla K20, we obtain:

```
Relaxation calculation on 4096 x 4096 mesh

CPU results

  Iteration    Max Residual
        10     0.023564
        20     0.011931
        30     0.008061
        40     0.006065
        50     0.004811
        60     0.004040
        70     0.003442
        80     0.003029
        90     0.002685
       100     0.002420

GPU global results

  Iteration    Max Residual
        10     0.023564
        20     0.011931
        30     0.008061
        40     0.006065
        50     0.004811
        60     0.004040
        70     0.003442
        80     0.003029
        90     0.002685
       100     0.002420
  Completed in      0.540 seconds

GPU shared results

  Iteration    Max Residual
        10     0.023564
        20     0.011931
        30     0.008061
        40     0.006065
        50     0.004811
        60     0.004040
        70     0.003442
        80     0.003029
        90     0.002685
       100     0.002420
```

```
    Completed in        0.496 seconds

GPU texture results

   Iteration    Max Residual
        10      0.023564
        20      0.011931
        30      0.008061
        40      0.006065
        50      0.004811
        60      0.004040
        70      0.003442
        80      0.003029
        90      0.002685
       100      0.002420
    Completed in        0.457 seconds
```

The maximum residual at each printed iteration is the same for all cases, so the results are in agreement. From the output we observe that the elapsed times for all of the GPU versions appear fairly similar. Of course, the reported elapsed times reflect not only the various kernels in the laplaceRoutines module but also the CUF kernels that perform the reduction as well as the array copy at the end of each iteration from aNew_d to a_d, along with the initial host-to-device transfers and the final device-to-host transfer of the result. Since the CUF kernels and the data copies are common to each approach, the difference in the kernel execution, percentage-wise, is larger than the overall time indicates. One could use CUDA events to time only the kernel executions, but here we instead opt for using the Command Line Profiler. The full output from the profiler lists the execution times of all kernel calls, including CUF kernels, and data transfers for each iteration. Here we list representative output from each kernel on the Tesla K20:

```
method=[ laplaceroutines_jacobiglobal_ ] gputime=[ 2179.072 ]
      cputime=[ 8.000 ] occupancy=[ 1.000 ]
method=[ laplaceroutines_jacobishared_ ] gputime=[ 1752.800 ]
      cputime=[ 8.000 ] occupancy=[ 1.000 ]
method=[ laplaceroutines_jacobitexture_ ] gputime=[ 1378.272 ]
      cputime=[ 12.000 ] occupancy=[ 1.000 ]
```

Comparing the global and texture memory versions, we see almost a factor of two in performance improvement by using textures. All things considered, the global memory case doesn't perform that badly. Recall that the Tesla K20 does not cache global variables in the L1 cache, so it is the L2 cache that is helping out the global memory version's performance. Although this is far from perfectly coalesced, there is enough locality in this compact stencil for the global version to perform reasonably well. However, the point we want to make here is that by using textures, with relative ease we can improve performance simply by replacing instances of the global variable on the right-hand side with texture pointers.

We might think that the shared memory version should be optimal, but the issue of populating a shared memory tile with more values than there are threads in a thread block introduces some inefficiency. We could use a larger thread block so that the shared memory tile can be populated with one instruction, but then some threads would remain dormant during the calculation of updated values. The shared memory version does outperform the global memory version, but the texture version is preferable to the shared memory version, in terms of both performance and ease of programming. Texture usage is at the moment limited to single precision, but this restriction will be removed in upcoming versions of the PGI compiler.

In closing, we should point out that for large meshes the convergence rate of an iterative method such as this is slow, and one would likely resort to a multigrid method. However, a discussion of multigrid methods is beyond the scope of this book. We refer the interested reader to the work that has been done in CUDA C on multigrid methods.

Applications of Fast Fourier Transform

CHAPTER OUTLINE HEAD

The Fourier Transform is of fundamental importance in several fields, from image processing to computational physics. The Discrete Fourier Transform (DFT) is an approximation in which discrete samples of a function $f(x)$ in physical space can be transformed to Fourier coefficients $\hat{f}$ via the relation:

$$\hat{f}_k = \frac{1}{N} \sum_{j=0}^{N-1} e^{-\frac{2\pi \iota}{N} jk} f_j$$

This formula could be rewritten as a matrix-vector multiplication, $\hat{f} = Wf$, where W is called the Fourier matrix:

$$(W_N)_{jk} = \frac{1}{N} e^{-\frac{2\pi \iota}{N} jk} = \frac{1}{N} \omega_N^{jk}$$

with ω_N being the primitive N^{th} root of unity. Instead of the expected arithmetic complexity of $O(N^2)$ operations typical of a matrix-vector product, Cooley and Tukey (1965) introduced the Fast Fourier Transform (FFT) algorithm based on a divide-and-conquer approach that results in an arithmetic complexity of $O(Nlog_2 N)$ operations. In addition to this original FFT algorithm (also called the *decimation-in-time algorithm*), there are now several other FFT algorithms (e.g., decimation in frequency, Bluestein, prime factor) that are commonly used. An extensive list of such algorithms can be found in Van Loan (1992).

7.1 CUFFT

Writing a high-performance FFT library is not a easy task. Fortunately, the CUDA C CUFFT library contains a simple interface to FFTs that can transform arrays containing up to 2^{27} single-precision or 2^{26}

Table 7.1 Possible types of transforms: R (single-precision real data), C (single-precision complex data), D (double-precision real data), Z (double-precision complex data).

	Output	
	Real	**Complex**
Input real	-	R2C/D2Z
Input complex	C2R/Z2D	C2C/Z2Z

double-precision elements on the GPU, provided enough device memory is available. If the array size can be expressed as $2^a \cdot 3^b \cdot 5^c \cdot 7^d$, the CUFFT library will execute highly optimized kernels.

The steps needed to call CUFFT are similar to those used by the FFTW library, a very well-known FFT library used on CPUs:

- *Create a plan.* This step will perform all the allocations and initializations needed by the library. Depending on the dimensionality of the input data, there are different functions that accomplish this task: `cufftPlan1d`, `cufftPlan2d`, and `cufftPlan3d`. In addition to these three functions, the function `cufftPlanMany` can be used to create a plan for performing multiple independent transforms for which the data are strided and/or offset in memory. For the 1D case, CUFFT can also transform multiple arrays at once, using a *batch* argument in `cufftPlan1d`.
- *Execute the plan.* Once a plan is created, a variety of routines can be called to compute the FFT of the input sequence. If the dimensions of the data do not change, the routine can be called multiple times without creating a new plan. The function names are `cuffExecuteX2Y`, where the last three letters depend on the data type shown in Table 7.1. For complex-to-complex transforms, we will also need to supply the direction `CUFFT_FORWARD` for transforms from physical to Fourier space or `CUFFT_INVERSE` for transforms from Fourier to physical space. Real-to-complex transforms have an implicit direction (`CUFFT_FORWARD`), as do complex-to-real transforms (`CUFFT_INVERSE`). The latter case also assumes the input data are Hermitian (to ensure that the inverse transform resulting in real values exists).
- *Destroy the plan.* This step will release the resources allocated when the plan was created. The function name is `cufftDestroy`.

Similar to what was done for the CURAND library in Chapter 5, we rely on the ISO_C_BINDING module to interface with the CUFFT C functions of the CUFFT library. This interface is more complex than the CURAND interface for several reasons. Unlike Fortran, C does not have native support for complex data types. Luckily, the layout choosen by the library and defined by the type `cuComplex` has the same layout of the native complex data type in Fortran.

We should mention a few issues involved in creating our interface. CUFFT uses plans, which are opaque objects, to store information about the transforms and auxiliary arrays. We will declare the plan as a `type(c_ptr)` variable in Fortran. The call to create a plan will generate all the proper information; the variable is just a pointer to the opaque object with the proper size. Declaring the variable as `type(c_ptr)` will also make the code portable between 32- and 64-bit systems. A second issue is that CUFFT uses several constants, e.g., `CUFFT_C2C` and `CUFFT_FORWARD`, which are defined in hexadecimal in CUDA C. To express hexadecimal numbers in Fortran, the Z prefix is used. For example, the constant in the CUFFT C header file CUFFT_R2C=0x2a will be defined as CUFFT_R2C=Z'2a' in the Fortran module. Finally, CUFFT expects multidimensional data in row-major order, as is the default in C, not column-major order as in Fortran. Since we are writing an interface to the library, we need to decide whether to use the C or Fortran order in our Fortran interface. To keep a familiar coding style, we decided to use the Fortran order.

We only show the interface for the creation of the 2D plan with cufftPlan2d that needs to swap the arguments for the dimensions. This is done with a declaration of a generic interface cufftPlan2D that contains a new subroutine cufftPlan2DSwap, declared as a module procedure. The native cufftPlan2D routine is renamed cufftPlan2DC, which is called by the routine cufftPlan2DSwap.

```
122    interface cufftPlan2d
123       module procedure cufftPlan2Dswap
124    end interface cufftPlan2d
125
126    interface cufftPlan2dC
127       subroutine cufftPlan2d(plan, nx, ny, type) &
128            bind(C,name='cufftPlan2d')
129          use iso_c_binding
130          type(c_ptr):: plan
131          integer(c_int),value:: nx, ny, type
132       end subroutine cufftPlan2d
133    end interface cufftPlan2dC
134
135 contains
136
137    subroutine cufftPlan2Dswap(plan,nx,ny, type)
138       use iso_c_binding
139       type(c_ptr):: plan
140       integer(c_int),value:: nx, ny, type
141       call cufftPlan2dC(plan,ny,nx,type)
142    end subroutine cufftPlan2Dswap
```

The CUFFT library is capable of doing transforms either "in place" (where the same memory is used for both the input and output arrays, i.e., the output array overwrites the input data) or "out of place" (where different memory is used for the input and output arrays). When doing transforms in place, we need to consider the different memory requirements that depend on the nature of the sequence (real or complex). A complex sequence of N points is transformed to a complex sequence of N points. If the input sequence is real, from a starting sequence of N real numbers we end up with a sequence of $N/2 + 1$ complex numbers. Due to the properties of the Fourier transform, the imaginary part of the zero-wave number and of the highest-wave number ($N/2$), also called the *Nyquist wave number*, are zero. As such, the content of the information is preserved (N real values are transformed to $N/2 - 1$ complex values plus 2 real values.) However, CUFFT explicitly stores these $N/2 + 1$ values. To do an in-place real-to-complex transform, the array needs to accommodate the largest case. A complex array of size $N/2 + 1$ has the same storage footprint of a real array of size $N + 2$.

Another important issue regarding FFTs is the normalization factor. With CUFFT, transforming an array back and forth between physical and Fourier space will give us the original data multiplied by the length of the transform:

$$IFFT(FFT(A)) = len(A)*A$$

To get back our original data after a round trip through Fourier space once must divide by the length of the array. There is also the possibility of adopting a data layout compatible[1] with FFTW (but we will not cover this option) and the choice of the stream in which the library calls will execute using the `cufftSetStream` function. This is a very important optimization for several use cases, as we will see later in the section illustrating convolutions.

Now that we have all the pieces in place, let's do a simple transform of a signal with period 2π:

$$f_j = cos(2x_j) + sin(3x_j)$$

defined on $x_j = (2\pi/N)j$, with $j = 0, N - 1$. Since the Fourier transform is defined as

$$\hat{f}_k = \frac{1}{N} \sum_{j=0}^{N-1} e^{-2\pi i \frac{jk}{N}} f_j = \frac{1}{N} \sum_{j=0}^{N-1} e^{-ikx_j} f_j \quad \text{for} \quad k = -\frac{N}{2}, -\frac{N}{2} + 1, \ldots, \frac{N}{2} - 1$$

and remembering that from Euler's formula $e^{ix} = cos\,x + i sin\,x$, $cos\,x = \frac{e^{ix}+e^{-ix}}{2}$ and $sin\,x = \frac{e^{ix}-e^{-ix}}{2i}$, we are expecting to see two nonzero real coefficients of value 0.5 at $k = \pm 2$ (corresponding to the cosine term) and two nonzero imaginary coefficients with conjugate symmetry of value ∓ 0.5 at $k = \pm 3$ (corresponding to the sine term). Transforming a signal with a known output is a good way to check the wave number layout of the library. Amplitudes for the positive wave numbers (from 0 to $N/2 - 1$) are returned in the positions 1 to $N/2$; amplitudes for the negative wave numbers (from -1 to $-N/2$) are returned in reverse order in the positions $N/2 + 1, \ldots, N$. This is a typical arrangement for several FFT libraries. The code that performs this test is:

```
1   program fft_test_c2c
2   use iso_c_binding
3   use precision_m
4   use cufft_m
5   implicit none
6   integer, allocatable :: kx(:)
7   complex(fp_kind), allocatable :: cinput(:), coutput(:)
8   complex(fp_kind), allocatable, device :: cinput_d(:), coutput_d(:)
9
10  integer :: i,n
11  type(c_ptr) :: plan
12  real(fp_kind) :: twopi=8._fp_kind*atan(1._fp_kind),h
13
```

[1]A detailed description is available in the CUFFT manual available online at http://docs.nvidia.com.

```
14  n=16
15  h=twopi/real(n,fp_kind)
16
17  ! allocate arrays on the host
18  allocate (cinput(n),coutput(n),kx(n))
19
20  ! allocate arrays on the device
21  allocate (cinput_d(n),coutput_d(n))
22
23  !initialize arrays on host
24  kx =(/ (i-1, i=1,n/2), (-n+i-1, i=n/2+1,n) /)
25
26  do i=1,n
27  cinput(i)=(cos(2*real(i-1,fp_kind)*h)+sin(3*real(i-1,fp_kind)*h))
28  end do
29
30  !copy arrays to device
31  cinput_d=cinput
32
33  ! Initialize the plan for complex to complex transform
34  if (fp_kind== singlePrecision) call cufftPlan1D(plan,n,CUFFT_C2C,1)
35  if (fp_kind== doublePrecision) call cufftPlan1D(plan,n,CUFFT_Z2Z,1)
36
37  ! Forward transform out of place
38   call cufftExec(plan,cinput_d,coutput_d,CUFFT_FORWARD)
39
40  ! Copy results back to host
41  coutput=coutput_d
42
43  print *," Transform from complex array"
44  do i=1,n
45   write(*,'(i2,1x,2(f8.4),2x,i2,2(f8.4))') i,cinput(i),kx(i),coutput(i)/n
46  end do
47
48  !release memory on the host and on the device
49  deallocate (cinput,coutput,kx,cinput_d,coutput_d)
50
51  ! Destroy the plans
52  call cufftDestroy(plan)
53
54  end program fft_test_c2c
```

Compiling and running the code, we check that the frequencies are in the expected positions:

```
% pgf90 -o fft_test_sp  precision_m.F90 cufft.cuf fft_test.cuf -lcufft
% pgf90 -DDOUBLE -o fft_test_dp precision_m.F90 cufft.cuf  \
           fft_test.cuf -lcufft
% ./fft_test_sp
 i    Re(in)  IM(in)  kx  Re(out)  Im(out)
 1    1.0000  0.0000   0   0.0000   0.0000
```

```
 2    1.6310   0.0000    1    0.0000    0.0000
 3    0.7071   0.0000    2    0.5000    0.0000
 4   -1.0898   0.0000    3    0.0000   -0.5000
 5   -2.0000   0.0000    4    0.0000    0.0000
 6   -1.0898   0.0000    5    0.0000    0.0000
 7    0.7071   0.0000    6    0.0000    0.0000
 8    1.6310   0.0000    7    0.0000    0.0000
 9    1.0000   0.0000   -8    0.0000    0.0000
10   -0.2168   0.0000   -7    0.0000    0.0000
11   -0.7071   0.0000   -6    0.0000    0.0000
12   -0.3244   0.0000   -5    0.0000    0.0000
13    0.0000   0.0000   -4    0.0000    0.0000
14   -0.3244   0.0000   -3    0.0000    0.5000
15   -0.7071   0.0000   -2    0.5000    0.0000
16   -0.2168   0.0000   -1    0.0000    0.0000
```

The code that performs a real-to-complex transform in place is:

```
1  program fft_test_r2c
2  use iso_c_binding
3  use cudafor
4  use precision_m
5  use cufft_m
6  implicit none
7  integer, allocatable:: kx(:)
8  real(fp_kind), allocatable:: rinput(:)
9  real(fp_kind), allocatable, device:: rinput_d(:)
10 complex(fp_kind),allocatable:: coutput(:)
11
12 type(c_ptr):: plan
13 integer:: i,n,istat
14 real(fp_kind):: twopi=8._fp_kind*atan(1._fp_kind),h
15
16 n=16
17 h=twopi/real(n,fp_kind)
18
19 ! allocate arrays on the host
20 allocate (rinput(n),coutput(n/2+1),kx(n/2+1))
21
22 ! allocate arrays on the device
23 allocate (rinput_d(n+2))
24
25 !initialize arrays on host
26 kx =(/ (i-1, i=1,n/2+1) /)
27
28 do i=1,n
29  rinput(i)=(cos(2*real(i-1,fp_kind)*h)+ &
30            sin(3*real(i-1,fp_kind)*h))
31 end do
```

```
32
33  !copy arrays to device
34  rinput_d=rinput
35
36  ! Initialize the plan for real to complex transform
37  if (fp_kind== singlePrecision) call cufftPlan1D(plan,n,CUFFT_R2C,1)
38  if (fp_kind== doublePrecision) call cufftPlan1D(plan,n,CUFFT_D2Z,1)
39
40  ! Execute Forward transform in place
41  call cufftExec(plan,rinput_d,rinput_d)
42
43  ! Copy results back to host
44  istat=cudaMemcpy(coutput,rinput_d,n+2,cudaMemcpyDeviceToHost)
45
46  print *," Transform from real array"
47  do i=1,n/2+1
48    write(*,'(i2,1x,i2,2(f8.4))') i,kx(i),coutput(i)/n
49  end do
50
51  !release memory on the host and on the device
52  deallocate (rinput,coutput,kx,rinput_d)
53
54  ! Destroy the plans
55  call cufftDestroy(plan)
56
57  end program fft_test_r2c
```

The input array on the device is of dimension $N+2$ to accommodate the extra elements in the output, since we are doing the transform in place. The input array on the host can be of dimension N, there is no need to add extra space, since the transform is done on the GPU. The first copy from host to device can be done with a simple assignment, even if there is a mismatch in the length of the array. The runtime will transfer N real elements from the host real array to the equivalent elements in the device array. Once the data are resident in device memory, a cufftExec call is invoked where the input and output arrays are the same. For the transfer of results back to the complex output array on the host, we cannot rely on the assignment, since there is a type mismatch and a call to cudaMemcpy is needed with an explicit declaration of the direction. The size of the payload needs to be specified in elements of the source array, in this case the number of elements in rinput_d. The output will produce only half of the wave numbers, from 0 to $N/2$; the other half could be obtained using Hermitian symmetry.

```
 Transform from real array
 1   0   0.0000   0.0000
 2   1   0.0000   0.0000
 3   2   0.5000   0.0000
 4   3   0.0000  -0.5000
 5   4   0.0000   0.0000
 6   5   0.0000   0.0000
 7   6   0.0000   0.0000
```

```
8   7   0.0000   0.0000
9   8   0.0000   0.0000
```

For several applications, it is much easier to work in Fourier space once the wave numbers are rearranged in a more natural layout, with the zero wave number at the center of the range. For example, MATLAB provides functions called FFTSHIFT and IFFTSHIFT to achieve this goal. CUFFT is missing this capability and we have to write our own. At first glance, we would think that the only way to achieve this is via a kernel that basically performs a copy while taking care of rearranging the wave numbers: part of the spectrum is shifted, the other one is shifted and reversed. This would be a completely memory-bound kernel. There is another way to achieve this shift that takes advantage of the GPU's floating-point performance. If we multiply the input by a function $shift(i) = (-1)^{(i+1)}$ (in 2D $shift(i, j) = (-1)^{(i+j)}$), the output of this modified input will give us a Fourier transform whereby the wave numbers are in natural order (Solomon and Brecon, 2011). Since the multiplication is element-wise and the access pattern is quite simple, we can achieve optimal throughput. We will check this method by adding the following lines to the `fft_test_c2c` code before the FFT transform on line 38. After the data are in device memory, we call a CUF kernel to multiply each element by the factor $(-1)^{(i+1)}$.

```
!$cuf kernel do   <<<*,*>>>
  do i=1,n
      cinput_d(i)=cinput_d(i)*((-1._fp_kind)**(i+1))
  end do
```

We also add a constant n to the function to better identify the zero-wave number that will contain the average of the function and print the wave numbers in natural order, starting from $-N/2$.

```
Transform from complex array
 1   17.0000   0.0000   -8   0.0000   0.0000
 2   17.6310   0.0000   -7   0.0000   0.0000
 3   16.7071   0.0000   -6   0.0000   0.0000
 4   14.9102   0.0000   -5   0.0000   0.0000
 5   14.0000   0.0000   -4   0.0000   0.0000
 6   14.9102   0.0000   -3   0.0000   0.5000
 7   16.7071   0.0000   -2   0.5000   0.0000
 8   17.6310   0.0000   -1   0.0000   0.0000
 9   17.0000   0.0000    0  16.0000   0.0000
10   15.7832   0.0000    1   0.0000   0.0000
11   15.2929   0.0000    2   0.5000   0.0000
12   15.6756   0.0000    3   0.0000  -0.5000
13   16.0000   0.0000    4   0.0000   0.0000
14   15.6756   0.0000    5   0.0000   0.0000
15   15.2929   0.0000    6   0.0000   0.0000
16   15.7832   0.0000    7   0.0000   0.0000
```

If we were to transform back this shifted sequence, we would need to multiply the output using the same CUF kernel to remove the shift function.

7.2 Spectral derivatives

In Chapter 6, we saw how finite differencing could be used to compute approximate derivatives. There is another way of computing derivatives, known as *spectral differentiation*. Despite being more expensive from a computational point of view and less flexible with respect to the boundary conditions, spectral methods are in many cases preferred as they have superior accuracy and are commonly used in several computational physics fields, from computational fluid dynamics to optics.

An excellent explanation of the properties of spectral differentiation can be found in the books by Moin (Moin, 2001) and Trefethen (Trefethen, 2000). Here we limit the description and examples to periodic functions and linear examples, but spectral derivatives could be extended to nonperiodic domains (using Chebyshev or Legendre polynomials) and nonlinear cases (with particular attention to aliasing effects).

Once we have the Fourier coefficients $\hat{f}$, we can express the original function $f(x_j)$ as:

$$f(x_j) = \sum_{k=-N/2}^{N/2-1} \hat{f}_k e^{\imath k x_j}$$

The Fourier series for the derivative is simply:

$$f'(x_j) = \sum_{k=-N/2}^{N/2-1} \imath k \hat{f}_k e^{\imath k x_j}$$

Although the concept is quite simple, there are few important details to consider in the implementation of such a method (Trefethen, 2000). The algorithm to compute the first derivative of a periodic function from samples f_i is:

- From f_i compute the Fourier coefficient $\hat{f}_i$ using FFT.
- Multiply the Fourier coefficient $\hat{f}_i$ by $\imath k_x$. If N is even, the coefficient of the derivative corresponding to $N/2 + 1$, the Nyquist frequency, needs to be multiplied by zero.[2] This step could also include the normalization factor.
- Transform back to the physical space using the inverse FFT to obtain f'_i.

The second derivative can be computed in a similar matter:

- From f_i compute the Fourier coefficient $\hat{f}_i$ using FFT.
- Multiply the Fourier coefficient $\hat{f}_i$ by the $-k_x^2$. Since the multiplication factor is now real, there is no need for a special treatment of the Nyquist frequency. This step could also include the normalization factor.
- Transform back to the physical space using the inverse FFT to obtain f''_i.

---

[2]The imaginary part equal to zero is needed to generate a real function. The real part equal to zero is needed to preserve some symmetry properties of the derivative operator.

Having discussed the procedure for calculating spectral derivatives, we now compute the derivative of the function used in the previous section:

$$f_j = cos(2x_j) + sin(3x_j)$$

defined on $x_j = (2\pi/N)j$, with $j = 0, N - 1$. The exact derivative is, of course:

$$f'_j = -2sin(2x_j) + 3sin(3x_j)$$

The code that performs this is:

```
1   program fft_derivative
2   use iso_c_binding
3   use precision_m
4   use cufft_m
5   implicit none
6   real(fp_kind), allocatable:: kx(:), derivative(:)
7   real(fp_kind), allocatable, device:: kx_d(:)
8
9   complex(fp_kind), allocatable:: cinput(:),output(:)
10  complex(fp_kind), allocatable, device:: cinput_d(:),output_d(:)
11
12  integer:: i,n
13  type(c_ptr):: plan
14  real(fp_kind):: twopi=8._fp_kind*atan(1._fp_kind),h
15
16  n=8
17  h=twopi/real(n,fp_kind)
18
19  ! allocate arrays on the host
20  allocate (cinput(n),coutput(n),derivative(n),kx(n))
21
22  ! allocate arrays on the device
23  allocate (cinput_d(n),coutput_d(n),kx_d(n))
24
25  ! initialize arrays on host
26  kx =(/ ((i-1), i=1,n/2), ((-n+i-1), i=n/2+1,n) /)
27
28  ! Set the wave number for the Nyquist frequency to zero
29  kx(n/2+1)=0._fp_kind
30
31  ! Copy the wave number vector to the device
32  kx_d=kx
33
34  do i=1,n
35    cinput(i)=(cos(2*real(i-1,fp_kind)*h) &
36            +sin(3*real(i-1,fp_kind)*h))
37    derivative(i)=(-2*sin(2*real(i-1,fp_kind)*h) &
38              +3*cos(3*real(i-1,fp_kind)*h))
39  end do
```

```
40
41  ! copy input to device
42    cinput_d=cinput
43
44  ! Initialize the plan for complex to complex transform
45  if (fp_kind== singlePrecision) call cufftPlan1D(plan,n,CUFFT_C2C,1)
46  if (fp_kind== doublePrecision) call cufftPlan1D(plan,n,CUFFT_Z2Z,1)
47
48  ! Forward transform out of place
49  call cufftExec(plan,cinput_d,coutput_d,CUFFT_FORWARD)
50
51  ! Compute the derivative in spectral space and normalize the FFT
52  !$cuf kernel do <<<*,*>>>
53  do i=1,n
54    coutput_d(i)=cmplx(0.,kx_d(i),fp_kind)*coutput_d(i)/n
55  end do
56
57  ! Inverse transform in place
58  call cufftExec(plan,coutput_d,coutput_d,CUFFT_INVERSE)
59
60  ! Copy results back to host
61  coutput=coutput_d
62
63  print *," First Derivative from complex array"
64  do i=1,n
65    write(*,'(i2,2(1x,f8.4),2x,e13.7)') i,real(coutput(i)),derivative(i) &
66                                    ,real(coutput(i))-derivative(i)
67  end do
68
69  !release memory on the host and on the device
70  deallocate (cinput,coutput,kx,derivative,cinput_d,coutput_d,kx_d)
71
72  ! Destroy the plans
73  call cufftDestroy(plan)
74
75  end program fft_derivative
```

After we compute the FFT, we multiply the data element-wise by $cmplx(0.,kx\_d(i),fp\_kind)$ on the device using a CUF kernel, taking particular care to define the multiplication factor of the right precision using fp_kind. If we were to use $cmplx(0.,kx\_d(i))$, we will lose double-precision accuracy in the final result. Finally, there is an additional in-place inverse transform to return to physical space. When we compile and run this code in both single and double precision and then compare the results to the analytic expression, we can verify that the result is correct to the round-off error. For double precision we have:

```
% pgf90 -DDOUBLE -o spectral_dp  precision_m.F90 cufft.cuf \
              fft_derivative.cuf -lcufft
% ./spectral_dp
```

```
 First  Derivative  from  complex  array
1     3.0000     3.0000    0.1332268E-14
2    -4.1213    -4.1213    -.8881784E-15
3     0.0000     0.0000    -.1419503E-15
4     4.1213     4.1213    0.8881784E-15
5    -3.0000    -3.0000    -.8881784E-15
6     0.1213     0.1213    0.3108624E-14
7     0.0000     0.0000    -.6466482E-15
8    -0.1213    -0.1213    -.1776357E-14
```

and for single precision:

```
% pgf90  -o  spectral_sp  precision_m.F90  cufft.cuf \
                fft_derivative.cuf  -lcufft
% ./spectral_sp
 First  Derivative  from  complex  array
1     3.0000     3.0000    -.2384186E-06
2    -4.1213    -4.1213    0.0000000E+00
3     0.0000     0.0000    -.2702248E-06
4     4.1213     4.1213    0.0000000E+00
5    -3.0000    -3.0000    0.0000000E+00
6     0.1213     0.1213    -.2384186E-06
7     0.0000     0.0000    0.4768569E-06
8    -0.1213    -0.1213    -.2145767E-05
```

7.3 Convolution

One of the most used properties of the FFT is that a convolution in the time domain can be expressed as the point-wise multiplication in Fourier space:

$$conv(A, B) = IFFT\big[FFT(A).*FFT(B)\big]$$

where .* denotes an element-wise multiplication. Another important operation, cross-correlation, can be implemented in a similar fashion by multiplying the conjugate transform of one array with the transform of the other:

$$crosscorr(A, B) = IFFT\big[conj(FFT(A)).*FFT(B)\big]$$

In this example, we convolve two series, S1 and S2, of P 2D complex matrices of dimension (M, N), focusing on minimizing the overall execution time. Each series is represented as a 3D array of dimension (M, N, P).

A naive implementation would transfer S1 and S2 to the GPU, perform FFT(S1) and FFT(S2), multiply the two transformed series element-wise, and transform the result back to physical space.

However, given the independence of the planes of data in S1 and S2, this is a situation where we can overlap data transfers and computation. Once plane n from S1, i.e., S1(:,:,n), and its corresponding plane S2(:,:,n) are in device memory, we can compute the correlation of these planes while transferring subsequent planes to the device. In addition, as soon as the convolution for slice n is complete, it can be transferred to host while overlapping the host-to-device transfer as well as another convolution computation. This approach is not only beneficial to overall execution time, but it also allows one to stage arrays on the GPU that do not fit in GPU memory. All that is required for optimal performance is enough planes resident in GPU memory to have effective overlap. Four planes are usually sufficient. The convolution code that performs this overlap is:

```
1  program fftOverlap
2  use cudafor
3  use precision_m
4  use cufft_m
5  implicit none
6
7  complex(fp_kind), allocatable,dimension(:,:,:),pinned :: A,B,C
8  complex(fp_kind), allocatable,dimension(:,:,:),device :: A_d,B_d
9  integer, parameter :: num_streams=4
10 integer:: nx, ny, nomega, ifr, i,j, stream_index
11 integer:: clock_start,clock_end,clock_rate, istat
12 integer(kind=cuda_stream_kind) :: stream(num_streams)
13 type(c_ptr):: plan
14 real:: elapsed_time
15 real(fp_kind):: scale
16
17 nx=512; ny=512;  nomega=196
18 scale=1./real(nx*ny,fp_kind)
19
20 ! Initialize FFT plan
21  call cufftPlan2d(plan,nx,ny,CUFFT_C2C)
22
23 ! Create streams
24  do i = 1,num_streams
25    istat= cudaStreamCreate(stream(i))
26  end do
27
28  call SYSTEM_CLOCK(COUNT_RATE=clock_rate) ! Find the rate
29
30 ! Allocate arrays on CPU and GPU
31  allocate(A(nx,ny,nomega),B(nx,ny,nomega),C(nx,ny,nomega))
32  allocate(A_d(nx,ny,num_streams),B_d(nx,ny,num_streams))
33
34 ! Initialize arrays on CPU
35  A=cmplx(1.,1.,fp_kind); B=cmplx(1.,1.,fp_kind); C=cmplx(0.,0.,fp_kind)
36
37 ! Measure only the transfer time
38  istat=cudaThreadSynchronize()
39
40  print *,"I/O only"
```

```
41    call SYSTEM_CLOCK(COUNT=clock_start) ! Start timing
42
43    do ifr=1,nomega
44     istat= cudaMemcpy(A_d(1,1,1),A(1,1,ifr),nx*ny)
45     istat= cudaMemcpy(B_d(1,1,1),B(1,1,ifr),nx*ny)
46     istat= cudaMemcpy(C(1,1,ifr),A_d(1,1,1),nx*ny)
47    end do
48
49    istat=cudaThreadSynchronize()
50    call SYSTEM_CLOCK(COUNT=clock_end) ! End timing
51    elapsed_time=REAL(clock_end-clock_start)/REAL(clock_rate)
52    print *,"Elapsed time :",elapsed_time
53
54 ! Measure the transfer time H2D, FFT , IFFT and transfer time D2H
55
56 print '(/a)',"Single stream  loop"
57 istat=cudaThreadSynchronize()
58 call SYSTEM_CLOCK(COUNT=clock_start) ! Start timing
59 stream_index = 1
60 call cufftSetStream(plan,stream(stream_index))
61 do ifr=1,nomega
62  istat= cudaMemcpy(A_d(1,1,stream_index),A(1,1,ifr),nx*ny)
63  istat= cudaMemcpy(B_d(1,1,stream_index),B(1,1,ifr),nx*ny)
64    call cufftExecC2C(plan ,A_d(1,1,stream_index),&
65                           A_d(1,1,stream_index),CUFFT_FORWARD)
66    call cufftExecC2C(plan ,B_d(1,1,stream_index),&
67                           B_d(1,1,stream_index),CUFFT_FORWARD)
68
69    ! Convolution and scaling of the  arrays
70    !$cuf kernel do(2) <<<*,(16,16),stream=stream(stream_index)>>>
71      do j=1,ny
72        do i=1,nx
73           B_d(i,j,stream_index)= A_d(i,j,stream_index)*&
74                               B_d(i,j,stream_index)*scale
75        end do
76      end do
77
78    call cufftExecC2C(plan ,B_d(1,1,stream_index),&
79                           B_d(1,1,stream_index),CUFFT_INVERSE)
80    istat=cudaMemcpy( C(1,1,ifr),B_d(1,1,stream_index),nx*ny)
81 end do
82
83 istat=cudaThreadSynchronize()
84 call SYSTEM_CLOCK(COUNT=clock_end) ! End timing
85 elapsed_time=REAL(clock_end-clock_start)/REAL(clock_rate)
86 print *,"Elapsed time :",elapsed_time
87
88 ! Overlap I/O and compute using multiple streams and async copies
89 print '(/a)',"Do loop with multiple streams"
90 call SYSTEM_CLOCK(COUNT=clock_start) ! Start timing
91
92 do ifr=1,nomega
```

```
 93
 94    ! assign a stream for the current plan
 95    stream_index = mod(ifr,num_streams)+1
 96
 97    ! Set the stream used by CUFFT
 98      call cufftSetStream(plan,stream(stream_index))
 99
100    ! Send A to GPU
101     istat= cudaMemcpyAsync(A_d(1,1,stream_index),A(1,1,ifr),&
102                             nx*ny, stream(stream_index))
103
104    ! Execute forward FFTs on GPU
105      call cufftExecC2C(plan ,A_d(1,1,stream_index),&
106                             A_d(1,1,stream_index),CUFFT_FORWARD)
107
108    ! Send B to GPU
109     istat= cudaMemcpyAsync(B_d(1,1,stream_index), &
110                             B(1,1,ifr),nx*ny, stream(stream_index))
111
112    ! Execute forward FFTs on GPU
113      call cufftExecC2C(plan ,B_d(1,1,stream_index),&
114                             B_d(1,1,stream_index),CUFFT_FORWARD)
115
116    ! Convolution and scaling of the   arrays
117     !$cuf kernel do(2) <<<*,(16,16),stream=stream(stream_index)>>>
118        do j=1,ny
119          do i=1,nx
120            B_d(i,j,stream_index)= A_d(i,j,stream_index)* &
121                                    B_d(i,j,stream_index)*scale
122          end do
123        end do
124
125    ! Execute inverse FFTs on GPU
126        call cufftExecC2C(plan ,B_d(1,1,stream_index), &
127                             B_d(1,1,stream_index),CUFFT_INVERSE)
128
129    ! Copy results back
130      istat=cudaMemcpyAsync( C(1,1,ifr),B_d(1,1,stream_index), &
131                             nx*ny, stream=stream(stream_index))
132
133    end do
134
135    istat=cudaThreadSynchronize()
136    call SYSTEM_CLOCK(COUNT=clock_end) ! Start timing
137    elapsed_time=REAL(clock_end-clock_start)/REAL(clock_rate)
138    print *,"Elapsed time :",elapsed_time
139
140    deallocate(A,B,C); deallocate(A_d,B_d)
141    call cufftDestroy(plan)
142
143    end program fftOverlap
```

The code has few points that need to be highlighted. The first point is that since we are planning to use asynchronous data transfers, we need to use pinned memory for the host arrays. We also create an array of streams that corresponds to different planes of S1 and S2. We do all the transforms in place, so there is no need to allocate a third array on the GPU. The first do loop on lines 43–47 transfers A and B to the device and transfers C back to CPU memory, one plane at the time. The transfer is timed and will give us an indication on how fast we can go, once we optimize the data transfer. The second loop on lines 61–81 does the convolution one plane at the time. The convolution is performed using a CUF kernel. The difference in time between these loops will indicate how much time is spent in the computation. The final loop starting on line 92 is the optimized implementation. Each iteration selects a stream in round-robin fashion, sends a plane from S1 and S2 to the GPU memory using cudaMemcpyAsync, sets the stream for FFT functions using cufftSetStream and transform them to Fourier space, performs the convolution using CUF kernel (this time we will need to specify the same stream of the other operations), transforms the result back to physical space, and sends it back to the CPU with another cudaMemcpyAsync call. All the work in one iteration is scheduled using the same stream. In theory, we should be able to achieve 2/3 of the I/O time (aside from the first two planes for S1 and S2 and the last one of the convolved matrix, the transfer back to CPU should be completely hidden) if the execution time is I/O limited, since we can hide all the computations. The optimized execution time can be written as $max(2/3*I/O\_time, compute\_time)$ to accommodate the case in which the compute time is the dominant factor.

If we compile and run on a Tesla K20x, we obtain:

```
% pgf90 -O3 -Minfo -o exampleOverlapFFT   precision_m.F90 cufft.cuf   \
       exampleOverlapFFT.cuf -lcufft
% ./exampleOverlapFFT
I/O only
  Elapsed time :    0.2232550

Single stream  loop
  Elapsed time :    0.2951850

Do loop with multiple streams
  Elapsed time :    0.1551300
```

where we observe that the overlap is very effective. From the elapsed time, our previous estimate gives us a time of 0.15 s, and we measured a time of 0.155 s. We can use the profiler to get better insight on the execution times and scheduling flow. Since our main interest is the transfer time and overlap, we generate a configuration file for the Command Line Profiler that will record the timestamps, the memory transfer size, and the stream information. We also want to use nvvp to visualize the traces, so the traces will need to be generated in CSV format.

```
% export CUDA_PROFILE=1
% export CUDA_PROFILE_CSV=1
% export CUDA_PROFILE_CONFIG=./cuda_prof_conf
```

```
% cat ./cuda_prof_conf
conckerneltrace
timestamp
gpustarttimestamp
gpuendtimestamp
memtransfersize
streamid
```

If we use the Command Line Profiler and `nvvp`, the output of which is shown in Figure 7.1, we see that the optimized version schedules the transfers and computations as expected, achieving a perfect overlap. Each FFT takes approximately 80 ms, whereas the convolution takes approximately 40 ms, for a total of 280 ms. Each plane transfer takes 380 ms, and we need at least one from S1 and one from S2 before we can start the convolution for a total of 760 ms. Improving the compute time will have no effect on the execution time: For this particular choice of N, M, and P, along with the PCI-e bandwidth of the system, the limiting factor is the data transfers. We are also able to explain the small discrepancy between expected and measured runtimes. On this particular system, transfers in one direction will achieve bandwidths of 5.5 GB/s for host-to-device transfers and 6.19 GB/s for device-to-host transfers. When we overlap both directions, the bandwidth drops to 5 GB/s.

Different parameter choices and different hardware can move the limiting factor from bandwidth to the computation. If we run the original code on a system with Gen3 PCIe bus and a Tesla K10 (also capable of supporting Gen3 speed), we observe the following output:

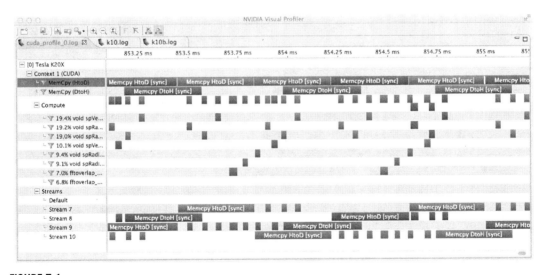

FIGURE 7.1

Kernel overlap for the K20x.

```
%  ./exampleOverlapFFT
I/O only
 Elapsed time :    0.1116750

Single stream  loop
 Elapsed time :    0.2037710

Do loop with multiple streams
 Elapsed time :    0.1334740
```

Here we notice a faster transfer time (0.11 s), because this chipset is able to transfer data at 10.7 GB/s in both directions, basically halving the I/O time. For this system configuration, the compute time, 0.092 s (obtained from the difference between the single stream loop time and the I/O only time), is larger than 2/3 of the I/O time, 0.074 s, so this will be our expected optimized runtime with a perfect scheduling. We also notice that the overlapping strategy does not seem to give the expected results.

The visualization of the profiler trace is able to shed some light, as we can see in Figure 7.2. The scheduling of kernels and transfers is different on a Tesla K20x (card with compute capability 3.5 and Hyper-Q) and a Tesla K10 (card with compute capability 3.0 with no Hyper-Q). In the multiple-streams do loop, the FFT after the memcopyAsync of A is blocking the memcopyAsync of B. A simple fix is to schedule the two memcopyAsync calls back to back, moving the memcopy of B just after A. After reloading the profiler trace into nvvp, we can visually inspect that now there is a proper scheduling of

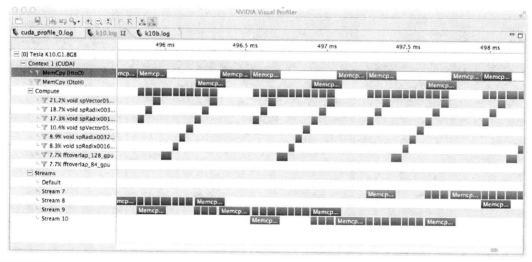

FIGURE 7.2

Kernel overlap for Tesla K10.

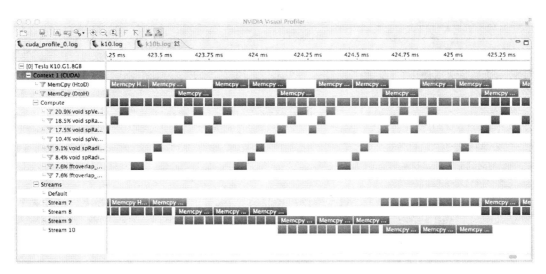

FIGURE 7.3

Kernel overlap for the Tesla K10 with modified source code.

memcopy and kernel, as observed in Figure 7.3. If we look at the output of the run, we now see that the optimized version is running in the expected time:

```
% ./exampleOverlapFFT
 I/O only
 Elapsed time :    0.1117420

Single stream  loop
 Elapsed time :    0.2038810

Do loop with multiple streams
 Elapsed time :    9.8977998E-02
```

7.4 Poisson Solver

Many problems in computational physics require the solution of a *Poisson equation*, an equation of the form:

$$\nabla^2 u = \rho$$

where ρ is a source term and ∇^2 is the Laplacian operator. The general form of the Laplacian operator in d Cartesian dimensions is:

$$\nabla^2 u = \sum_{i=1}^{d} \frac{\partial^2 u}{\partial x_i^2}$$

but here we focus on a two-dimensional problem where the Poisson equation is:

$$\frac{\partial^2 u}{\partial x^2} + \frac{\partial^2 u}{\partial y^2} = \rho$$

In addition to satisfying the preceding equation, the solution must also satisfy boundary conditions, which can be of several forms. Dirichlet boundary conditions specify u along the boundary, and Neumann boundary conditions specify the derivative of u along the boundary. There can also be a mixture of these two types.

If the domain shape and the boundary conditions are appropriate, spectral methods can be used to find the solution to the Poisson equation very efficiently and accurately. This solution utilizes the calculation of the second derivative, which we presented for one-dimensional data in Section 7.2. In one dimension, we observed that the spectral derivative for a function f is calculated by taking the inverse Fourier transform of the product of the Fourier coefficient of the function $\hat{f}_{k_x}$ with the negative square of the wavenumber, $-k_x^2$. Taking the Fourier transform of our 2D Poisson equation, we obtain a set of algebraic equations for each pair of wavenumbers k_x, k_y:

$$-\left(k_x^2 + k_y^2\right) \hat{u}_{k_x,k_y} = \hat{\rho}_{k_x,k_y}$$

Each $\hat{u}_{k_x,k_y}$ Fourier coefficient can be found by solving this simple algebraic equation, and with an inverse transform we obtain the solution in physical space.

The steps to solve a $2D$ Poisson equation using a spectral method can be summarized as:

- Find $\hat{\rho}_{k_x,k_y}$, the Fourier coefficients of ρ using a 2D FFT.
- Obtain $\hat{u}_{k_x,k_y}$, the Fourier coefficients of u, as $-\frac{\hat{\rho}_{k_x,k_y}}{(k_x^2+k_y^2)}$. This solution is undefined at $k_x = k_y = 0$, corresponding to an unknown constant c that must be specified. This is evident from the fact that if u is a solution to the Poisson equation, $u + c$ is also a solution. For problems with Dirichlet boundary conditions, the constant can be readily obtained.
- Transform $\hat{u}_{k_x,k_y}$ back to physical space using an inverse 2D FFT and apply the boundary conditions.

We present a code that solves the 2D Poisson equation:

$$\frac{\partial^2 u}{\partial x^2} + \frac{\partial^2 u}{\partial y^2} = \frac{(r^2 - 2\alpha^2)}{\alpha^4} e^{-\frac{r^2}{2\alpha^2}}$$

on a square domain of size L centered around the origin with Dirichlet boundary condition $u = 0$ on the boundary. In our source term on the right-hand side, $r = \sqrt{x^2 + y^2}$ and α is a parameter. In the limit of $\alpha \to 0$ the solution of u converges to:

$$u = e^{-r^2/(2\alpha^2)}$$

which we use to calculate the error of the spectral method solution. The complete code is listed in Appendix D.6. The set-up and execution of the FFTs in the Poisson code is similar to the previous codes presented in this chapter. The only difference is in the definition of the wave numbers; since the domain length is not 2π, there is a scaling factor $\frac{2\pi}{L}$. We define a `poisson_m` module that contains several utility routines in addition to a short Poisson solver:

```
1  module poisson_m
2    use precision_m
3
4    complex(fp_kind),device ::ref_sol
5
6  contains
7
8    attributes(global) subroutine real2complex(a, b, N, M)
9      implicit none
10     real(fp_kind):: a(N,M)
11     complex(fp_kind):: b(N,M)
12     integer, value:: N,M
13     integer:: i,j
14
15     i=threadIdx%x+(blockIdx%x-1)*blockDim%x
16     j=threadIdx%y+(blockIdx%y-1)*blockDim%y
17
18     if ( i .le. N .and. j .le. M) then
19        b(i,j) = cmplx( a(i,j), 0._fp_kind,fp_kind )
20     end if
21    end subroutine real2complex
22
23    attributes(global) subroutine real2complex1D(a, b, N, M)
24      implicit none
25      real(fp_kind):: a(N*M)
26      complex(fp_kind):: b(N*M)
27      integer, value:: N,M
28      integer:: i,index
29
30      index=threadIdx%x+(blockIdx%x-1)*blockDim%x
31
32      do i=index,N*M,blockDim%x*GridDim%x
33         b(i) = cmplx( a(i), 0._fp_kind,fp_kind )
34      end do
35    end subroutine real2complex1D
36
37    attributes(global) subroutine &
38        complex2real(input, output, ref_sol, N, M)
39      implicit none
40      complex (fp_kind):: input(N,M),ref_sol
41      real (fp_kind):: output(N,M)
42      integer, value:: N,M
```

```
43      integer:: i,j
44      real(fp_kind):: scale
45
46      i=threadIdx%x+(blockIdx%x-1)*blockDim%x
47      j=threadIdx%y+(blockIdx%y-1)*blockDim%y
48
49      scale = 1._fp_kind/real(N*M,fp_kind)
50      if ( i .le. N .and. j .le. M) then
51         output(i,j) = (real(input(i,j)) -real(ref_sol))*scale
52      end if
53    end subroutine complex2real
54
55    attributes(global) subroutine &
56         solve_poisson( phi, kx,ky, N, M)
57      implicit none
58      complex (fp_kind):: phi(N,M)
59      real(fp_kind):: kx(N),ky(M)
60      integer, value:: N,M
61      integer:: i,j
62      real(fp_kind):: scale
63
64      i=threadIdx%x+(blockIdx%x-1)*blockDim%x
65      j=threadIdx%y+(blockIdx%y-1)*blockDim%y
66
67      if ( i .le. N .and. j .le. M) then
68         scale =   (kx(i)*kx(i)+ky(j)*ky(j))
69         if ( i .eq. 1 .and. j .eq. 1) scale = 1._fp_kind
70         phi(i,j) = -phi(i,j)/scale
71      end if
72    end subroutine solve_poisson
73
74  end module poisson_m
```

The portion of the host code that performs the solution procedure outlined here is:

```
150    ! Set up execution configuration
151    Block = dim3(16,16,1)
152    grid  = dim3(ceiling(real(n)/Block%x), &
153    ceiling(real(m)/Block%y), 1 )
154
155    ! Transform real array to complex
156    !call real2complex<<<grid,Block>>>(rinput_d,cinput_d,N,M)
157    call real2complex1D<<<64,128>>>(rinput_d,cinput_d,N,M)
158
159    ! Execute forward transform in place
```

```
160    if ( fp_kind == singlePrecision) &
161         call cufftExecC2C(plan,cinput_d,cinput_d,CUFFT_FORWARD)
162    if ( fp_kind == doublePrecision) &
163         call cufftExecZ2Z(plan,cinput_d,cinput_d,CUFFT_FORWARD)
164
165    !Call kernel to solve the Poisson equation in Fourier space
166    call solve_poisson<<<grid,Block>>>(cinput_d,kx_d,ky_d,N,M)
167
168    !Execute backward transform in place
169    if ( fp_kind == singlePrecision) &
170         call cufftExecC2C(plan,cinput_d,cinput_d,CUFFT_INVERSE)
171    if ( fp_kind == doublePrecision) &
172         call cufftExecZ2Z(plan,cinput_d,cinput_d,CUFFT_INVERSE)
173
174    ! Transform complex array to real and scale
175    istat =  cudaMemcpy(ref_sol,cinput_d(1,1),1)
176    call complex2real<<<grid,Block>>>(cinput_d,rinput_d, &
177         ref_sol,N,M)
178
179    ! Copy result back to host
180    routput=rinput_d
```

The code declares two real matrices on the CPU: `rinput(N,M)`, used to store the source term, and `routput(N,M)`, which stores the solution. These two matrices are declared with the `pinned` variable attribute to get the best possible transfer time. To keep the code simple, we use complex-to-complex transforms, so we will allocate one real array `rinput_d(N,M)` and one complex array `cinput_d(N,M)` on the device. After we transfer the source term and the arrays with the wave numbers to the GPU, the first thing we do is trasform `rinput_d` to a complex array `cinput_d`. We perform this operation with a simple kernel `real2complex`, using 2D addressing, after we compute an execution configuration using a block with 16×16 threads. The FFT set-up and invocation are similar to the other codes presented in this chapter. The kernel performing the solution of the Laplace operator also uses 2D addressing and it is straightforward. Once the global indices i and j are computed from the local thread indices, there is a check to ensure we are operating on valid data, and a scaling factor is applied to the transformed source term, taking care of the special situation $k_x = k_y = 0$. The last kernel extracts the real part of the solution, applies the normalization factor for the FFT, and subtracts the value of the solution in the first corner, corresponding to the indices $(1, 1)$, to the whole solution. We need to take particular care in doing this last operation. We cannot use the value `cinput_d(1,1)` directly because doing so would result in a race condition; we do not know when the thread block that updates this value will execute in relation to the other thread blocks. To avoid such a race condition, we save the value to a separate device variable, `ref_sol`, before invoking the kernel. We perform a `cudaMempcpy` on line 175 and then pass the `ref_sol` to the `complex2real` subroutine, where the offset in the solution is computed. Note that there is no `value` variable attribute in the `ref_sol` scalar variable declaration, since this variable resides on the device.

Once we run the code, we can see that the spectral solution to the Poisson equation discretized on a 1024 × 1024 point mesh is solved in less than 6 ms on a Tesla K20x.

```
% pgf90 -DDOUBLE -O3 -o poisson_dp precision_m.F90 cufft.cuf \
      poisson.cuf -lcufft
% ./poisson_dp
 Poisson equation on a mesh :           1024           1024
 Elapsed time (ms) :      5.749312
 L infinity norm:      2.3077315062211532E-005
 L2 norm      :      5.6284773431400125E-009
```

If we run the code through nvprof, we can see where the time is spent.

```
% nvprof ./poisson_dp
======== NVPROF is profiling poisson_dp...
======== Command: poisson_dp
 Poisson equation on a mesh :           1024           1024
 Elapsed time (ms) :      5.819744
 L infinity norm:      2.3077315062211532E-005
 L2 norm      :      5.6284773431400125E-009
======== Profiling result:
 Time(%)   Time Calls     Avg       Min       Max   Name
 30.64   1.41ms    3   469.18us    2.34us    1.40ms   [CUDA memcpy HtoD]
 27.28   1.25ms    1    1.25ms    1.25ms    1.25ms   [CUDA memcpy DtoH]
  8.75 401.73us    2   200.87us  193.57us  208.16us   dpRadix0032B::<fftDir=-1>
  8.72 400.71us    2   200.35us  193.86us  206.85us   dpRadix0032B::<fftDir=1>
  6.58 302.34us    1   302.34us  302.34us  302.34us   dpVector1024D:<fftDir=-1>
  6.51 298.95us    1   298.95us  298.95us  298.95us   dpVector1024D:<fftDir=1>
  4.48 205.95us    1   205.95us  205.95us  205.95us   poisson_m_solve_laplacian_
  3.88 178.40us    1   178.40us  178.40us  178.40us   poisson_m_real2complex_
  3.05 140.32us    1   140.32us  140.32us  140.32us   poisson_m_complex2real_
  0.11   4.86us    1    4.86us    4.86us    4.86us   [CUDA memcpy DtoD]
```

The first two calls on the nvprof output are the copies to and from device memory. The host-to-device copy is slightly slower than the device-to-host due to the asymmetry in the two directions in PCIe bandwidth, but they are performing at the expected rate ($1024 * 1024 * 8B/0.00140$ s/$(1000^3) =$ 6 GB/s H2D and $1024 * 1024 * 8B/0.00125$ s/$(1000^3) = 6.7$ GB/s D2H). The next four calls are the forward and inverse 2D FFT; the profiler is showing the internal kernels that CUFFT executes to perform the 1024^2 transform. Each FFT executes in 700 ms. From the formula $5NMlog_2(NM)$ expressing the number of operations needed for 2D FFT, we can compute the GFlops rate at 150 GFlops. For the very simple kernels, real2complex and complex2real, we could also use a 1D thread block, considering the 2D array of shape (N, M) as a 1D array of shape (N*M), as we can see in the listing for real2complex1D. Since there are minimum computations in the kernel, this will reduce the address computation and it will give us a 10% speed improvement.

Appendices

Tesla Specifications

Floating-point performance								
Tesla Products	**C870**	**C1060**	**C2050**	**C2070**	**M2090**	**K10**	**K20**	**K20X**
Compute capability	1.0	1.3	2.0			3.0	3.5	
Number of multiprocessors	16	30	14	14	16	2 × 8	13	14
Core clock (GHz)	1.35	1.296	1.15	1.15	1.3	0.745	0.706	0.732
Single-precision cores per multiprocessor	8	8	32			192	192	
Total single-precision cores	128	240	448	448	512	2 × 1536	2496	2688
Single-precision GFlops (Multiply + Add)	346	622	1030	1030	1331	2 × 2289	3524	3935
Double-precision cores per multiprocessor	–	1	16*			8	64	
Total double-precision cores	–	30	224*	224*	256*	2 × 64	832	896
Double-precision GFlops (Multiply + Add)	–	78	515*	515*	665*	2 × 95	1175	1312
*GeForce GPUs have fewer double-precision units.								

Memory

Tesla Products	C870	C1060	C2050	C2070	M2090	K10	K20	K20X
Compute capability	1.0	1.3	2.0			3.0	3.5	
Device Memory (DRAM)								
Total global memory (GB)	1.5	4	3*	6*	6*	2 × 4*	5*	6*
Constant memory (KB)	64							
Memory clock (MHz)	800	800	1,500	1,566	1,848	2,500	2,600	2,600
Bus width (bits)	384	512	384	384	384	2 × 256	320	384
Theoretical peak bandwidth (GB/s)	76.8	102.4	144*	150.3*	177.4*	2 × 160*	208*	249.6*
On-Chip Memory								
32-bit registers per multiprocessor	8 K	16 K	32 K	32 K	32 K	64 K	64 K	64 K
Maximum registers per thread	127	127	63	63	63	63	255	255
Shared memory per multiprocessor	16 K	16 K	48 K/16 K	48 K/16 K	48 K/16 K	48 K/32 K/16 K	48 K/32 K/16 K	48 K/32 K/16 K
L1 cache per multiprocessor	–	–	16 K/48 K	16 K/48 K	16 K/48 K	16 K/32 K/48 K**	16 K/32 K/48 K**	16 K/32 K/48 K**
Constant memory cache per multiprocessor (KB)	8							

*With ECC enabled the available global memory and peak bandwidth will be less than the numbers listed.
**For the K10, K20, and K20X GPUs, the L1 cache is used for local memory only.

Execution configuration limits

Compute capability	1.0	1.3	2.0			3.0	3.5	
Tesla products	C870	C1060	C2050 M2050	C2070 M2070	M2090	K10	K20	K20X
Maximum thread blocks per multiprocessor	8	8	8			16	16	
Maximum threads per thread block	512	512	1024			1024	1024	
Maximum threads (warps) per multiprocessor	768 (24)	1024 (32)	1536 (48)			2048 (64)	2048 (64)	
Maximum grid dimensions	65536 × 65536 × 1	65536 × 65536 × 1	65536 × 65536 × 65536			2147483647 × 65536 × 65536	2147483647 × 65536 × 65536	
Maximum block dimensions	512 × 512 × 64	512 × 512 × 64	1024 × 1024 × 64			1024 × 1024 × 64	1024 × 1024 × 64	

System and Environment Management

B.1 Environment variables

A variety of environment variables can control certain aspects of CUDA Fortran compilation and execution. We group them here in terms of general environment variables, those related to the Command Line Profiler, and those related to just-in-time compilation of device code.

B.1.1 General

CUDA_LAUNCH_BLOCKING, when set to 1, forces execution of kernels to be synchronous. That is, after launching a kernel, control will return to the CPU only after the kernel has completed. This provides an efficient way to check whether host-device synchronization errors are responsible for unexpected behavior. By default, launch blocking is off.

CUDA_VISIBLE_DEVICES can be used to make certain devices invisible on the system and to change the enumeration of devices. A comma-separated list of integers is assigned to this variable, which contains the visible devices and their enumeration as shown by the subsequent execution of CUDA

Fortran programs. Recall that device enumeration begins with 0. (We can use the deviceQuery code presented earlier or the utility pgaccelinfo to obtain the default enumeration of devices.)

B.1.2 **Command Line Profiler**

COMPUTE_PROFILE, when set to 1, turns profiling by the Command Line Profiler on. When it's set to 0, profiling is off. By default, profiling is off.

COMPUTE_PROFILE_LOG is set to the desired file path for profiling output. For runs with multiple devices, the string %d must be added to the filename, which will be used to create separate profiler output files for each device. Likewise, in the case of multiple host processes (e.g., MPI), the string %p must appear in the filename. By default, profiler output will appear in the file cuda_profile_%d.log in the local directory.

COMPUTE_PROFILE_CSV, when set to 0 or 1, either disables or enables a comma-separated version of the profiler output. This is a convenient feature for importing the file into a spreadsheet.

COMPUTE_PROFILE_CONFIG is used to specify a configuration file containing options for tracing execution (collecting timeline data) as well as collecting hardware counters. A list of the options for tracing execution, as well as their interpretation, is given in the *CUDA Profiler Users Guide* provided with the CUDA Toolkit, which can also be obtained online. A list of hardware counters that can be profiled can be obtained from the nvprof profiling tool by issuing the command nvprof--query-events. The nvprof profiling tool is distributed in the CUDA Toolkit.

B.1.3 **Just-in-time compilation**

CUDA_CACHE_DISABLE, when set to 1, disables caching, meaning that no binary code is added to or retrieved from the cache.

CUDA_CACHE_MAXSIZE specifies the size of the compute cache in bytes. By default it is 32 MB, and the maximum value is 4 GB. Binary codes that exceed this limit are not cached, and older binary codes are evicted from the cache as needed.

CUDA_CACHE_PATH controls the location of the compute cache. By default, the cache is located at ~/.nv/ComputeCache on Linux, $HOME/Library/Application\ Support/NVIDIA/ComputeCache on MacOS, and %APPDATA%\NVIDIA\ComputeCache in Windows.

CUDA_FORCE_PTX_JIT, when set to 1, forces the driver to ignore all embedded binary code in an application and to just-in-time compile embedded PTX code. This option is useful for testing whether an application has embedded PTX code and whether the embedded code works. If this environment variable is set to 1 and a kernel does not have embedded PTX code, it will fail to load.

B.2 nvidia-smi System Management Interface

Additional control of devices on a system is available through the System Management Interface utility, nvidia-smi, which is bundled with the NVIDIA driver on all Linux platforms. The man pages for nvidia-smi contain an extensive list of options. In this section we demonstrate some of the more common uses of the utility.

Without any options, `nvidia-smi` lists some basic information on all attached NVIDIA GPUs, as shown in Figure B.1. Although `nvidia-smi` lists all devices, it only provides detailed information on Tesla and high-end Quadro devices. The Quadro NVS 285 listed in the output of Figure B.1 is not a high-end card, and consequently little information is provided.

```
% nvidia-smi
Thu Apr 25 14:48:10 2013
+-------------------------------------------------------------------+
| NVIDIA-SMI 4.304.52    Driver Version: 304.52          |
|-------------------------------+----------------------+------------------------|
| GPU  Name                     | Bus-Id        Disp.  | Volatile Uncorr. ECC |
| Fan  Temp  Perf  Pwr:Usage/Cap| Memory-Usage         | GPU-Util  Compute M.  |
|===============================+======================+======================|
|   0  Tesla K20                | 0000:80:00.0    Off  |                   0  |
| 30%   30C    P8    16W / 225W |   0%    13MB / 4799MB |   0%      Default  |
+-------------------------------+----------------------+------------------------+
|   1  Quadro NVS 285           | 0000:60:00.0    N/A  |                 N/A  |
| N/A   60C   N/A    N/A /  N/A |  45%    55MB /  123MB |  N/A          N/A  |
+-------------------------------+----------------------+------------------------+

+-------------------------------------------------------------------+
| Compute processes:                                    GPU Memory |
|  GPU       PID  Process name                          Usage      |
|===================================================================|
|   1              Not Supported                                    |
+-------------------------------------------------------------------+
%
```

FIGURE B.1

Default output of `nvidia-smi` on a system with a Tesla K20 and a Quadro NVS 285. The limited output for the Quadro NVS 285 is because the GPU is not CUDA-capable.

A simple list of devices on the system can be obtained from the output of `nvidia-smi -L`:

```
% nvidia-smi -L
GPU 0: Tesla K20 (S/N: 0324612033969)
GPU 1: Quadro NVS 285 (UUID: N/A)
```

B.2.1 Enabling and disabling ECC

There are several ways we can determine whether ECC is enabled or disabled on a device. The field `ECCEnabled` of the `cudaDeviceProp` derived type can used to query the ECC status of the current device, and the utility `pgiaccelinfo` also displays whether ECC is enabled or disabled for all attached devices.

From `nvidia-smi` one can obtain more detailed information about ECC as well as enable or disable ECC. Querying the ECC status for a device using `nvidia-smi` is done as follows:

```
% nvidia-smi -i 0 -q -d ECC

=============NVSMI LOG=============

Timestamp                          : Tue Apr 16 16:43:35 2013

Driver Version                     : 304.52

Attached GPUs                      : 2
GPU 0000:80:00.0
    Ecc Mode
        Current                    : Enabled
        Pending                    : Enabled
    ECC Errors
        Volatile
            Single Bit
                Device Memory  : 0
                Register File  : 0
                L1 Cache       : 0
                L2 Cache       : 0
                Texture Memory : 0
                Total          : 0
            Double Bit
                Device Memory  : 0
                Register File  : 0
                L1 Cache       : 0
                L2 Cache       : 0
                Texture Memory : 0
                Total          : 0
        Aggregate
            Single Bit
                Device Memory  : 0
                Register File  : 0
                L1 Cache       : 0
                L2 Cache       : 0
                Texture Memory : 0
                Total          : 0
            Double Bit
                Device Memory  : 0
                Register File  : 0
                L1 Cache       : 0
                L2 Cache       : 0
                Texture Memory : 0
                Total          : 0
```

where device 0 is specified by the `-i 0` option, and the ECC output is specified by the `-d ECC` option. Most of the output from this command lists the errors for the different memory types. Single-bit errors are corrected; double-bit errors are uncorrectable. Volatile error counters track the number of errors since the last driver load, and aggregate errors persist indefinitely.

The ECC mode near the top of this output displays both the current and pending fields. The pending ECC mode will become the current ECC mode upon reboot or reset. The ECC mode can be disabled as follows (assuming root privileges):

```
% nvidia-smi -i 0 -e 0
Disabled ECC support for GPU 0000:80:00.0.
All done.
Reboot required.
```

At this point the ECC mode status printed by `nvidia-smi -i 0 -q -d ECC` is:

```
Ecc Mode
    Current              : Enabled
    Pending              : Disabled
```

For the pending change to take effect, a reboot of the machine is required, after which the ECC mode status is:

```
Ecc Mode
    Current              : Disabled
    Pending              : Disabled
```

B.2.2 Compute mode

The compute mode determines whether multiple host processes or threads can use the same GPU. The four compute modes, from least to most restrictive, are:

default: 0 In this mode multiple host threads can use the same device.

exclusive thread: 1 In this mode only a single context can be created by a single process systemwide, and this context can be current to at most one thread of the process at a time.

prohibited: 2 In this mode no contexts can be created on the device.

exclusive process: 3 In this mode only a single context can be created by a single process systemwide, and this context can be current to all threads of that process

As with the ECC status, the compute mode can be determined using the `cudaDeviceProp` derived type via the `computeMode` field and by the `pgaccelinfo` utility. Using `nvidia-smi`, we can query the compute mode as follows:

```
% nvidia-smi -q -i 0 -d COMPUTE

==============NVSMI LOG==============

Timestamp                           : Thu Apr 18 13:38:29 2013
Driver Version                      : 304.52

Attached GPUs                       : 2
GPU 0000:80:00.0
    Compute Mode                    : Default
```

which indicates that device 0 is in default compute mode. The compute mode can be changed (assuming root privileges) by using the `-c` option:

```
% nvidia-smi -i 0 -c 1
Set compute mode to EXCLUSIVE_THREAD for GPU 0000:80:00.0.
All done.
```

The effect of changing the compute mode is immediate:

```
% nvidia-smi -q -i 0 -d COMPUTE

==============NVSMI LOG==============

Timestamp                           : Thu Apr 18 13:49:40 2013
Driver Version                      : 304.52

Attached GPUs                       : 2
GPU 0000:80:00.0
    Compute Mode                    : Exclusive_Thread
```

Upon reboot or reset of the device, the compute mode will reset to the default compute mode.

B.2.3 Persistence mode

When persistence mode is enabled on a GPU, the driver remains initialized, even when there are no active clients, and as a result the driver latency is minimized when we run CUDA applications. On systems running the X Window System, this is not an issue, since the X Window client is always active, but on headless systems where X is not running, it is important to avoid driver reinitialization when launching CUDA applications by enabling persistence mode.

Persistence mode is disabled by default and reverts to disabled when the device is reset or the system is rebooted. We can determine whether persistence mode is enabled or not from the general query output of `nvidia-smi`:

```
% nvidia-smi -q -i 0

==============NVSMI LOG==============

Timestamp                         : Thu Apr 18 14:17:25 2013
Driver Version                    : 304.52

Attached GPUs                     : 2
GPU 0000:80:00.0
    Product Name                  : Tesla K20
    Display Mode                  : Disabled
    Persistence Mode              : Disabled
    . . .
```

Persistence mode can be enabled (assuming root privileges) using the `-pm` option to `nvidia-smi` as follows:

```
% nvidia-smi -i 0 -pm 1
Enabled persistence mode for GPU 0000:80:00.0.
All done.
```

Calling CUDA C from CUDA Fortran

There are several reasons one would want to call CUDA C code from CUDA Fortran: (1) to leverage code already written in CUDA C, especially libraries where an explicit CUDA Fortran interface is not available, and (2) to write CUDA C code that uses features that are not available in CUDA Fortran. We provide an example for each of these use cases in this appendix.

C.1 Calling CUDA C libraries

With the advent of the `iso_c_binding` module in Fortran 2003, calling CUDA C from CUDA Fortran is straightforward. We demonstrate the procedure for specifying an interface using the CUBLAS library. Note that this is not needed as of the 11.7 release of the compilers, since one simply has to use the `cublas` module included with the compiler, as on line 2 in the following code that performs a matrix multiplication via the CUBLAS version of SGEMM:

```
1   program sgemmDevice
2     use cublas
3     use cudafor
4     implicit none
5     integer, parameter :: m = 100, n = 100, k = 100
6     real :: a(m,k), b(k,n), c(m,n)
7     real, device :: a_d(m,k), b_d(k,n), c_d(m,n)
8     real, parameter :: alpha = 1.0, beta = 0.0
9     integer :: lda = m, ldb = k, ldc = m
10    integer :: istat
11
12    a = 1.0; b = 2.0; c = 0.0
13    a_d = a; b_d = b; c_d = c
14
15    istat = cublasInit()
```

```
16   call cublasSgemm('n','n',m,n,k, &
17        alpha,a_d,lda,b_d,ldb,beta,c_d,ldc)
18
19   c = c_d
20   write(*,*) 'Max error =', maxval(c-k*2.0)
21
22  end program sgemmDevice
```

Here the cublas module defines the interfaces for all the CUBLAS routines, including cublasInit() and cublasSgemm(). Prior to the cublas module introduced in the 11.7 compilers, one had to explicitly interface with the C routines in the CUBLAS library, as in this user-defined cublas_m module:

```
1  module cublas_m
2     interface cublasInit
3        integer function cublasInit() &
4              bind(C,name='cublasInit')
5        end function cublasInit
6     end interface
7
8     interface cublasSgemm
9        subroutine cublasSgemm(cta,ctb,m,n,k, &
10             alpha,A,lda,B,ldb,beta,C,ldc) &
11             bind(C,name='cublasSgemm')
12          use iso_c_binding
13          character(1,c_char), value :: cta, ctb
14          integer(c_int), value :: k,m,n,lda,ldb,ldc
15          real(c_float), value :: alpha, beta
16          real(c_float), device :: &
17               A(lda,*), B(ldb,*), C(ldc,*)
18        end subroutine cublasSgemm
19     end interface cublasSgemm
20  end module cublas_m
21
22
23  program sgemmDevice
24     use cublas_m
25     use cudafor
26     implicit none
27     integer, parameter :: m = 100, n = 100, k = 100
28     real :: a(m,k), b(k,n), c(m,n)
29     real, device :: a_d(m,k), b_d(k,n), c_d(m,n)
30     real, parameter :: alpha = 1.0, beta = 0.0
31     integer :: lda = m, ldb = k, ldc = m
32     integer :: istat
33
```

```
34   a = 1.0; b = 2.0; c = 0.0
35   a_d = a; b_d = b; c_d = c
36
37   istat = cublasInit()
38   call cublasSgemm('n','n',m,n,k, &
39        alpha,a_d,lda,b_d,ldb,beta,c_d,ldc)
40
41   c = c_d
42   write(*,*) 'Max error = ', maxval(c-k*2.0)
43
44 end program sgemmDevice
```

The only difference in the main program between these two codes is that the user-defined `cublas_m` on line 24 in the latter code replaces the `cublas` module on line 2 in the former code. The `cublas_m` module defined on lines 1–20 includes only interfaces to the two functions used in this application, `cublasInit()` and `cublasSgemm()`. The interface for `cublasInit()` defined on lines 2–6 is straightforward, since this function has no arguments. Within the interface, the function is listed and bound to the C function using the `bind` keyword. `bind()` takes two arguments; the first is the language in which the routine being called is written, in this case C, and the second is the name of the routine being called.

The interface to `cublasSgemm()` is more complicated due to the subroutine arguments. Each dummy argument is declared in the interface using the kinds `c_int`, `c_char`, and `c_float`, which are defined in the `iso_c_binding` module. In addition to the `iso_c_binding` kinds, these declarations make use of the `device` and `value` variable attributes as needed.

One can develop a generic interface for `sgemm`, which has been implemented in the `cublas` module, by including the declaration for both the host `sgemm()` and the device `cublasSgemm()` in the interface block and changing the interface name in line 8 to `sgemm`. In such cases, the actual routine used will depend on whether device or host arrays are used as arguments when `sgemm` is called from host code.

One final note on developing interfaces to libraries is the use of the `!pgi$ ignore_tkr` directive. This directive can be used to have the compiler ignore any combination of the variable type, kind, and rank, as well as ignoring the presence or absence of the `device` attribute. For example, the following lines of code are used in the Monte Carlo chapter to interface with the CURAND library routines:

```
!pgi$ ignore_tkr (tr) odata
real(c_float), device:: odata(*)
```

Here the type and rank of variable `odata` are ignored. Any combination of `(tkrd)` can be used and applied to individual variables in a comma-separated list:

```
!pgi$ ignore_tkr (tr) a, (k) b
real(c_float), device :: a(*), b(*)
```

where the type and rank of a and the kind of b are ignored. The default case, where qualifiers in the parentheses are not included, corresponds to (tkr).

C.2 Calling User-Written CUDA C Code

Interfacing CUDA Fortran with user-written CUDA C routines is very similar to interfacing with CUDA C libraries as we have done. In fact, from the CUDA Fortran perspective, the procedure is identical: We write an interface to the CUDA C routine using kinds in the iso_c_binding module to declare the dummy arguments. From the CUDA C perspective there are a couple of issues we should be aware of.

To demonstrate this, we use CUDA Fortran to call a CUDA C routine that zeroes a small array. The CUDA C kernel is:

```
extern "C" __global__ void zero (float *a)
{
   a[blockIdx.x*blockDim.x+threadIdx.x] = 0.0f;
}
```

CUDA C and Fortran kernel code share quite a bit in common: Both have automatically defined variables blockIdx, blockDim, and threadIdx, though with different offsets, and the __global__ in CUDA C is equivalent to CUDA Fortran's attributes(global). Of note here is the extern "C", which is required for CUDA Fortran to interface with this routine because it prevents name mangling. As long as the extern "C" is specified, the CUDA Fortran code is straightforward:

```
1  module kernel_m
2    interface zero
3      attributes(global) subroutine zero(a) &
4           bind(C,name='zero')
5        use iso_c_binding
6        real(c_float) :: a(*)
7      end subroutine zero
8    end interface
9  end module kernel_m
10
11 program fCallingC
12   use cudafor
13   use kernel_m
14   integer, parameter :: n = 4
15   real, device :: a_d(n)
16   real :: a(n)
17
18   a_d = 1.0
19   call zero<<<1,n>>>(a_d)
20   a = a_d
```

```
21     write(*,*) a
22  end program fCallingC
```

where the interface specified on lines 2–8 is similar to that of the CUBLAS example. The CUDA C and CUDA Fortran routines are in separate files, `zero.cu` and `fCallingC.cuf`, respectively, and compiled as follows:

```
nvcc -c zero.cu
pgf90 -Mcuda -o fCallingC fCallingC.cuf zero.o
```

where the `nvcc` compiler is used for compiling `zero.cu`.

Source Code

D

CHAPTER OUTLINE HEAD

CUDA Fortran source code that was deemed too long to include in its entirety in earlier chapters is listed in this appendix. Each section in this appendix contains all the relevant code, both host code and device code, for the particular application.

D.1 Texture memory

The following is the CUDA Fortran code used in Section 3.2.3 to discuss how textures can be advantageous in accessing neighboring data on a 2D mesh using four- and eight-point stencils:

```
1   module kernels_m
2     real, texture, pointer :: aTex(:,:)
3     integer, parameter :: n = 2048
4     integer, parameter :: nTile = 32
5   contains
6     attributes(global) subroutine average4(b, a)
7       implicit none
8       real :: b(n,n), a(0:n+1,0:n+1)
9       integer :: i, j
10      i = blockDim%x*(blockIdx%x-1)+threadIdx%x
11      j = blockDim%y*(blockIdx%y-1)+threadIdx%y
```

```fortran
12       b(i,j) = 0.25*( &
13                    a(i-1,j)+ &
14           a(i,j-1)+              a(i,j+1)+&
15                    a(i+1,j))
16    end subroutine average4
17
18    attributes(global) subroutine average8(b, a)
19      implicit none
20      real :: b(n,n), a(0:n+1,0:n+1)
21      integer :: i, j
22      i = blockDim%x*(blockIdx%x-1)+threadIdx%x
23      j = blockDim%y*(blockIdx%y-1)+threadIdx%y
24      b(i,j) = 0.125*( &
25           a(i-1,j-1)+a(i-1,j)+a(i-1,j+1)+ &
26           a(i,j-1)+              a(i,j+1)+&
27           a(i+1,j-1)+a(i+1,j)+a(i+1,j+1))
28    end subroutine average8
29
30    attributes(global) subroutine average4Tex(b)
31      implicit none
32      real :: b(n,n)
33      integer :: i, j
34      i = blockDim%x*(blockIdx%x-1)+threadIdx%x
35      j = blockDim%y*(blockIdx%y-1)+threadIdx%y
36      b(i,j) = 0.25*( &
37                    aTex(i-1,j)+ &
38           aTex(i,j-1)+              aTex(i,j+1)+ &
39                    aTex(i+1,j))
40    end subroutine average4Tex
41
42    attributes(global) subroutine average8Tex(b)
43      implicit none
44      real :: b(n,n)
45      integer :: i, j
46      i = blockDim%x*(blockIdx%x-1)+threadIdx%x
47      j = blockDim%y*(blockIdx%y-1)+threadIdx%y
48      b(i,j) = 0.125*( &
49           aTex(i-1,j-1)+aTex(i-1,j)+aTex(i-1,j+1)+ &
50           aTex(i,j-1)+              aTex(i,j+1)+ &
51           aTex(i+1,j-1)+aTex(i+1,j)+aTex(i+1,j+1))
52    end subroutine average8Tex
53 end module kernels_m
54
55 program average
56   use cudafor
57   use kernels_m
58
```

```
59   implicit none
60
61   real :: b(n,n), res4(n,n), res8(n,n)
62   real, device :: b_d(n,n)
63   real :: a(0:n+1,0:n+1)
64   real, device, target :: a_d(0:n+1,0:n+1)
65   type(cudaEvent) :: startEvent, stopEvent
66   type(cudaDeviceProp) :: prop
67   integer :: i, j, istat
68   real :: time
69   type(dim3) :: grid, tBlock
70
71   tBlock = dim3(nTile,nTile,1)
72   grid = dim3(n/nTile, n/nTile, 1)
73
74   istat = cudaGetDeviceProperties(prop, 0)
75   write(*,'(/,"Device: ",a,/)') trim(prop%name)
76
77   call random_number(a)
78   a_d = a
79
80   do j = 1, n
81      do i = 1, n
82         res4(i,j) = 0.25*( &
83                              a(i-1,j)+ &
84                 a(i,j-1)+                a(i,j+1)+&
85                              a(i+1,j))
86
87         res8(i,j) = 0.125*( &
88                 a(i-1,j-1)+a(i-1,j)+a(i-1,j+1)+ &
89                 a(i,j-1)+                a(i,j+1)+&
90                 a(i+1,j-1)+a(i+1,j)+a(i+1,j+1))
91      enddo
92   enddo
93
94   istat = cudaEventCreate(startEvent)
95   istat = cudaEventCreate(stopEvent)
96
97   ! 4pt averages
98
99   write(*,*) '4-point versions'
100
101  ! global
102
103  call average4<<<grid, tBlock>>>(b_d, a_d)
104
105  istat = cudaEventRecord(startEvent,0)
```

```
106     call average4<<<grid,tBlock>>>(b_d, a_d)
107     istat = cudaEventRecord(stopEvent,0)
108     istat = cudaEventSynchronize(stopEvent)
109     istat = cudaEventElapsedTime(time, startEvent, stopEvent)
110     write(*,*) '  Global Bandwidth  (GB/s):', &
111          4*(n**2 + (n+2)**2)/time*1.e-6
112     b = b_d
113     write(*,*) '     Max Error: ', maxval(b-res4)
114
115     ! texture
116
117     ! bind the texture
118     aTex => a_d
119
120     call average4Tex<<<grid,tBlock>>>(b_d)
121
122     istat = cudaEventRecord(startEvent,0)
123     call average4Tex<<<grid,tBlock>>>(b_d)
124     istat = cudaEventRecord(stopEvent,0)
125     istat = cudaEventSynchronize(stopEvent)
126     istat = cudaEventElapsedTime(time, startEvent, stopEvent)
127     write(*,*) '  Texture Bandwidth (GB/s):', &
128          4*(n**2 + (n+2)**2)/time*1.e-6
129     b = b_d
130     write(*,*) '     Max Error: ', maxval(b-res4)
131
132     ! 8pt averages
133
134     write(*,*)
135     write(*,*) '8-point versions'
136
137     ! global
138
139     call average8<<<grid, tBlock>>>(b_d, a_d)
140
141     istat = cudaEventRecord(startEvent,0)
142     call average8<<<grid,tBlock>>>(b_d, a_d)
143     istat = cudaEventRecord(stopEvent,0)
144     istat = cudaEventSynchronize(stopEvent)
145     istat = cudaEventElapsedTime(time, startEvent, stopEvent)
146     write(*,*) '  Global Bandwidth  (GB/s):', &
147          4*(n**2 + (n+2)**2)/time*1.e-6
148     b = b_d
149     write(*,*) '     Max Error: ', maxval(b-res8)
150
151     ! texture
152
```

```
153   call average8Tex<<<grid,tBlock>>>(b_d)
154
155   istat = cudaEventRecord(startEvent,0)
156   call average8Tex<<<grid,tBlock>>>(b_d)
157   istat = cudaEventRecord(stopEvent,0)
158   istat = cudaEventSynchronize(stopEvent)
159   istat = cudaEventElapsedTime(time, startEvent, stopEvent)
160   write(*,*) '  Texture Bandwidth (GB/s):', &
161        4*(n**2 + (n+2)**2)/time*1.e-6
162   b = b_d
163   write(*,*) '     Max Error: ', maxval(b-res8)
164
165   ! unbind the texture
166   nullify(aTex)
167
168   istat = cudaEventDestroy(startEvent)
169   istat = cudaEventDestroy(stopEvent)
170 end program average
```

D.2 Matrix transpose

The following is the complete matrix transpose CUDA Fortran code discussed at length in Section 3.4.

```
1  !this program demonstates various memory optimzation techniques
2  !applied to a matrix transpose.
3
4  module dimensions_m
5
6    implicit none
7
8    integer, parameter :: TILE_DIM = 32
9    integer, parameter :: BLOCK_ROWS = 8
10   integer, parameter :: NUM_REPS = 100
11   integer, parameter :: nx = 1024, ny = 1024
12   integer, parameter :: mem_size = nx*ny*4
13
14 end module dimensions_m
15
16
17
18 module kernels_m
19
20   use dimensions_m
```

```fortran
21     implicit none
22
23   contains
24
25     ! copy kernel using shared memory
26     !
27     ! used as reference case
28
29     attributes(global) subroutine copySharedMem(odata, idata)
30
31       real, intent(out) :: odata(nx,ny)
32       real, intent(in) :: idata(nx,ny)
33
34       real, shared :: tile(TILE_DIM, TILE_DIM)
35       integer :: x, y, j
36
37       x = (blockIdx%x-1) * TILE_DIM + threadIdx%x
38       y = (blockIdx%y-1) * TILE_DIM + threadIdx%y
39
40       do j = 0, TILE_DIM-1, BLOCK_ROWS
41          tile(threadIdx%x, threadIdx%y+j) = idata(x,y+j)
42       end do
43
44       call syncthreads()
45
46       do j = 0, TILE_DIM-1, BLOCK_ROWS
47          odata(x,y+j) = tile(threadIdx%x, threadIdx%y+j)
48       end do
49     end subroutine copySharedMem
50
51     ! naive transpose
52     !
53     ! simplest transpose - doesn't use shared memory
54     ! reads from global memory are coalesced but not writes
55
56     attributes(global) &
57          subroutine transposeNaive(odata, idata)
58
59       real, intent(out) :: odata(ny,nx)
60       real, intent(in) :: idata(nx,ny)
61
62       integer :: x, y, j
63
64       x = (blockIdx%x-1) * TILE_DIM + threadIdx%x
65       y = (blockIdx%y-1) * TILE_DIM + threadIdx%y
66
67       do j = 0, TILE_DIM-1, BLOCK_ROWS
```

```
68          odata(y+j,x) = idata(x,y+j)
69       end do
70    end subroutine transposeNaive
71
72    ! coalesced transpose
73    !
74    ! uses shared memory to achieve coalesing
75    ! in both reads and writes
76    !
77    ! tile size causes shared memory bank conflicts
78
79    attributes(global) &
80         subroutine transposeCoalesced(odata, idata)
81
82      real, intent(out) :: odata(ny,nx)
83      real, intent(in) :: idata(nx,ny)
84      real, shared :: tile(TILE_DIM, TILE_DIM)
85      integer :: x, y, j
86
87      x = (blockIdx%x-1) * TILE_DIM + threadIdx%x
88      y = (blockIdx%y-1) * TILE_DIM + threadIdx%y
89
90      do j = 0, TILE_DIM-1, BLOCK_ROWS
91         tile(threadIdx%x, threadIdx%y+j) = idata(x,y+j)
92      end do
93
94      call syncthreads()
95
96      x = (blockIdx%y-1) * TILE_DIM + threadIdx%x
97      y = (blockIdx%x-1) * TILE_DIM + threadIdx%y
98
99      do j = 0, TILE_DIM-1, BLOCK_ROWS
100        odata(x,y+j) = tile(threadIdx%y+j, threadIdx%x)
101     end do
102   end subroutine transposeCoalesced
103
104   ! no bank-conflict transpose
105   !
106   ! like transposeCoalesced except the first tile dim
107   ! is padded to avoid shared memory bank conflicts
108
109   attributes(global) &
110        subroutine transposeNoBankConflicts(odata, idata)
111
112     real, intent(out) :: odata(ny,nx)
113     real, intent(in) :: idata(nx,ny)
114     real, shared :: tile(TILE_DIM+1, TILE_DIM)
```

```
115        integer :: x, y, j
116
117      x = (blockIdx%x-1) * TILE_DIM + threadIdx%x
118      y = (blockIdx%y-1) * TILE_DIM + threadIdx%y
119
120      do j = 0, TILE_DIM-1, BLOCK_ROWS
121         tile(threadIdx%x, threadIdx%y+j) = idata(x,y+j)
122      end do
123
124      call syncthreads()
125
126      x = (blockIdx%y-1) * TILE_DIM + threadIdx%x
127      y = (blockIdx%x-1) * TILE_DIM + threadIdx%y
128
129      do j = 0, TILE_DIM-1, BLOCK_ROWS
130         odata(x,y+j) = tile(threadIdx%y+j, threadIdx%x)
131      end do
132    end subroutine transposeNoBankConflicts
133
134    ! Diagonal reordering
135    !
136    ! This version should be used on cards of CC 1.3
137    ! to avoid partition camping.  It reschedules the
138    ! order in which blocks are executed so requests
139    ! for global memory access by active blocks are
140    ! spread evenly amongst partitions
141
142    attributes(global) &
143         subroutine transposeDiagonal(odata, idata)
144
145      real, intent(out) :: odata(ny,nx)
146      real, intent(in) :: idata(nx,ny)
147      real, shared :: tile(TILE_DIM+1, TILE_DIM)
148      integer :: x, y, j
149      integer :: blockIdx_x, blockIdx_y
150
151      if (nx==ny) then
152         blockIdx_y = blockIdx%x
153         blockIdx_x = &
154             mod(blockIdx%x+blockIdx%y-2,gridDim%x)+1
155      else
156         x = blockIdx%x + gridDim%x*(blockIdx%y-1)
157         blockIdx_y = mod(x-1,gridDim%y)+1
158         blockIdx_x = &
159             mod((x-1)/gridDim%y+blockIdx_y-1,gridDim%x)+1
160      endif
161
```

```fortran
162        x = (blockIdx_x-1) * TILE_DIM + threadIdx%x
163        y = (blockIdx_y-1) * TILE_DIM + threadIdx%y
164
165        do j = 0, TILE_DIM-1, BLOCK_ROWS
166           tile(threadIdx%x, threadIdx%y+j) = idata(x,y+j)
167        end do
168
169        call syncthreads()
170
171        x = (blockIdx_y-1) * TILE_DIM + threadIdx%x
172        y = (blockIdx_x-1) * TILE_DIM + threadIdx%y
173
174        do j = 0, TILE_DIM-1, BLOCK_ROWS
175           odata(x,y+j) = tile(threadIdx%y+j, threadIdx%x)
176        end do
177      end subroutine transposeDiagonal
178
179   end module kernels_m
180
181
182
183   program transposeTest
184
185      use cudafor
186      use kernels_m
187      use dimensions_m
188
189      implicit none
190
191      type (dim3) :: grid, tBlock
192      type (cudaEvent) :: startEvent, stopEvent
193      type (cudaDeviceProp) :: prop
194      real :: time
195
196      real :: in_h(nx,ny), copy_h(nx,ny), trp_h(ny,nx)
197      real :: gold(ny,nx)
198      real, device :: in_d(nx,ny), copy_d(nx,ny), trp_d(ny,nx)
199
200      integer :: i, j, istat
201
202      ! check parameters and calculate execution configuration
203
204      if (mod(nx, TILE_DIM) /= 0 &
205          .or. mod(ny, TILE_DIM) /= 0) then
206        write(*,*) 'nx and ny must be a multiple of TILE_DIM'
207        stop
208      end if
```

```fortran
209
210    if (mod(TILE_DIM, BLOCK_ROWS) /= 0) then
211       write(*,*) 'TILE_DIM must be a multiple of BLOCK_ROWS'
212       stop
213    end if
214
215    grid = dim3(nx/TILE_DIM, ny/TILE_DIM, 1)
216    tBlock = dim3(TILE_DIM, BLOCK_ROWS, 1)
217
218    ! write parameters
219
220    i = cudaGetDeviceProperties(prop, 0)
221    write(*,"(/,'Device Name: ',a)") trim(prop%name)
222    write(*,"('Compute Capability: ',i0,'.',i0)") &
223         prop%major, prop%minor
224
225
226    write(*,*)
227    write(*,"('Matrix size:', i5, i5, ',   Block size:', &
228         i3, i3, ',   Tile size:', i3, i3)") &
229         nx, ny, TILE_DIM, BLOCK_ROWS, TILE_DIM, TILE_DIM
230
231    write(*,"('grid:', i4,i4,i4, ',    tBlock:', i4,i4,i4)") &
232         grid%x, grid%y, grid%z, tBlock%x, tBlock%y, tBlock%z
233
234    ! initialize data
235
236    ! host
237
238    do j = 1, ny
239       do i = 1, nx
240          in_h(i,j) = i+(j-1)*nx
241       enddo
242    enddo
243
244    gold = transpose(in_h)
245
246    ! device
247
248    in_d = in_h
249    trp_d = -1.0
250    copy_d = -1.0
251
252    ! events for timing
253
254    istat = cudaEventCreate(startEvent)
255    istat = cudaEventCreate(stopEvent)
```

```
256
257     ! ------------
258     ! time kernels
259     ! ------------
260
261     write(*,'(/,a25,a25)') 'Routine', 'Bandwidth (GB/s)'
262
263     ! ------------
264     ! copySharedMem
265     ! ------------
266
267     write(*,'(a25)', advance='NO') 'shared memory copy'
268
269     copy_d = -1.0
270     ! warmup
271     call copySharedMem<<<grid, tBlock>>>(copy_d, in_d)
272
273     istat = cudaEventRecord(startEvent, 0)
274     do i=1, NUM_REPS
275        call copySharedMem<<<grid, tBlock>>> (copy_d, in_d)
276     end do
277     istat = cudaEventRecord(stopEvent, 0)
278     istat = cudaEventSynchronize(stopEvent)
279     istat = cudaEventElapsedTime(time, startEvent, stopEvent)
280
281     copy_h = copy_d
282     call postprocess(in_h, copy_h, time)
283
284     ! --------------
285     ! transposeNaive
286     ! --------------
287
288     write(*,'(a25)', advance='NO') 'naive transpose'
289
290     trp_d = -1.0
291     ! warmup
292     call transposeNaive<<<grid, tBlock>>>(trp_d, in_d)
293
294     istat = cudaEventRecord(startEvent, 0)
295     do i=1, NUM_REPS
296        call transposeNaive<<<grid, tBlock>>>(trp_d, in_d)
297     end do
298     istat = cudaEventRecord(stopEvent, 0)
299     istat = cudaEventSynchronize(stopEvent)
300     istat = cudaEventElapsedTime(time, startEvent, stopEvent)
301
302     trp_h = trp_d
```

```fortran
303     call postprocess(gold, trp_h, time)
304
305     ! ------------------
306     ! transposeCoalesced
307     ! ------------------
308
309     write(*,'(a25)', advance='NO') 'coalesced transpose'
310
311     trp_d = -1.0
312     ! warmup
313     call transposeCoalesced<<<grid, tBlock>>>(trp_d, in_d)
314
315     istat = cudaEventRecord(startEvent, 0)
316     do i=1, NUM_REPS
317        call transposeCoalesced<<<grid, tBlock>>>(trp_d, in_d)
318     end do
319     istat = cudaEventRecord(stopEvent, 0)
320     istat = cudaEventSynchronize(stopEvent)
321     istat = cudaEventElapsedTime(time, startEvent, stopEvent)
322
323     trp_h = trp_d
324     call postprocess(gold, trp_h, time)
325
326     ! ----------------------
327     ! transposeNoBankConflicts
328     ! ----------------------
329
330     write(*,'(a25)', advance='NO') 'conflict-free transpose'
331
332     trp_d = -1.0
333     ! warmup
334     call transposeNoBankConflicts<<<grid, tBlock>>>(trp_d, in_d)
335
336     istat = cudaEventRecord(startEvent, 0)
337     do i=1, NUM_REPS
338        call transposeNoBankConflicts &
339             <<<grid, tBlock>>>(trp_d, in_d)
340     end do
341     istat = cudaEventRecord(stopEvent, 0)
342     istat = cudaEventSynchronize(stopEvent)
343     istat = cudaEventElapsedTime(time, startEvent, stopEvent)
344
345     trp_h = trp_d
346     call postprocess(gold, trp_h, time)
347
348     ! --------------
349     ! transposeDigonal
```

```
350    ! ---------------
351
352    write(*,'(a25)', advance='NO') 'diagonal transpose'
353
354    trp_d = -1.0
355    ! warmup
356    call transposeDiagonal<<<grid, tBlock>>>(trp_d, in_d)
357
358    istat = cudaEventRecord(startEvent, 0)
359    do i=1, NUM_REPS
360       call transposeDiagonal<<<grid, tBlock>>>(trp_d, in_d)
361    end do
362    istat = cudaEventRecord(stopEvent, 0)
363    istat = cudaEventSynchronize(stopEvent)
364    istat = cudaEventElapsedTime(time, startEvent, stopEvent)
365
366    trp_h = trp_d
367    call postprocess(gold, trp_h, time)
368
369    ! cleanup
370
371    write(*,*)
372
373    istat = cudaEventDestroy(startEvent)
374    istat = cudaEventDestroy(stopEvent)
375
376 contains
377
378    subroutine postprocess(ref, res, t)
379       real, intent(in) :: ref(:,:), res(:,:), t
380       if (all(res == ref)) then
381          write(*,'(f20.2)') 2.0*mem_size*1.0e-6/(t/NUM_REPS)
382       else
383          write(*,'(a20)') '*** Failed ***'
384       end if
385    end subroutine postprocess
386
387 end program transposeTest
```

D.3 Thread- and instruction-level parallelism

The following is the complete CUDA Fortran code used to discuss thread- and instruction-level parallelism in Section 3.5.2:

```fortran
1   ! This code demonstrates use of thread- and instruction-
2   ! level parallelism and their effect on performance
3
4   module copy_m
5     integer, parameter :: N = 1024*1024
6     integer, parameter :: ILP=4
7   contains
8
9     ! simple copy code that requires thread-level paralellism
10    ! to hide global memory latencies
11
12    attributes(global) subroutine copy(odata, idata)
13      use precision_m
14      implicit none
15      real(fp_kind) :: odata(*), idata(*), tmp
16      integer :: i
17
18      i = (blockIdx%x-1)*blockDim%x + threadIdx%x
19      tmp = idata(i)
20      odata(i) = tmp
21    end subroutine copy
22
23    ! copy code which uses instruction-level parallelism
24    ! in addition to thread-level parallelism to hide
25    ! global memory latencies
26
27    attributes(global) subroutine copy_ILP(odata, idata)
28      use precision_m
29      implicit none
30      real(fp_kind) :: odata(*), idata(*), tmp(ILP)
31      integer :: i,j
32
33      i = (blockIdx%x-1)*blockDim%x*ILP + threadIdx%x
34
35      do j = 1, ILP
36          tmp(j) = idata(i+(j-1)*blockDim%x)
37      enddo
38
39      do j = 1, ILP
40          odata(i+(j-1)*blockDim%x) = tmp(j)
41      enddo
42    end subroutine copy_ILP
43
44  end module copy_m
45
46  program parallelism
```

```fortran
47   use cudafor
48   use precision_m
49   use copy_m
50
51   implicit none
52
53   type(dim3) :: grid, threadBlock
54   type(cudaEvent) :: startEvent, stopEvent
55   type(cudaDeviceProp) :: prop
56
57   real(fp_kind) :: a(N), b(N)
58   real(fp_kind), device :: a_d(N), b_d(N)
59
60   real :: time
61   integer :: i, smBytes, istat
62
63
64   istat = cudaGetDeviceProperties(prop, 0)
65   write(*,"(/,'Device Name: ',a)") trim(prop%name)
66   write(*,"('Compute Capability: ',i0,'.',i0)") &
67        prop%major, prop%minor
68   if (fp_kind == singlePrecision) then
69      write(*,"('Single Precision')")
70   else
71      write(*,"('Double Precision')")
72   end if
73
74   a = 1.0
75   a_d = a
76
77   smBytes = prop%sharedMemPerBlock
78
79   istat = cudaEventCreate(startEvent)
80   istat = cudaEventCreate(stopEvent)
81
82   write(*,'(/,"Thread-level parallelism runs")')
83
84   write(*,'(/," Multiple Blocks per Multiprocessor")')
85   write(*,'(a20,a25)') 'Threads/Block', 'Bandwidth (GB/s)'
86
87   do i = prop%warpSize, prop%maxThreadsPerBlock, prop%warpSize
88      if (mod(N,i) /= 0) cycle
89
90      b_d = 0.0
91
92      grid = dim3(ceiling(real(N)/i),1,1)
93      threadBlock = dim3(i,1,1)
```

```fortran
 94
 95       istat = cudaEventRecord(startEvent,0)
 96       call copy<<<grid, threadBlock>>>(b_d, a_d)
 97       istat = cudaEventRecord(stopEvent,0)
 98       istat = cudaEventSynchronize(stopEvent)
 99       istat = cudaEventElapsedTime(time, startEvent, stopEvent)
100
101     b = b_d
102     if (all(b==a)) then
103        write(*,'(i20, f20.2)') &
104             i, 2.*1000*sizeof(a)/(1024**3*time)
105     else
106        write(*,'(a20)') '*** Failed ***'
107     end if
108   end do
109
110   write(*,'(/," Single Block per Multiprocessor")')
111   write(*,'(a20,a25)') 'Threads/Block', 'Bandwidth (GB/s)'
112
113   do i = prop%warpSize, prop%maxThreadsPerBlock, prop%warpSize
114     if (mod(N,i) /= 0) cycle
115
116     b_d = 0.0
117
118     grid = dim3(ceiling(real(N)/i),1,1)
119     threadBlock = dim3(i,1,1)
120
121     istat = cudaEventRecord(startEvent,0)
122     call copy<<<grid, threadBlock, 0.9*smBytes>>>(b_d, a_d)
123     istat = cudaEventRecord(stopEvent,0)
124     istat = cudaEventSynchronize(stopEvent)
125     istat = cudaEventElapsedTime(time, startEvent, stopEvent)
126
127     b = b_d
128     if (all(b==a)) then
129        write(*,'(i20, f20.2)') i, 2.*sizeof(a)*1.0e-6/time
130     else
131        write(*,'(a20)') '*** Failed ***'
132     end if
133   end do
134
135   write(*,'(/,"Intruction-level parallelism runs")')
136
137   write(*,'(/," ILP=", i0, &
138        ", Single Block per Multiprocessor")') ILP
139   write(*,'(a20,a25)') 'Threads/Block', 'Bandwidth (GB/s)'
140
```

```
141    do i = prop%warpSize, prop%maxThreadsPerBlock, prop%warpSize
142       if (mod(N,i) /= 0) cycle
143
144       b_d = 0.0
145
146       grid = dim3(ceiling(real(N)/(i*ILP)),1,1)
147       threadBlock = dim3(i,1,1)
148
149       istat = cudaEventRecord(startEvent,0)
150       call copy_ILP<<<grid, threadBlock, &
151                         0.9*smBytes>>>(b_d, a_d)
152       istat = cudaEventRecord(stopEvent,0)
153       istat = cudaEventSynchronize(stopEvent)
154       istat = cudaEventElapsedTime(time, startEvent, stopEvent)
155
156       b = b_d
157       if (all(b==a)) then
158          write(*,'(i20, f20.2)') i, 2.*sizeof(a)*1.0e-6/time
159       else
160          write(*,'(a20)') '*** Failed ***'
161       end if
162    end do
163
164 end program parallelism
```

D.4 Multi-GPU programming

The following are the complete peer-to-peer and MPI matrix transpose codes discussed in Sections 4.1.3 and 4.2.2.

We use a wall-clock timer for timing these applications, since timing using cudaEvents is not possible across nodes in the MPI case. This timer uses the C function gettimeofday():

```
1  #include <time.h>
2  #include <sys/types.h>
3  #include <sys/times.h>
4  #include <sys/time.h>
5
6  double wallclock()
7  {
8    struct timeval tv;
9    struct timezone tz;
10   double t;
11
12   gettimeofday(&tv, &tz);
```

```
13
14    t = (double)tv.tv_sec;
15    t += ((double)tv.tv_usec)/1000000.0;
16
17    return t;
18 }
```

and is accessed in Fortran through the `timing` module:

```
1 module timing
2    interface wallclock
3       function wallclock() result(res) bind(C, name='wallclock')
4          use iso_c_binding
5          real (c_double) :: res
6       end function wallclock
7    end interface wallclock
8 end module timing
```

D.4.1 Peer-to-peer transpose

```
1  ! multi-GPU transpose using CUDA's peer-to-peer capability
2  !
3  ! This code requires all visible devices have direct access
4  ! with each other.  Use CUDA_VISIBLE_DEVICES to enumerate a
5  ! list of devices that are P2P accessible with each other.
6  ! Run the p2pAccess to see which devices have direct access
7  ! with each other.
8
9  module transpose_m
10    integer, parameter :: cudaTileDim = 32
11    integer, parameter :: blockRows = 8
12 contains
13
14    attributes(global) subroutine cudaTranspose( &
15         odata, ldo, idata, ldi)
16      implicit none
17      real, intent(out) :: odata(ldo,*)
18      real, intent(in) :: idata(ldi,*)
19      integer, value, intent(in) :: ldo, ldi
20      real, shared :: tile(cudaTileDim+1, cudaTileDim)
21      integer :: x, y, j
22
23      x = (blockIdx%x-1) * cudaTileDim + threadIdx%x
```

```
24       y = (blockIdx%y-1) * cudaTileDim + threadIdx%y
25
26       do j = 0, cudaTileDim-1, blockRows
27          tile(threadIdx%x, threadIdx%y+j) = idata(x,y+j)
28       end do
29
30       call syncthreads()
31
32       x = (blockIdx%y-1) * cudaTileDim + threadIdx%x
33       y = (blockIdx%x-1) * cudaTileDim + threadIdx%y
34
35       do j = 0, cudaTileDim-1, blockRows
36          odata(x,y+j) = tile(threadIdx%y+j, threadIdx%x)
37       end do
38    end subroutine cudaTranspose
39
40  end module transpose_m
41
42  !
43  ! Main code
44  !
45
46  program transposeP2P
47    use cudafor
48    use transpose_m
49    use timing
50
51    implicit none
52
53    ! global array size
54    integer, parameter :: nx = 1024, ny = 768
55
56    ! toggle async
57    logical, parameter :: asyncVersion = .true.
58
59    ! host arrays (global)
60    real :: h_idata(nx,ny), h_tdata(ny,nx), gold(ny,nx)
61    real (kind=8) :: timeStart, timeStop
62
63    ! CUDA vars and device arrays
64    type (dim3) :: dimGrid, dimBlock
65    integer(kind=cuda_stream_kind), allocatable :: &
66        streamID(:,:)  ! (device, stage)
67
68    ! distributed arrays
69    type deviceArray
70       real, device, allocatable :: v(:,:)
```

```fortran
71    end type deviceArray
72
73    type (deviceArray), allocatable :: &
74         d_idata(:), d_tdata(:), d_rdata(:)   ! (0:nDevices-1)
75
76    integer :: nDevices
77    type (cudaDeviceProp) :: prop
78    integer, allocatable :: devices(:)
79
80    integer :: p2pTileDimX, p2pTileDimY
81    integer :: i, j, nyl, jl, jg, p, access, istat
82    integer :: xOffset, yOffset
83    integer :: rDev, sDev, stage
84
85    ! determine number of devices
86
87    istat = cudaGetDeviceCount(nDevices)
88    write(*,"('Number of CUDA-capable devices: ', i0,/)") &
89         nDevices
90
91    do i = 0, nDevices-1
92       istat = cudaGetDeviceProperties(prop, i)
93       write(*,"('  Device ', i0, ': ', a)") i, trim(prop%name)
94    end do
95
96    ! check to make sure all devices are P2P accessible with
97    ! each other and enable peer access, if not exit
98
99    do j = 0, nDevices-1
100      do i = j+1, nDevices-1
101         istat = cudaDeviceCanAccessPeer(access, j, i)
102         if (access /= 1) then
103            write(*,*) &
104                 'Not all devices are P2P accessible ', &
105                 'with each other.'
106            write(*,*) &
107                 'Use the p2pAccess code to determine ', &
108                 'a subset that can do P2P and set'
109            write(*,*) &
110                 'the environment variable', &
111                 'CUDA_VISIBLE_DEVICES accordingly'
112            stop
113         end if
114         istat = cudaSetDevice(j)
115         istat = cudaDeviceEnablePeerAccess(i, 0)
116         istat = cudaSetDevice(i)
117         istat = cudaDeviceEnablePeerAccess(j, 0)
```

```
118        end do
119    end do
120
121    ! determine partition sizes and check tile sizes
122
123    if (mod(nx,nDevices) == 0 .and. mod(ny,nDevices) == 0) then
124       p2pTileDimX = nx/nDevices
125       p2pTileDimY = ny/nDevices
126    else
127       write(*,*) 'nx, ny must be multiples of nDevices'
128       stop
129    endif
130
131    if (mod(p2pTileDimX, cudaTileDim) /= 0 .or. &
132         mod(p2pTileDimY, cudaTileDim) /= 0) then
133       write(*,*) 'p2pTileDim* must be multiples of cudaTileDim'
134       stop
135    end if
136
137    if (mod(cudaTileDim, blockRows) /= 0) then
138       write(*,*) 'cudaTileDim must be a multiple of blockRows'
139       stop
140    end if
141
142    dimGrid = dim3(p2pTileDimX/cudaTileDim, &
143         p2pTileDimY/cudaTileDim, 1)
144    dimBlock = dim3(cudaTileDim, blockRows, 1)
145
146    ! write parameters
147
148    write(*,*)
149    write(*,"(/,'Array size: ', i0,'x',i0,/)") nx, ny
150
151    write(*,"('CUDA block size: ', i0,'x',i0, &
152         ',  CUDA tile size: ', i0,'x',i0)") &
153         cudaTileDim, blockRows, cudaTileDim, cudaTileDim
154
155    write(*,"('dimGrid: ', i0,'x',i0,'x',i0, &
156         ',    dimBlock: ', i0,'x',i0,'x',i0,/)") &
157         dimGrid%x, dimGrid%y, dimGrid%z, &
158         dimBlock%x, dimBlock%y, dimBlock%z
159
160    write(*,"('nDevices: ', i0, ', Local input array size: ', &
161         i0,'x',i0)") nDevices, nx, p2pTileDimY
162    write(*,"('p2pTileDim: ', i0,'x',i0,/)") &
163         p2pTileDimX, p2pTileDimY
164
```

```
165    write(*,"('async mode: ', l,//)") asyncVersion
166
167    ! allocate and initialize arrays
168
169    call random_number(h_idata)
170    gold = transpose(h_idata)
171
172    ! A stream is associated with a device,
173    ! so first index of streamID is the device (0:nDevices-1)
174    ! and second is the stage, which also spans (0:nDevices-1)
175    !
176    ! The 0th stage corresponds to the local transpose (on
177    ! diagonal tiles), and 1:nDevices-1 are the stages with
178    ! P2P communication
179
180    allocate(streamID(0:nDevices-1,0:nDevices-1))
181    do p = 0, nDevices-1
182       istat = cudaSetDevice(p)
183       do stage = 0, nDevices-1
184          istat = cudaStreamCreate(streamID(p,stage))
185       enddo
186    enddo
187
188    ! device data allocation and initialization
189
190    allocate(d_idata(0:nDevices-1),&
191         d_tdata(0:nDevices-1), d_rdata(0:nDevices-1))
192
193    do p = 0, nDevices-1
194       istat = cudaSetDevice(p)
195       allocate(d_idata(p)%v(nx,p2pTileDimY), &
196            d_rdata(p)%v(nx,p2pTileDimY), &
197            d_tdata(p)%v(ny,p2pTileDimX))
198
199       yOffset = p*p2pTileDimY
200       d_idata(p)%v(:,:) = h_idata(:, &
201            yOffset+1:yOffset+p2pTileDimY)
202       d_rdata(p)%v(:,:) = -1.0
203       d_tdata(p)%v(:,:) = -1.0
204    enddo
205
206    ! ---------
207    ! transpose
208    ! ---------
209
210    do p = 0, nDevices-1
211       istat = cudaSetDevice(p)
```

```
212        istat = cudaDeviceSynchronize()
213     enddo
214     timeStart = wallclock()
215
216     ! Stage 0:
217     ! transpose diagonal blocks (local data) before kicking off
218     ! transfers and transposes of other blocks
219
220     do p = 0, nDevices-1
221        istat = cudaSetDevice(p)
222        if (asyncVersion) then
223           call cudaTranspose &
224                <<<dimGrid, dimBlock, 0, streamID(p,0)>>> &
225                (d_tdata(p)%v(p*p2pTileDimY+1,1), ny, &
226                d_idata(p)%v(p*p2pTileDimX+1,1), nx)
227        else
228           call cudaTranspose<<<dimGrid, dimBlock>>> &
229                (d_tdata(p)%v(p*p2pTileDimY+1,1), ny, &
230                d_idata(p)%v(p*p2pTileDimX+1,1), nx)
231        endif
232     enddo
233
234     ! now send data to blocks to the right of diagonal
235     ! (using mod for wrapping) and transpose
236
237     do stage = 1, nDevices-1      ! stages = offset diagonals
238        do rDev = 0, nDevices-1   ! device that receives
239           sDev = mod(stage+rDev, nDevices)   ! dev that sends
240
241           if (asyncVersion) then
242              istat = cudaSetDevice(rDev)
243              istat = cudaMemcpy2DAsync( &
244                   d_rdata(rDev)%v(sDev*p2pTileDimX+1,1), nx, &
245                   d_idata(sDev)%v(rDev*p2pTileDimX+1,1), nx, &
246                   p2pTileDimX, p2pTileDimY, &
247                   stream=streamID(rDev,stage))
248           else
249              istat = cudaMemcpy2D( &
250                   d_rdata(rDev)%v(sDev*p2pTileDimX+1,1), nx, &
251                   d_idata(sDev)%v(rDev*p2pTileDimX+1,1), nx, &
252                   p2pTileDimX, p2pTileDimY)
253           end if
254
255           istat = cudaSetDevice(rDev)
256           if (asyncVersion) then
257              call cudaTranspose &
258                   <<<dimGrid, dimBlock, 0, &
```

```
259                        streamID(rDev,stage)>>>   &
260                 (d_tdata(rDev)%v(sDev*p2pTileDimY+1,1), ny, &
261                 d_rdata(rDev)%v(sDev*p2pTileDimX+1,1), nx)
262            else
263               call cudaTranspose<<<dimGrid, dimBlock>>> &
264                 (d_tdata(rDev)%v(sDev*p2pTileDimY+1,1), ny, &
265                 d_rdata(rDev)%v(sDev*p2pTileDimX+1,1), nx)
266            endif
267         enddo
268      enddo
269
270      ! wait for execution to complete and get wallclock
271      do p = 0, nDevices-1
272         istat = cudaSetDevice(p)
273         istat = cudaDeviceSynchronize()
274      enddo
275      timeStop = wallclock()
276
277      ! transfer results to host and check for errors
278
279      do p = 0, nDevices-1
280         xOffset = p*p2pTileDimX
281         istat = cudaSetDevice(p)
282         h_tdata(:, xOffset+1:xOffset+p2pTileDimX) = &
283              d_tdata(p)%v(:,:)
284      end do
285
286      if (all(h_tdata == gold)) then
287         write(*,"('Bandwidth (GB/s): ', f7.2,/)") &
288              2.*(nx*ny*4)/(1.0e+9*(timeStop-timeStart))
289      else
290         write(*,"(' *** Failed ***',/)")
291      endif
292
293      ! cleanup
294
295      do p = 0, nDevices-1
296         istat = cudaSetDevice(p)
297         deallocate(d_idata(p)%v, d_tdata(p)%v, d_rdata(p)%v)
298         do stage = 0, nDevices-1
299            istat = cudaStreamDestroy(streamID(p,stage))
300         enddo
301      end do
302      deallocate(d_idata, d_tdata, d_rdata)
303
304 end program transposeP2P
```

D.4.2 MPI transpose with host MPI transfers

This version of the MPI transpose uses MPI_SENDRECV on host data:

```fortran
module transpose_m

  implicit none
  integer, parameter :: cudaTileDim = 32
  integer, parameter :: blockRows = 8

contains

  attributes(global) &
       subroutine cudaTranspose(odata, ldo, idata, ldi)
    real, intent(out) :: odata(ldo,*)
    real, intent(in) :: idata(ldi,*)
    integer, value, intent(in) :: ldo, ldi
    real, shared :: tile(cudaTileDim+1, cudaTileDim)
    integer :: x, y, j

    x = (blockIdx%x-1) * cudaTileDim + threadIdx%x
    y = (blockIdx%y-1) * cudaTileDim + threadIdx%y

    do j = 0, cudaTileDim-1, blockRows
       tile(threadIdx%x, threadIdx%y+j) = idata(x,y+j)
    end do

    call syncthreads()

    x = (blockIdx%y-1) * cudaTileDim + threadIdx%x
    y = (blockIdx%x-1) * cudaTileDim + threadIdx%y

    do j = 0, cudaTileDim-1, blockRows
       odata(x,y+j) = tile(threadIdx%y+j, threadIdx%x)
    end do
  end subroutine cudaTranspose

end module transpose_m

!
! Main code
!

program transposeMPI
  use cudafor
  use mpi
```

```fortran
43    use mpiDeviceUtil
44    use transpose_m
45
46    implicit none
47
48    ! global array size
49    integer, parameter :: nx = 2048, ny = 2048
50
51    ! host arrays
52    real :: h_idata(nx,ny), h_tdata(ny,nx), gold(ny,nx)
53    real, pinned, allocatable :: sTile(:,:), rTile(:,:)
54
55    ! CUDA vars and device arrays
56    integer :: deviceID
57    type (dim3) :: dimGrid, dimBlock
58    real, device, allocatable :: &
59         d_idata(:,:), d_tdata(:,:), d_rTile(:,:)
60
61    ! MPI stuff
62    integer :: mpiTileDimX, mpiTileDimY
63    integer :: myrank, nprocs, tag, ierr
64    integer :: nstages, stage, sRank, rRank
65    integer :: status(MPI_STATUS_SIZE)
66    real(8) :: timeStart, timeStop
67
68    integer :: i, j, nyl, jl, jg, p
69    integer :: xOffset, yOffset
70
71    ! MPI initialization
72
73    call MPI_init(ierr)
74    call MPI_comm_rank(MPI_COMM_WORLD, myrank, ierr)
75    call MPI_comm_size(MPI_COMM_WORLD, nProcs, ierr)
76
77    ! get and set device
78
79    call assignDevice(deviceID)
80
81    ! check parameters and calculate execution configuration
82
83    if (mod(nx,nProcs) == 0 .and. mod(ny,nProcs) == 0) then
84       mpiTileDimX = nx/nProcs
85       mpiTileDimY = ny/nProcs
86    else
87       write(*,*) 'ny must be an integral multiple of nProcs'
88       call MPI_Finalize(ierr)
89       stop
```

```
90    endif
91
92    if (mod(mpiTileDimX, cudaTileDim) /= 0 .or. &
93          mod(mpiTileDimY, cudaTileDim) /= 0) then
94        write(*,*) 'mpiTileDimX and mpitileDimY must be an ', &
95                'integral multiple of cudaTileDim'
96        call MPI_Finalize(ierr)
97        stop
98    end if
99
100   if (mod(cudaTileDim, blockRows) /= 0) then
101       write(*,*) 'cudaTileDim must be a multiple of blockRows'
102       call MPI_Finalize(ierr)
103       stop
104   end if
105
106   dimGrid = dim3(mpiTileDimX/cudaTileDim, &
107         mpiTileDimY/cudaTileDim, 1)
108   dimBlock = dim3(cudaTileDim, blockRows, 1)
109
110   ! write parameters
111
112   if (myrank == 0) then
113       write(*,*)
114       write(*,"(/,'Array size: ', i0,'x',i0,/)") nx, ny
115
116       write(*,"('CUDA block size: ', i0,'x',i0, &
117           ',   CUDA tile size: ', i0,'x',i0)") &
118           cudaTileDim, blockRows, cudaTileDim, cudaTileDim
119
120       write(*,"('dimGrid: ', i0,'x',i0,'x',i0, &
121           ',   dimBlock: ', i0,'x',i0,'x',i0,/)") &
122           dimGrid%x, dimGrid%y, dimGrid%z, &
123           dimBlock%x, dimBlock%y, dimBlock%z
124
125       write(*,"('nprocs: ', i0, ',   Local input array size: ', &
126           i0,'x',i0)") nprocs, nx, mpiTileDimY
127       write(*,"('mpiTileDim: ', i0,'x',i0,/)") &
128           mpiTileDimX, mpiTileDimY
129   endif
130
131   ! initialize data
132
133   ! host - each process has entire array on host
134
135   do p = 0, nProcs-1
136     do jl = 1, mpiTileDimY
```

```
137            jg = p*mpiTileDimY + jl
138            do i = 1, nx
139                h_idata(i,jg) = i+(jg-1)*nx
140            enddo
141        enddo
142     enddo
143
144     gold = transpose(h_idata)
145
146     ! device - each process has
147     ! nx*mpiTileDimY = ny*mpiTileDimX  elements
148
149     allocate(d_idata(nx, mpiTileDimY), &
150          sTile(mpiTileDimX,mpiTileDimY), &
151          rTile(mpiTileDimX, mpiTileDimY), &
152          d_rTile(mpiTileDimX, mpiTileDimY), &
153          d_tdata(ny, mpiTileDimX))
154
155     yOffset = myrank*mpiTileDimY
156     d_idata(1:nx,1:mpiTileDimY) = &
157          h_idata(1:nx,yOffset+1:yOffset+mpiTileDimY)
158
159     d_tdata = -1.0
160
161     ! ---------
162     ! transpose
163     ! ---------
164
165     call MPI_BARRIER(MPI_COMM_WORLD, ierr)
166     timeStart = MPI_Wtime()
167
168     ! 0th stage - local transpose
169
170     call cudaTranspose<<<dimGrid, dimBlock>>> &
171          (d_tdata(myrank*mpiTileDimY+1,1), ny, &
172          d_idata(myrank*mpiTileDimX+1,1), nx)
173
174     ! other stages that involve MPI transfers
175
176     do stage = 1, nProcs-1
177        ! sRank = the rank to which myrank sends data
178        ! rRank = the rank from which myrank receives data
179        sRank = modulo(myrank-stage, nProcs)
180        rRank = modulo(myrank+stage, nProcs)
181
182        call MPI_BARRIER(MPI_COMM_WORLD, ierr)
183
```

```fortran
184        ! D2H transfer - pack into contiguous host array
185        ierr = cudaMemcpy2D(sTile, mpiTileDimX, &
186              d_idata(sRank*mpiTileDimX+1,1), nx, &
187              mpiTileDimX, mpiTileDimY)
188
189        ! MPI transfer
190        call MPI_SENDRECV(sTile, mpiTileDimX*mpiTileDimY, &
191              MPI_REAL, sRank, myrank, &
192              rTile, mpiTileDimX*mpiTileDimY, MPI_REAL, &
193              rRank, rRank, MPI_COMM_WORLD, status, ierr)
194
195        ! H2D transfer
196        d_rTile = rTile
197
198        ! do transpose from receive tile into final array
199        call cudaTranspose<<<dimGrid, dimBlock>>> &
200              (d_tdata(rRank*mpiTileDimY+1,1), ny, &
201              d_rTile, mpiTileDimX)
202     end do
203
204     call MPI_BARRIER(MPI_COMM_WORLD, ierr)
205     timeStop = MPI_Wtime()
206
207     ! check results
208
209     h_tdata = d_tdata
210
211     xOffset = myrank*mpiTileDimX
212     if (all(h_tdata(1:ny,1:mpiTileDimX) == &
213        gold(1:ny, xOffset+1:xOffset+mpiTileDimX))) then
214        if (myrank == 0) then
215           write(*,"('Bandwidth (GB/s): ', f7.2,/)") &
216                 2.*(nx*ny*4)/(1.0e+9*(timeStop-timeStart))
217        endif
218     else
219        write(*,"('[',i0,']', *** Failed ***,/)") myrank
220     endif
221
222     ! cleanup
223
224     deallocate(d_idata, d_tdata, sTile, rTile, d_rTile)
225
226     call MPI_Finalize(ierr)
227
228  end program transposeMPI
```

D.4.3 MPI transpose with device MPI transfers

The following version uses MVAPICH, whereby one can specify MPI_SENDRECV transfers on device data. When the devices in question are peer-to-peer capable with each other, the transfer is done through CUDA's peer-to-peer functionality. Otherwise the copy proceeds through the host.

```fortran
module transpose_m

  implicit none
  integer, parameter :: cudaTileDim = 32
  integer, parameter :: blockRows = 8

contains

  attributes(global) &
       subroutine cudaTranspose(odata, ldo, idata, ldi)
    real, intent(out) :: odata(ldo,*)
    real, intent(in) :: idata(ldi,*)
    integer, value, intent(in) :: ldo, ldi
    real, shared :: tile(cudaTileDim+1, cudaTileDim)
    integer :: x, y, j

    x = (blockIdx%x-1) * cudaTileDim + threadIdx%x
    y = (blockIdx%y-1) * cudaTileDim + threadIdx%y

    do j = 0, cudaTileDim-1, blockRows
       tile(threadIdx%x, threadIdx%y+j) = idata(x,y+j)
    end do

    call syncthreads()

    x = (blockIdx%y-1) * cudaTileDim + threadIdx%x
    y = (blockIdx%x-1) * cudaTileDim + threadIdx%y

    do j = 0, cudaTileDim-1, blockRows
       odata(x,y+j) = tile(threadIdx%y+j, threadIdx%x)
    end do
  end subroutine cudaTranspose

end module transpose_m

!
! Main code
!

program transposeMPI
```

```
41   use cudafor
42   use mpi
43   use transpose_m
44
45   implicit none
46
47   ! global array size
48   integer, parameter :: nx = 2048, ny = 2048
49
50   ! host arrays (global)
51   real :: h_idata(nx,ny), h_tdata(ny,nx), gold(ny,nx)
52
53   ! CUDA vars and device arrays
54   integer :: deviceID
55   type (dim3) :: dimGrid, dimBlock
56   real, device, allocatable :: &
57        d_idata(:,:), d_tdata(:,:), d_sTile(:,:), d_rTile(:,:)
58
59   ! MPI stuff
60   integer :: mpiTileDimX, mpiTileDimY
61   integer :: myrank, nprocs, tag, ierr, localRank
62   integer :: nstages, stage, sRank, rRank
63   integer :: status(MPI_STATUS_SIZE)
64   real(8) :: timeStart, timeStop
65   character (len=10) :: localRankStr
66
67   integer :: i, j, nyl, jl, jg, p
68   integer :: xOffset, yOffset
69
70   ! for MVAPICH set device before MPI initialization
71
72   call get_environment_variable('MV2_COMM_WORLD_LOCAL_RANK', &
73        localRankStr)
74   read(localRankStr,'(i10)') localRank
75   ierr = cudaSetDevice(localRank)
76
77   ! MPI initialization
78
79   call MPI_init(ierr)
80   call MPI_comm_rank(MPI_COMM_WORLD, myrank, ierr)
81   call MPI_comm_size(MPI_COMM_WORLD, nProcs, ierr)
82
83   ! check parameters and calculate execution configuration
84
85   if (mod(nx,nProcs) == 0 .and. mod(ny,nProcs) == 0) then
86      mpiTileDimX = nx/nProcs
87      mpiTileDimY = ny/nProcs
```

```
88    else
89       write(*,*) 'ny must be an integral multiple of nProcs'
90       call MPI_Finalize(ierr)
91       stop
92    endif
93
94    if (mod(mpiTileDimX, cudaTileDim) /= 0 .or. &
95          mod(mpiTileDimY, cudaTileDim) /= 0) then
96       write(*,*) 'mpiTileDimX and mpitileDimY must be an ', &
97             'integral multiple of cudaTileDim'
98       call MPI_Finalize(ierr)
99       stop
100   end if
101
102   if (mod(cudaTileDim, blockRows) /= 0) then
103      write(*,*) 'cudaTileDim must be a multiple of blockRows'
104      call MPI_Finalize(ierr)
105      stop
106   end if
107
108   dimGrid = dim3(mpiTileDimX/cudaTileDim, &
109        mpiTileDimY/cudaTileDim, 1)
110   dimBlock = dim3(cudaTileDim, blockRows, 1)
111
112   ! write parameters
113
114   if (myrank == 0) then
115      write(*,*)
116      write(*,"(/,'Array size: ', i0,'x',i0,/)") nx, ny
117
118      write(*,"('CUDA block size: ', i0,'x',i0, &
119            ',   CUDA tile size: ', i0,'x',i0)") &
120            cudaTileDim, blockRows, cudaTileDim, cudaTileDim
121
122      write(*,"('dimGrid: ', i0,'x',i0,'x',i0, &
123            ',   dimBlock: ', i0,'x',i0,'x',i0,/)") &
124            dimGrid%x, dimGrid%y, dimGrid%z, &
125            dimBlock%x, dimBlock%y, dimBlock%z
126
127      write(*,"('nprocs: ', i0, ',   Local input array size: ', &
128            i0,'x',i0)") nprocs, nx, mpiTileDimY
129      write(*,"('mpiTileDim: ', i0,'x',i0,/)") &
130            mpiTileDimX, mpiTileDimY
131   endif
132
133   ! initialize data
134
```

```
135   ! host - each process has entire array on host (for now)
136
137   do p = 0, nProcs-1
138      do jl = 1, mpiTileDimY
139         jg = p*mpiTileDimY + jl
140         do i = 1, nx
141            h_idata(i,jg) = i+(jg-1)*nx
142         enddo
143      enddo
144   enddo
145
146   gold = transpose(h_idata)
147
148   ! device - each process has
149   ! nx*mpiTileDimY = ny*mpiTileDimX  elements
150
151   allocate(d_idata(nx, mpiTileDimY), &
152        d_tdata(ny, mpiTileDimX), &
153        d_sTile(mpiTileDimX,mpiTileDimY), &
154        d_rTile(mpiTileDimX, mpiTileDimY))
155
156   yOffset = myrank*mpiTileDimY
157   d_idata(1:nx,1:mpiTileDimY) = &
158        h_idata(1:nx,yOffset+1:yOffset+mpiTileDimY)
159
160   d_tdata = -1.0
161
162
163   ! ---------
164   ! transpose
165   ! ---------
166
167   call MPI_BARRIER(MPI_COMM_WORLD, ierr)
168   timeStart = MPI_Wtime()
169
170   ! 0th stage - local transpose
171
172   call cudaTranspose<<<dimGrid, dimBlock>>> &
173        (d_tdata(myrank*mpiTileDimY+1,1), ny, &
174        d_idata(myrank*mpiTileDimX+1,1), nx)
175
176   ! other stages that involve MPI transfers
177
178   do stage = 1, nProcs-1
179      ! sRank = the rank to which myrank sends data
180      ! rRank = the rank from which myrank receives data
181      sRank = modulo(myrank-stage, nProcs)
```

```
182      rRank = modulo(myrank+stage, nProcs)
183
184      call MPI_BARRIER(MPI_COMM_WORLD, ierr)
185
186      ! pack tile so data to be sent is contiguous
187
188      !$cuf kernel do(2) <<<*,*>>>
189      do j = 1, mpiTileDimY
190         do i = 1, mpiTileDimX
191            d_sTile(i,j) = d_idata(sRank*mpiTileDimX+i,j)
192         enddo
193      enddo
194
195      call MPI_SENDRECV(d_sTile, mpiTileDimX*mpiTileDimY, &
196            MPI_REAL, sRank, myrank, &
197            d_rTile, mpiTileDimX*mpiTileDimY, MPI_REAL, &
198            rRank, rRank, MPI_COMM_WORLD, status, ierr)
199
200      ! do transpose from receive tile into final array
201      ! (no need to unpack)
202
203      call cudaTranspose<<<dimGrid, dimBlock>>> &
204            (d_tdata(rRank*mpiTileDimY+1,1), ny, &
205            d_rTile, mpiTileDimX)
206
207   end do ! stage
208
209   call MPI_BARRIER(MPI_COMM_WORLD, ierr)
210   timeStop = MPI_Wtime()
211
212   ! check results
213
214   h_tdata = d_tdata
215
216   xOffset = myrank*mpiTileDimX
217   if (all(h_tdata(1:ny,1:mpiTileDimX) == &
218         gold(1:ny, xOffset+1:xOffset+mpiTileDimX))) then
219      if (myrank == 0) then
220         write(*,"('Bandwidth (GB/s): ', f7.2,/)") &
221               2.*(nx*ny*4)/(1.0e+9*(timeStop-timeStart))
222      endif
223   else
224      write(*,"('[',i0,']', *** Failed ***,/)") myrank
225   endif
226
227   ! cleanup
228
```

```
229    deallocate(d_idata, d_tdata, d_sTile, d_rTile)
230
231    call MPI_Finalize(ierr)
232
233  end program transposeMPI
```

D.5 Finite difference code

The following is the complete CUDA Fortran code used in the Finite Difference case study of Chapter 6. For the one-dimensional derivative, the derivative module containing the kernels is:

```
1  ! This file contains the setup host code and kernels for
2  ! calculating derivatives using a 9-point finite difference
3  ! stencil
4
5  module derivative_m
6    use cudafor
7    use precision_m
8
9    integer, parameter :: mx = 64, my = 64, mz = 64
10   real(fp_kind) :: x(mx), y(my), z(mz)
11
12   ! shared memory tiles will be m*-by-*Pencils
13   ! sPencils is used when each thread calculates
14   !    the derivative at one point
15   ! lPencils is used for coalescing in y and z
16   !    where each thread has to calculate the
17   !    derivative at mutiple points
18
19   integer, parameter :: sPencils = 4    ! small # pencils
20   integer, parameter :: lPencils = 32   ! large # pencils
21
22   type(dim3) :: g_sp(3), b_sp(3)
23   type(dim3) :: g_lp(3), b_lp(3)
24
25   ! stencil coefficients
26
27   real(fp_kind), constant :: ax_c, bx_c, cx_c, dx_c
28   real(fp_kind), constant :: ay_c, by_c, cy_c, dy_c
29   real(fp_kind), constant :: az_c, bz_c, cz_c, dz_c
30
31  contains
32
```

```fortran
33    ! host routine to set constant data
34
35    subroutine setDerivativeParameters()
36
37      implicit none
38
39      real(fp_kind) :: dsinv
40      integer :: i, j, k
41
42      ! check to make sure dimensions are multiples of sPencils
43      if (mod(my,sPencils) /= 0) then
44         write(*,*) '"my" must be a multiple of sPencils'
45         stop
46      end if
47
48      if (mod(mx,sPencils) /= 0) then
49         write(*,*) '"mx" must be a multiple of sPencils', &
50               ' (for y-deriv)'
51         stop
52      end if
53
54      if (mod(mz,sPencils) /= 0) then
55         write(*,*) '"mz" must be a multiple of sPencils', &
56               ' (for z-deriv)'
57         stop
58      end if
59
60      if (mod(mx,lPencils) /= 0) then
61         write(*,*) '"mx" must be a multiple of lPencils'
62         stop
63      end if
64
65      if (mod(my,lPencils) /= 0) then
66         write(*,*) '"my" must be a multiple of lPencils'
67         stop
68      end if
69
70      ! stencil weights (for unit length problem)
71
72      dsinv = real(mx-1)
73      do i = 1, mx
74         x(i) = (i-1.)/(mx-1.)
75      enddo
76      ax_c =   4./  5. * dsinv
77      bx_c =  -1./  5. * dsinv
78      cx_c =   4./105. * dsinv
79      dx_c =  -1./280. * dsinv
```

```
80
81       dsinv = real(my-1)
82       do j = 1, my
83          y(j) = (j-1.)/(my-1.)
84       enddo
85       ay_c =   4./  5. * dsinv
86       by_c =  -1./  5. * dsinv
87       cy_c =   4./105. * dsinv
88       dy_c =  -1./280. * dsinv
89
90       dsinv = real(mz-1)
91       do k = 1, mz
92          z(k) = (k-1.)/(mz-1.)
93       enddo
94       az_c =   4./  5. * dsinv
95       bz_c =  -1./  5. * dsinv
96       cz_c =   4./105. * dsinv
97       dz_c =  -1./280. * dsinv
98
99       ! Execution configurations for small and
100      ! large pencil tiles
101
102      g_sp(1) = dim3(my/sPencils,mz,1)
103      b_sp(1) = dim3(mx,sPencils,1)
104
105      g_lp(1) = dim3(my/lPencils,mz,1)
106      b_lp(1) = dim3(mx,sPencils,1)
107
108      g_sp(2) = dim3(mx/sPencils,mz,1)
109      b_sp(2) = dim3(sPencils,my,1)
110
111      g_lp(2) = dim3(mx/lPencils,mz,1)
112      ! we want to use the same number of threads as above.
113      ! so if we use lPencils instead of sPencils in one
114      ! dimension, we multiply the other by sPencils/lPencils
115      b_lp(2) = dim3(lPencils, my*sPencils/lPencils,1)
116
117      g_sp(3) = dim3(mx/sPencils,my,1)
118      b_sp(3) = dim3(sPencils,mz,1)
119
120      g_lp(3) = dim3(mx/lPencils,my,1)
121      b_lp(3) = dim3(lPencils, mz*sPencils/lPencils,1)
122
123    end subroutine setDerivativeParameters
124
125    ! -------------
126    ! x derivatives
```

```fortran
127    ! -------------
128
129    attributes(global) subroutine deriv_x(f, df)
130      implicit none
131
132      real(fp_kind), intent(in) :: f(mx,my,mz)
133      real(fp_kind), intent(out) :: df(mx,my,mz)
134
135      real(fp_kind), shared :: f_s(-3:mx+4,sPencils)
136
137      integer :: i,j,k,j_l
138
139      i = threadIdx%x
140      j = (blockIdx%x-1)*blockDim%y + threadIdx%y
141      ! j_l is local variant of j for accessing shared memory
142      j_l = threadIdx%y
143      k = blockIdx%y
144
145      f_s(i,j_l) = f(i,j,k)
146
147      call syncthreads()
148
149      ! fill in periodic images in shared memory array
150
151      if (i <= 4) then
152         f_s(i-4, j_l) = f_s(mx+i-5,j_l)
153         f_s(mx+i,j_l) = f_s(i+1,   j_l)
154      endif
155
156      call syncthreads()
157
158      df(i,j,k) = &
159          (ax_c *( f_s(i+1,j_l) - f_s(i-1,j_l) )   &
160          +bx_c *( f_s(i+2,j_l) - f_s(i-2,j_l) )   &
161          +cx_c *( f_s(i+3,j_l) - f_s(i-3,j_l) )   &
162          +dx_c *( f_s(i+4,j_l) - f_s(i-4,j_l) ))
163
164    end subroutine deriv_x
165
166    ! this version avoids the first syncthreads() call
167    ! in the above version by using the same thread
168    ! to write and read the same shared memory value
169
170    attributes(global) subroutine deriv_x_1sync(f, df)
171      implicit none
172
173      real(fp_kind), intent(in) :: f(mx,my,mz)
```

```
174        real(fp_kind), intent(out) :: df(mx,my,mz)
175
176        real(fp_kind), shared :: f_s(-3:mx+4,sPencils)
177
178        integer :: i,j,k,j_l
179
180        i = threadIdx%x
181        j = (blockIdx%x-1)*blockDim%y + threadIdx%y
182        ! j_l is local variant of j for accessing shared memory
183        j_l = threadIdx%y
184        k = blockIdx%y
185
186        f_s(i,j_l) = f(i,j,k)
187
188        ! fill in periodic images in shared memory array
189        ! Use the same thread, (i,j_l), on the RHS that was used
190        ! to read the value in, so no syncthreads is needed
191
192        if (i>mx-5 .and. i<mx) f_s(i-(mx-1),j_l) = f_s(i,j_l)
193        if (i>1    .and. i<6 ) f_s(i+(mx-1),j_l) = f_s(i,j_l)
194
195        call syncthreads()
196
197        df(i,j,k) = &
198             (ax_c *( f_s(i+1,j_l) - f_s(i-1,j_l) )    &
199             +bx_c *( f_s(i+2,j_l) - f_s(i-2,j_l) )    &
200             +cx_c *( f_s(i+3,j_l) - f_s(i-3,j_l) )    &
201             +dx_c *( f_s(i+4,j_l) - f_s(i-4,j_l) ))
202
203      end subroutine deriv_x_1sync
204
205      ! this version uses a 64x32 shared memory tile,
206      ! still with 64*sPencils threads
207
208      attributes(global) subroutine deriv_x_1Pencils(f, df)
209        implicit none
210
211        real(fp_kind), intent(in) :: f(mx,my,mz)
212        real(fp_kind), intent(out) :: df(mx,my,mz)
213
214        real(fp_kind), shared :: f_s(-3:mx+4,lPencils)
215
216        integer :: i,j,k,j_l,jBase
217
218        i = threadIdx%x
219        jBase = (blockIdx%x-1)*lPencils
220        k = blockIdx%y
```

```
221
222        do j_l = threadIdx%y, lPencils, blockDim%y
223           j = jBase + j_l
224           f_s(i,j_l) = f(i,j,k)
225        enddo
226
227        call syncthreads()
228
229        ! fill in periodic images in shared memory array
230
231        if (i <= 4) then
232           do j_l = threadIdx%y, lPencils, blockDim%y
233              f_s(i-4, j_l) = f_s(mx+i-5,j_l)
234              f_s(mx+i,j_l) = f_s(i+1,    j_l)
235           enddo
236        endif
237
238        call syncthreads()
239
240        do j_l = threadIdx%y, lPencils, blockDim%y
241           j = jBase + j_l
242           df(i,j,k) = &
243                (ax_c *( f_s(i+1,j_l) - f_s(i-1,j_l) )   &
244                +bx_c *( f_s(i+2,j_l) - f_s(i-2,j_l) )   &
245                +cx_c *( f_s(i+3,j_l) - f_s(i-3,j_l) )   &
246                +dx_c *( f_s(i+4,j_l) - f_s(i-4,j_l) ))
247        enddo
248
249     end subroutine deriv_x_lPencils
250
251     ! -------------
252     ! y derivatives
253     ! -------------
254
255     attributes(global) subroutine deriv_y(f, df)
256        implicit none
257
258        real(fp_kind), intent(in) :: f(mx,my,mz)
259        real(fp_kind), intent(out) :: df(mx,my,mz)
260
261        real(fp_kind), shared :: f_s(sPencils,-3:my+4)
262
263        integer :: i,i_l,j,k
264
265        i = (blockIdx%x-1)*blockDim%x + threadIdx%x
266        i_l = threadIdx%x
267        j = threadIdx%y
```

```
268        k = blockIdx%y
269
270        f_s(i_l,j) = f(i,j,k)
271
272        call syncthreads()
273
274        if (j <= 4) then
275           f_s(i_l,j-4) = f_s(i_l,my+j-5)
276           f_s(i_l,my+j) = f_s(i_l,j+1)
277        endif
278
279        call syncthreads()
280
281        df(i,j,k) = &
282             (ay_c *( f_s(i_l,j+1) - f_s(i_l,j-1) )    &
283             +by_c *( f_s(i_l,j+2) - f_s(i_l,j-2) )    &
284             +cy_c *( f_s(i_l,j+3) - f_s(i_l,j-3) )    &
285             +dy_c *( f_s(i_l,j+4) - f_s(i_l,j-4) ))
286
287     end subroutine deriv_y
288
289     ! y derivative using a tile of 32x64
290     ! launch with thread block of 32x8
291
292     attributes(global) subroutine deriv_y_1Pencils(f, df)
293       implicit none
294
295       real(fp_kind), intent(in) :: f(mx,my,mz)
296       real(fp_kind), intent(out) :: df(mx,my,mz)
297
298       real(fp_kind), shared :: f_s(1Pencils,-3:my+4)
299
300       integer :: i,j,k,i_l
301
302       i_l = threadIdx%x
303       i = (blockIdx%x-1)*blockDim%x + threadIdx%x
304       k = blockIdx%y
305
306       do j = threadIdx%y, my, blockDim%y
307          f_s(i_l,j) = f(i,j,k)
308       enddo
309
310       call syncthreads()
311
312       j = threadIdx%y
313       if (j <= 4) then
314          f_s(i_l,j-4) = f_s(i_l,my+j-5)
```

```
315          f_s(i_l,my+j) = f_s(i_l,j+1)
316      endif
317
318      call syncthreads()
319
320      do j = threadIdx%y, my, blockDim%y
321         df(i,j,k) = &
322              (ay_c *( f_s(i_l,j+1) - f_s(i_l,j-1) )   &
323              +by_c *( f_s(i_l,j+2) - f_s(i_l,j-2) )   &
324              +cy_c *( f_s(i_l,j+3) - f_s(i_l,j-3) )   &
325              +dy_c *( f_s(i_l,j+4) - f_s(i_l,j-4) ))
326      enddo
327
328    end subroutine deriv_y_1Pencils
329
330    ! ------------
331    ! z derivative
332    ! ------------
333
334    attributes(global) subroutine deriv_z(f, df)
335      implicit none
336
337      real(fp_kind), intent(in) :: f(mx,my,mz)
338      real(fp_kind), intent(out) :: df(mx,my,mz)
339
340      real(fp_kind), shared :: f_s(sPencils,-3:mz+4)
341
342      integer :: i,i_l,j,k
343
344      i = (blockIdx%x-1)*blockDim%x + threadIdx%x
345      i_l = threadIdx%x
346      j = blockIdx%y
347      k = threadIdx%y
348
349      f_s(i_l,k) = f(i,j,k)
350
351      call syncthreads()
352
353      if (k <= 4) then
354         f_s(i_l,k-4) = f_s(i_l,mz+k-5)
355         f_s(i_l,mz+k) = f_s(i_l,k+1)
356      endif
357
358      call syncthreads()
359
360      df(i,j,k) = &
361           (az_c *( f_s(i_l,k+1) - f_s(i_l,k-1) )   &
```

```
362              +bz_c *( f_s(i_l,k+2) - f_s(i_l,k-2) )    &
363              +cz_c *( f_s(i_l,k+3) - f_s(i_l,k-3) )    &
364              +dz_c *( f_s(i_l,k+4) - f_s(i_l,k-4) ))
365
366    end subroutine deriv_z
367
368
369    attributes(global) subroutine deriv_z_lPencils(f, df)
370      implicit none
371
372      real(fp_kind), intent(in) :: f(mx,my,mz)
373      real(fp_kind), intent(out) :: df(mx,my,mz)
374
375      real(fp_kind), shared :: f_s(lPencils,-3:mz+4)
376
377      integer :: i,i_l,j,k
378
379      i = (blockIdx%x-1)*blockDim%x + threadIdx%x
380      i_l = threadIdx%x
381      j = blockIdx%y
382
383      do k = threadIdx%y, mz, blockDim%y
384         f_s(i_l,k) = f(i,j,k)
385      enddo
386
387      call syncthreads()
388
389      k = threadIdx%y
390      if (k <= 4) then
391         f_s(i_l,k-4) = f_s(i_l,mz+k-5)
392         f_s(i_l,mz+k) = f_s(i_l,k+1)
393      endif
394
395      call syncthreads()
396
397      do k = threadIdx%y, mz, blockDim%y
398         df(i,j,k) = &
399              (az_c *( f_s(i_l,k+1) - f_s(i_l,k-1) )    &
400              +bz_c *( f_s(i_l,k+2) - f_s(i_l,k-2) )    &
401              +cz_c *( f_s(i_l,k+3) - f_s(i_l,k-3) )    &
402              +dz_c *( f_s(i_l,k+4) - f_s(i_l,k-4) ))
403      enddo
404    end subroutine deriv_z_lPencils
405
406 end module derivative_m
```

and the host code is:

```
1   ! This the main host code for the finite difference
2   ! example.  The kernels are contained in the derivative_m
3   ! module
4
5   program derivativeTest
6     use cudafor
7     use precision_m
8     use derivative_m
9
10    implicit none
11
12    real(fp_kind), parameter :: fx = 1.0, fy = 1.0, fz = 1.0
13    integer, parameter :: nReps = 20
14
15    real(fp_kind) :: f(mx,my,mz), df(mx,my,mz), sol(mx,my,mz)
16    real(fp_kind), device :: f_d(mx,my,mz), df_d(mx,my,mz)
17    real(fp_kind) :: twopi, error, maxError
18    type(cudaEvent) :: startEvent, stopEvent
19    type(cudaDeviceProp) :: prop
20
21    real :: time
22    integer :: i, j, k, istat
23
24    ! Print device and precision
25
26    istat = cudaGetDeviceProperties(prop, 0)
27    write(*,"(/,'Device Name: ',a)") trim(prop%name)
28    write(*,"('Compute Capability: ',i0,'.',i0)") &
29         prop%major, prop%minor
30    if (fp_kind == singlePrecision) then
31       write(*,"('Single Precision')")
32    else
33       write(*,"('Double Precision')")
34    end if
35
36    ! initialize
37
38    twopi = 8.*atan(1.d0)
39    call setDerivativeParameters()
40
41    istat = cudaEventCreate(startEvent)
42    istat = cudaEventCreate(stopEvent)
43
44    ! x-derivative using 64x4 tile
```

```
45
46   write(*,"(/,'x derivatives')")
47
48   do i = 1, mx
49      f(i,:,:) = cos(fx*twopi*(i-1.)/(mx-1))
50   enddo
51   f_d = f
52   df_d = 0
53
54   call deriv_x<<<g_sp(1),b_sp(1)>>>(f_d, df_d)
55   istat = cudaEventRecord(startEvent,0)
56   do i = 1, nReps
57      call deriv_x<<<g_sp(1),b_sp(1)>>>(f_d, df_d)
58   enddo
59   istat = cudaEventRecord(stopEvent,0)
60   istat = cudaEventSynchronize(stopEvent)
61   istat = cudaEventElapsedTime(time, startEvent, stopEvent)
62
63   df = df_d
64
65   do i = 1, mx
66      sol(i,:,:) = -fx*twopi*sin(fx*twopi*(i-1.)/(mx-1))
67   enddo
68
69   error = sqrt(sum((sol-df)**2)/(mx*my*mz))
70   maxError = maxval(abs(sol-df))
71
72   write(*,"(/,' Using shared memory tile of x-y: ', &
73      i0, 'x', i0)") mx, sPencils
74   write(*,*) '  RMS error: ', error
75   write(*,*) '  MAX error: ', maxError
76   write(*,*) '  Average time (ms): ', time/nReps
77   write(*,*) '  Average Bandwidth (GB/s): ', &
78      2.*1.e-6*sizeof(f)/(time/nReps)
79
80   ! x-deriv - similar to above but first
81   ! syncthreads removed
82
83   do i = 1, mx
84      f(i,:,:) = cos(fx*twopi*(i-1.)/(mx-1))
85   enddo
86   f_d = f
87   df_d = 0
88
89   call deriv_x_1sync<<<g_sp(1),b_sp(1)>>>(f_d, df_d)
90   istat = cudaEventRecord(startEvent,0)
91   do i = 1, nReps
```

```
 92        call deriv_x_1sync <<<g_sp(1),b_sp(1)>>>(f_d, df_d)
 93     enddo
 94     istat = cudaEventRecord(stopEvent,0)
 95     istat = cudaEventSynchronize(stopEvent)
 96     istat = cudaEventElapsedTime(time, startEvent, stopEvent)
 97
 98     df = df_d
 99
100     do i = 1, mx
101        sol(i,:,:) = -fx*twopi*sin(fx*twopi*(i-1.)/(mx-1))
102     enddo
103
104     error = sqrt(sum((sol-df)**2)/(mx*my*mz))
105     maxError = maxval(abs(sol-df))
106
107     write(*,"(/,a,a, i0, 'x', i0)") &
108          '  Single syncthreads,', &
109          ' using shared memory tile of x-y: ', &
110         mx, sPencils
111     write(*,*) '  RMS error: ', error
112     write(*,*) '  MAX error: ', maxError
113     write(*,*) '  Average time (ms): ', time/nReps
114     write(*,*) '  Average Bandwidth (GB/s): ', &
115          2.*1.e-6*sizeof(f)/(time/nReps)
116
117     ! x-deriv - uses extended tile (lPencils)
118
119     do i = 1, mx
120        f(i,:,:) = cos(fx*twopi*(i-1.)/(mx-1))
121     enddo
122     f_d = f
123     df_d = 0
124
125     call deriv_x_1Pencils <<<g_lp(1),b_lp(1)>>>(f_d, df_d)
126     istat = cudaEventRecord(startEvent,0)
127     do i = 1, nReps
128        call deriv_x_1Pencils <<<g_lp(1),b_lp(1)>>>(f_d, df_d)
129     enddo
130     istat = cudaEventRecord(stopEvent,0)
131     istat = cudaEventSynchronize(stopEvent)
132     istat = cudaEventElapsedTime(time, startEvent, stopEvent)
133
134     df = df_d
135
136     do i = 1, mx
137        sol(i,:,:) = -fx*twopi*sin(fx*twopi*(i-1.)/(mx-1))
138     enddo
```

```
139
140    error = sqrt(sum((sol-df)**2)/(mx*my*mz))
141    maxError = maxval(abs(sol-df))
142
143    write(*,"(/,'  Using shared memory tile of x-y: ', &
144          i0, 'x', i0)") mx, lPencils
145    write(*,*) '  RMS error: ', error
146    write(*,*) '  MAX error: ', maxError
147    write(*,*) '  Average time (ms): ', time/nReps
148    write(*,*) '  Average Bandwidth (GB/s): ', &
149          2.*1.e-6*sizeof(f)/(time/nReps)
150
151    ! y-derivative
152
153    write(*,"(/,'y derivatives')")
154
155    do j = 1, my
156        f(:,j,:) = cos(fy*twopi*(j-1.)/(my-1))
157    enddo
158    f_d = f
159    df_d = 0
160
161    call deriv_y<<<g_sp(2), b_sp(2)>>>(f_d, df_d)
162    istat = cudaEventRecord(startEvent,0)
163    do i = 1, nReps
164        call deriv_y<<<g_sp(2), b_sp(2)>>>(f_d, df_d)
165    enddo
166    istat = cudaEventRecord(stopEvent,0)
167    istat = cudaEventSynchronize(stopEvent)
168    istat = cudaEventElapsedTime(time, startEvent, stopEvent)
169
170    df = df_d
171
172    do j = 1, my
173        sol(:,j,:) = -fy*twopi*sin(fy*twopi*(j-1.)/(my-1))
174    enddo
175
176    error = sqrt(sum((sol-df)**2)/(mx*my*mz))
177    maxError = maxval(abs(sol-df))
178
179    write(*,"(/,'  Using shared memory tile of x-y: ', &
180          i0, 'x', i0)") sPencils, my
181    write(*,*) '  RMS error: ', error
182    write(*,*) '  MAX error: ', maxError
183    write(*,*) '  Average time (ms): ', time/nReps
184    write(*,*) '  Average Bandwidth (GB/s): ', &
185          2.*1.e-6*sizeof(f)/(time/nReps)
```

```
186
187     ! y-derivative lPencils
188
189     do j = 1, my
190        f(:,j,:) = cos(fy*twopi*(j-1.)/(my-1))
191     enddo
192     f_d = f
193     df_d = 0
194
195     call deriv_y_1Pencils<<<g_lp(2), b_lp(2)>>>(f_d, df_d)
196     istat = cudaEventRecord(startEvent,0)
197     do i = 1, nReps
198        call deriv_y_1Pencils<<<g_lp(2), b_lp(2)>>>(f_d, df_d)
199     enddo
200     istat = cudaEventRecord(stopEvent,0)
201     istat = cudaEventSynchronize(stopEvent)
202     istat = cudaEventElapsedTime(time, startEvent, stopEvent)
203
204     df = df_d
205
206     do j = 1, my
207        sol(:,j,:) = -fy*twopi*sin(fy*twopi*(j-1.)/(my-1))
208     enddo
209
210     error = sqrt(sum((sol-df)**2)/(mx*my*mz))
211     maxError = maxval(abs(sol-df))
212
213     write(*,"(/,'  Using shared memory tile of x-y: ', &
214        i0, 'x', i0)") lPencils, my
215     write(*,*) '  RMS error: ', error
216     write(*,*) '  MAX error: ', maxError
217     write(*,*) '  Average time (ms): ', time/nReps
218     write(*,*) '  Average Bandwidth (GB/s): ', &
219        2.*1.e-6*sizeof(f)/(time/nReps)
220
221     ! z-derivative
222
223     write(*,"(/,'z derivatives')")
224
225     do k = 1, mz
226        f(:,:,k) = cos(fz*twopi*(k-1.)/(mz-1))
227     enddo
228     f_d = f
229     df_d = 0
230
231     call deriv_z<<<g_sp(3),b_sp(3)>>>(f_d, df_d)
232     istat = cudaEventRecord(startEvent,0)
```

```
233    do i = 1, nReps
234        call deriv_z<<<g_sp(3),b_sp(3)>>>(f_d, df_d)
235    enddo
236    istat = cudaEventRecord(stopEvent,0)
237    istat = cudaEventSynchronize(stopEvent)
238    istat = cudaEventElapsedTime(time, startEvent, stopEvent)
239
240    df = df_d
241
242    do k = 1, mz
243        sol(:,:,k) = -fz*twopi*sin(fz*twopi*(k-1.)/(mz-1))
244    enddo
245
246    error = sqrt(sum((sol-df)**2)/(mx*my*mz))
247    maxError = maxval(abs(sol-df))
248
249    write(*,"(/,'  Using shared memory tile of x-z: ', &
250        i0, 'x', i0)") sPencils, mz
251    write(*,*) '  RMS error: ', error
252    write(*,*) '  MAX error: ', maxError
253    write(*,*) '  Average time (ms): ', time/nReps
254    write(*,*) '  Average Bandwidth (GB/s): ', &
255        2.*1.e-6*sizeof(f)/(time/nReps)
256
257    ! z-derivative 1Pencils
258
259    do k = 1, mz
260        f(:,:,k) = cos(fz*twopi*(k-1.)/(mz-1))
261    enddo
262    f_d = f
263    df_d = 0
264
265    call deriv_z_1Pencils<<<g_lp(3),b_lp(3)>>>(f_d, df_d)
266    istat = cudaEventRecord(startEvent,0)
267    do i = 1, nReps
268        call deriv_z_1Pencils<<<g_lp(3),b_lp(3)>>>(f_d, df_d)
269    enddo
270    istat = cudaEventRecord(stopEvent,0)
271    istat = cudaEventSynchronize(stopEvent)
272    istat = cudaEventElapsedTime(time, startEvent, stopEvent)
273
274    df = df_d
275
276    do k = 1, mz
277        sol(:,:,k) = -fz*twopi*sin(fz*twopi*(k-1.)/(mz-1))
278    enddo
279
```

```
280   error = sqrt(sum((sol-df)**2)/(mx*my*mz))
281   maxError = maxval(abs(sol-df))
282
283   write(*,"(/,'  Using shared memory tile of x-z: ', &
284        i0, 'x', i0)") lPencils, mz
285   write(*,*) '  RMS error: ', error
286   write(*,*) '  MAX error: ', maxError
287   write(*,*) '  Average time (ms): ', time/nReps
288   write(*,*) '  Average Bandwidth (GB/s): ', &
289        2.*1.e-6*sizeof(f)/(time/nReps)
290   write(*,*)
291
292 end program derivativeTest
```

The two-dimensional Laplace solver is:

```
1  module laplaceRoutines
2
3    integer, parameter :: nx = 4096, ny = 4096
4    integer, parameter :: fp_kind = kind(1.0)
5    integer, parameter :: BLOCK_X = 32, BLOCK_Y = 16
6
7    real(fp_kind), texture, pointer :: aTex(:,:)
8
9  contains
10
11   subroutine initialize(a, aNew)
12     implicit none
13     real(fp_kind), parameter :: &
14         pi = 2.0_fp_kind*asin(1.0_fp_kind)
15     real(fp_kind) :: a(nx,ny), aNew(nx,ny)
16     real(fp_kind) :: y0(nx)
17     integer :: i
18
19     do i = 1, nx
20        y0(i) = sin(pi*(i-1)/(nx-1))
21     enddo
22     a = 0.0_fp_kind
23     a(:,1) = y0
24     a(:,ny) = y0*exp(-pi)
25     aNew = a
26   end subroutine initialize
27
28   ! Global memory version
29
```

```
30    attributes(global) subroutine jacobiGlobal(a, aNew)
31      real(fp_kind) :: a(nx,ny), aNew(nx,ny)
32      integer :: i, j
33
34      i = (blockIdx%x-1)*blockDim%x + threadIdx%x
35      j = (blockIdx%y-1)*blockDim%y + threadIdx%y
36
37      if (i>1 .and. i<nx .and. j>1 .and. j<ny) then
38         aNew(i,j) = &
39               0.2_fp_kind * ( &
40               a(i-1,j) + a(i+1,j) + &
41               a(i,j-1) + a(i,j+1)) + &
42               0.05_fp_kind * (&
43               a(i-1,j-1) + a(i+1,j-1) + &
44               a(i-1,j+1) + a(i+1,j+1))
45      endif
46    end subroutine jacobiGlobal
47
48    ! Shared memory version
49
50    attributes(global) subroutine jacobiShared(a, aNew)
51      real(fp_kind) :: a(nx,ny), aNew(nx,ny)
52      real(fp_kind), shared :: t(0:BLOCK_X+1, 0:BLOCK_Y+1)
53      integer :: i, j, is, js
54
55      i = (blockIdx%x-1)*blockDim%x + threadIdx%x
56      j = (blockIdx%y-1)*blockDim%y + threadIdx%y
57      is = threadIdx%x
58      js = threadIdx%y
59
60      if (i > 1 .and. j > 1) &
61           t(is-1, js-1) = a(i-1, j-1)
62      if (i > 1 .and. j < ny .and. js >= BLOCK_Y-2) &
63           t(is-1, js+1) = a(i-1, j+1)
64      if (i < nx .and. j > 1 .and. is >= BLOCK_X-2) &
65           t(is+1,js-1) = a(i+1,j-1)
66      if (i < nx .and. j < ny .and. &
67           is >= BLOCK_X-2 .and. js >= BLOCK_Y-2) &
68           t(is+1,js+1) = a(i+1,j+1)
69
70      call syncthreads()
71
72      if (i > 1 .and. i < nx .and. j > 1 .and. j < ny) then
73         aNew(i,j) = 0.2_fp_kind * ( &
74               t(is,js-1) + t(is-1,js) + &
75               t(is+1,js) + t(is,js+1)) &
76               + 0.05_fp_kind * ( &
```

```
77                        t(is-1,js-1) + t(is+1,js-1) + &
78                        t(is-1,js+1) + t(is+1,js+1))
79            endif
80
81        end subroutine jacobiShared
82
83        ! Texture version
84
85        attributes(global) subroutine jacobiTexture(aNew)
86            real(fp_kind) :: aNew(nx,ny)
87            integer :: i, j
88
89            i = (blockIdx%x-1)*blockDim%x + threadIdx%x
90            j = (blockIdx%y-1)*blockDim%y + threadIdx%y
91
92            if (i > 1 .and. i < nx .and. j > 1 .and. j < ny) then
93                aNew(i,j) = 0.2_fp_kind * ( &
94                        aTex(i-1,j) + aTex(i+1,j) + &
95                        aTex(i,j-1) + aTex(i,j+1) ) &
96                        + 0.05_fp_kind * (&
97                        aTex(i-1,j-1) + aTex(i+1,j-1) + &
98                        aTex(i-1,j+1) + aTex(i+1,j+1))
99            endif
100       end subroutine jacobiTexture
101
102   end module laplaceRoutines
103
104
105   program laplace
106       use cudafor
107       use laplaceRoutines
108       implicit none
109       integer, parameter :: iterMax = 100
110       integer, parameter :: reportInterval = 10
111       real(fp_kind), parameter :: tol = 1.0e-5_fp_kind
112
113       real(fp_kind) :: a(nx,ny), aNew(nx,ny)
114       real(fp_kind), device, target :: a_d(nx,ny)
115       real(fp_kind), device :: aNew_d(nx,ny)
116
117       real(fp_kind) :: maxResidual = 2*tol
118       real :: start_time, stop_time
119       integer :: i, j, iter
120
121       type(dim3) :: grid, tBlock
122
123       write(*,'(/,a,i0,a,i0,a)') &
```

```fortran
124              'Relaxation calculation on ', nx, ' x ', ny, ' mesh'
125
126      ! CPU version
127
128      write(*,"(/,a,/)") 'CPU results'
129      write(*,*) 'Iteration   Max Residual'
130
131      call initialize(a, aNew)
132
133      iter=0
134      do while ( maxResidual > tol .and. iter <= iterMax )
135         maxResidual = 0.0_fp_kind
136
137         do j=2,ny-1
138            do i=2,nx-1
139               aNew(i,j) = 0.2_fp_kind * &
140                  (a(i,j-1)+a(i-1,j)+a(i+1,j)+a(i,j+1)) + &
141                  0.05_fp_kind * &
142                  (a(i-1,j-1)+a(i+1,j-1)+a(i-1,j+1)+a(i+1,j+1))
143
144               maxResidual = &
145                    max(maxResidual, abs(aNew(i,j)-a(i,j)))
146            end do
147         end do
148
149         iter = iter + 1
150         if(mod(iter,reportInterval) == 0) &
151            write(*,'(i8,3x,f10.6)'), iter, maxResidual
152         a = aNew
153      end do
154
155      ! GPU global version
156
157      write(*,"(/,a,/)") 'GPU global results'
158      write(*,*) 'Iteration   Max Residual'
159
160      tBlock = dim3(BLOCK_X,BLOCK_Y,1)
161      grid = dim3(ceiling(real(nx)/tBlock%x), &
162           ceiling(real(ny)/tBlock%y), 1)
163
164      call initialize(a, aNew)
165
166      call cpu_time(start_time)
167
168      a_d = a
169      aNew_d = aNew
170
```

```
171    iter=0
172    do while ( maxResidual > tol .and. iter <= iterMax )
173       maxResidual = 0.0_fp_kind
174
175       call jacobiGlobal<<<grid, tBlock>>>(a_d, aNew_d)
176
177       !$CUF kernel do <<<*,*>>>
178       do j = 1, ny
179          do i = 1, nx
180             maxResidual = &
181                   max(maxResidual, abs(a_d(i,j)-aNew_d(i,j)))
182          enddo
183       enddo
184
185       iter = iter + 1
186       if(mod(iter,reportInterval) == 0) &
187             write(*,'(i8,3x,f10.6)'), iter, maxResidual
188       a_d = aNew_d
189    end do
190
191    a = aNew_d
192    call cpu_time(stop_time)
193    write(*,'(a,f10.3,a)') '  Completed in ', &
194         stop_time-start_time, ' seconds'
195
196    !
197    ! GPU shared memory version
198    !
199
200    write(*,"(/,a,/)") 'GPU shared results'
201    write(*,*) 'Iteration   Max Residual'
202
203    call initialize(a, aNew)
204
205    call cpu_time(start_time)
206
207    a_d = a
208    aNew_d = aNew
209
210    iter=0
211    do while ( maxResidual > tol .and. iter <= iterMax )
212       maxResidual = 0.0_fp_kind
213
214       call jacobiShared<<<grid, tBlock>>>(a_d, aNew_d)
215
216       !$CUF kernel do <<<*,*>>>
217       do j = 1, ny
```

```
218            do i = 1, nx
219               maxResidual = &
220                  max(maxResidual, abs(a_d(i,j)-aNew_d(i,j)))
221            enddo
222         enddo
223
224         iter = iter + 1
225         if(mod(iter,reportInterval) == 0) &
226              write(*,'(i8,3x,f10.6)'), iter, maxResidual
227         a_d = aNew_d
228      end do
229
230      a = aNew_d
231      call cpu_time(stop_time)
232      write(*,'(a,f10.3,a)')   '  Completed in ', &
233           stop_time-start_time, ' seconds'
234
235      !
236      ! GPU texture version
237      !
238
239      write(*,"(/,a,/)") 'GPU texture results'
240      write(*,*) 'Iteration   Max Residual'
241
242      ! only single precision textures supported currently
243      if (fp_kind == kind(1.0)) then
244
245         call initialize(a, aNew)
246
247         call cpu_time(start_time)
248
249         a_d = a
250         aNew_d = aNew
251
252         ! bind the texture
253         aTex => a_d
254
255         iter=0
256         do while ( maxResidual > tol .and. iter <= iterMax )
257            maxResidual = 0.0_fp_kind
258
259            call jacobiTexture<<<grid, tBlock>>>(aNew_d)
260
261            !$CUF kernel do <<<*,*>>>
262            do j = 1, ny
263               do i = 1, nx
264                  maxResidual = &
```

```
265                        max(maxResidual, abs(a_d(i,j)-aNew_d(i,j)))
266             enddo
267         enddo
268
269         iter = iter + 1
270         if(mod(iter,reportInterval) == 0) &
271             write(*,'(i8,3x,f10.6)'), iter, maxResidual
272         a_d = aNew_d
273       end do
274
275       a = aNew_d
276       call cpu_time(stop_time)
277       write(*,'(a,f10.3,a)')  '  Completed in ', &
278             stop_time-start_time, ' seconds'
279
280     end if
281
282     ! cleanup
283
284     nullify(aTex)
285
286  end program laplace
```

D.6 Spectral Poisson Solver

The following is the CUDA Fortran code used to solve the Poisson equation in Section 7.4.

```
1   module poisson_m
2     use precision_m
3
4     complex(fp_kind),device ::ref_sol
5
6   contains
7
8     attributes(global) subroutine real2complex(a, b, N, M)
9       implicit none
10      real(fp_kind):: a(N,M)
11      complex(fp_kind):: b(N,M)
12      integer, value:: N,M
13      integer:: i,j
14
15      i=threadIdx%x+(blockIdx%x-1)*blockDim%x
16      j=threadIdx%y+(blockIdx%y-1)*blockDim%y
```

```
17
18        if ( i .le. N .and. j .le. M) then
19           b(i,j) = cmplx( a(i,j), 0._fp_kind,fp_kind )
20        end if
21     end subroutine real2complex
22
23     attributes(global) subroutine real2complex1D(a, b, N, M)
24        implicit none
25        real(fp_kind):: a(N*M)
26        complex(fp_kind):: b(N*M)
27        integer, value:: N,M
28        integer:: i,index
29
30        index=threadIdx%x+(blockIdx%x-1)*blockDim%x
31
32        do i=index,N*M,blockDim%x*GridDim%x
33           b(i) = cmplx( a(i), 0._fp_kind,fp_kind )
34        end do
35     end subroutine real2complex1D
36
37     attributes(global) subroutine &
38         complex2real(input, output, ref_sol, N, M)
39        implicit none
40        complex (fp_kind):: input(N,M),ref_sol
41        real (fp_kind):: output(N,M)
42        integer, value:: N,M
43        integer:: i,j
44        real(fp_kind):: scale
45
46        i=threadIdx%x+(blockIdx%x-1)*blockDim%x
47        j=threadIdx%y+(blockIdx%y-1)*blockDim%y
48
49        scale = 1._fp_kind/real(N*M,fp_kind)
50        if ( i .le. N .and. j .le. M) then
51           output(i,j) = (real(input(i,j)) -real(ref_sol))*scale
52        end if
53     end subroutine complex2real
54
55     attributes(global) subroutine &
56         solve_poisson( phi, kx,ky, N, M)
57        implicit none
58        complex (fp_kind):: phi(N,M)
59        real(fp_kind):: kx(N),ky(M)
60        integer, value:: N,M
61        integer:: i,j
62        real(fp_kind):: scale
63
```

```fortran
64       i=threadIdx%x+(blockIdx%x-1)*blockDim%x
65       j=threadIdx%y+(blockIdx%y-1)*blockDim%y
66
67     if ( i .le. N .and. j .le. M) then
68        scale =  (kx(i)*kx(i)+ky(j)*ky(j))
69        if ( i .eq. 1 .and. j .eq. 1) scale = 1._fp_kind
70        phi(i,j) = -phi(i,j)/scale
71     end if
72   end subroutine solve_poisson
73
74 end module poisson_m
75
76 program poisson
77   use iso_c_binding
78   use precision_m
79   use cufft_m
80   use poisson_m
81   use cudafor
82   implicit none
83
84   real(fp_kind), allocatable :: kx(:), ky(:), x(:), y(:)
85   real(fp_kind), allocatable, device :: &
86        kx_d(:), ky_d(:), x_d(:), y_d(:)
87
88   real(fp_kind), allocatable, pinned :: &
89        rinput(:,:), routput(:,:)
90   real(fp_kind), allocatable, device :: rinput_d(:,:)
91   complex(fp_kind), allocatable, device :: cinput_d(:,:)
92
93   real(fp_kind):: ref
94   integer:: i, j, n, m, istat
95   type(c_ptr):: plan
96   real(fp_kind):: twopi=8._fp_kind*atan(1._fp_kind)
97   real(fp_kind):: hx, hy, alpha, L, r, norm_inf,norm_l2,err
98   type(dim3):: grid, Block
99
100   type(cudaEvent):: startEvent, stopEvent
101   real:: time
102   character(len=12) :: arg
103
104   istat=cudaEventCreate(startEvent)
105   istat=cudaEventCreate(stopEvent)
106
107
108   n=1024; m= 1024; L=1._fp_kind
109   alpha=(0.1_fp_kind)**2
110
```

```
111    print *,"Poisson equation on a mesh :",n,m
112
113    !allocate arrays on the host
114    allocate(rinput(n,m),routput(n,m),kx(n),ky(m),x(n),y(m))
115
116    !allocate arrays on the device
117    allocate(rinput_d(n,m),cinput_d(n,m),kx_d(n),ky_d(m))
118
119    !initialize arrays on the host
120    kx= twopi/L* (/ (i-1, i=1,n/2),(-n+i-1, i=n/2+1,n) /)
121    ky= twopi/L* (/ (j-1, j=1,m/2),(-m+j-1, j=m/2+1,m) /)
122
123    hx=L/real(n,fp_kind)
124    hy=L/real(m,fp_kind)
125
126    x=-L/2+hx* (/ (i-1, i=1,n) /)
127    y=-L/2+hy* (/ (j-1, j=1,m) /)
128
129    do j=1,m
130       do i=1,n
131          r =  x(i)**2 +  y(j)**2
132          rinput(i,j) = exp(-r/(2*alpha)) &
133                 * (r-2*alpha)/(alpha*alpha)
134       end do
135    end do
136
137    istat=cudaEventRecord(startEvent,0) !start timing
138
139    !Copy arrays to device
140    rinput_d=rinput
141    kx_d = kx
142    ky_d = ky
143
144    !Initialize the plan for complex to complex transforms
145    if ( fp_kind == singlePrecision) &
146         call cufftPlan2D(plan,n,m,CUFFT_C2C)
147    if ( fp_kind == doublePrecision) &
148         call cufftPlan2D(plan,n,m,CUFFT_Z2Z)
149
150    ! Set up execution configuration
151    Block = dim3(16,16,1)
152    grid  = dim3(ceiling(real(n)/Block%x), &
153         ceiling(real(m)/Block%y), 1 )
154
155    ! Transform real array to complex
156    !call real2complex<<<grid,Block>>>(rinput_d,cinput_d,N,M)
157    call real2complex1D<<<64,128>>>(rinput_d,cinput_d,N,M)
```

```
158
159    ! Execute forward transform in place
160    if ( fp_kind == singlePrecision) &
161        call cufftExecC2C(plan,cinput_d,cinput_d,CUFFT_FORWARD)
162    if ( fp_kind == doublePrecision) &
163        call cufftExecZ2Z(plan,cinput_d,cinput_d,CUFFT_FORWARD)
164
165    !Call kernel to solve the Poisson equation in Fourier space
166    call solve_poisson<<<grid,Block>>>(cinput_d,kx_d,ky_d,N,M)
167
168    !Execute backward transform in place
169    if ( fp_kind == singlePrecision) &
170        call cufftExecC2C(plan,cinput_d,cinput_d,CUFFT_INVERSE)
171    if ( fp_kind == doublePrecision) &
172        call cufftExecZ2Z(plan,cinput_d,cinput_d,CUFFT_INVERSE)
173
174    ! Transform complex array to real and scale
175    istat = cudaMemcpy(ref_sol,cinput_d(1,1),1)
176    call complex2real<<<grid,Block>>>(cinput_d,rinput_d, &
177        ref_sol,N,M)
178
179    ! Copy result back to host
180    routput=rinput_d
181
182    istat=cudaEventRecord(stopEvent,0)
183    istat=cudaEventSynchronize(stopEvent)
184    istat=cudaEventElapsedTime(time,startEvent,stopEvent)
185
186    print *,"Elapsed time (ms) :",time
187
188
189    ! Compute L1 and L_infinity norms of the error on CPU
190    norm_inf = 0._fp_kind
191    norm_L2  = 0._fp_kind
192    do j=1,m
193       do i=1,n
194          r =  x(i)**2 +  y(j)**2
195          rinput(i,j) = exp(-r/(2*alpha))
196          err = routput(i,j)-rinput(i,j)
197          norm_inf = max(abs(err),norm_inf)
198          norm_L2  = norm_L2+err*err
199       end do
200    end do
201    norm_L2=sqrt(norm_L2)/(n*m)
202
203    print *,"L infinity norm:",norm_inf
204    print *,"L2 norm        :",norm_L2
```

```
205
206     deallocate(rinput,routput,kx,ky,x,y)
207     deallocate(rinput_d,cinput_d,kx_d,ky_d)
208
209     call cufftDestroy(plan)
210 end program poisson
```

References

Barone, L., Marinari, E., Organtini, G., Ricci-Tersenghi, F., 2006. Programmazione Scientifica. Linguaggio C, algoritmi e modelli nella scienza. Pearson Education, Milan, Italy.

Cooley, J., Tukey, J., 1965. An Algorithm for the Machine Calculation of Complex Fourier Series. Bell Telephone Laboratories, New York, NY.

Dowd, K., Severance, C.R., 1998. High Performance Computing, 2nd edn. O'Reilly & Associates, Cambridge.

Ferziger, J.H., 1981. Numerical Methods for Engineering Application. Wiley, New York.

Ferziger, J.H., Perić, M., 2001. Computational Methods for Fluid Dynamics, third ed. Springer, Berlin, Germany.

Garg, R.P., Sharapov, I.A., 2002. Techniques for Optimizing Applications: High-Performance Computing. Prentice Hall PTR, Upper Saddle River, NJ.

Gropp, W., Lusk, E., Skjellum, A., 1999. Using MPI: Portable Parallel Programming with the Message-Passing Interface. MIT Press, Cambridge, MA.

Higham, D., 2002. Accuracy and Stability of Numerical Algorithms. SIAM: Society for Industrial and Applied Mathematics, Philadelphia, PA.

Higham, D., 2004. An Introduction to Financial Option Valuation: Mathematics, Stochastics, and Computation. Cambridge University Press.

Kahan, W., 1965. Further remarks on reducing truncation errors. Communications of the ACM 8 (1), 40.

Kirk, D., Hwu, W., 2012. Programming Massively Parallel Processors. A Hands-on Approach, second ed. Morgan Kaufmann Elsevier, Burlington, MA.

Metcalf, M., Reid, J., Cohen, M., 2011. Modern Fortran Explained. Oxford University Press, Oxford, UK.

Moin, P., 2001. Fundamentals of Engineering Numerical Analysis. Cambridge University Press.

Sanders, J., Kandrot, E., 2011. CUDA by Example: An Introduction to General-Purpose GPU Programming. Addison-Wesley, Upper Saddle River, NJ.

Snir, M., 1996. MPI: The Complete Reference. MIT Press, Cambridge, MA.

Solomon, C., Brecon, T., 2011. Fundamentals of Digital Image Processing: A Practical Approach with Examples. Wiley, New York.

Trefethen, L., 2000. Spectral Methods in MATLAB. SIAM: Society for Industrial and Applied Mathematics, Philadelphia, PA.

Van, L.C.F., 1992. Computational Frameworks for the Fast Fourier Transform. SIAM: Society for Industrial and Applied Mathematics, Philadelphia, PA.

Willmott, P., Howison, S., Dewynne, J., 1995. The Mathematics of Financial Derivatives: A Student Introduction. Cambridge University Press.

Wilt, N., 2013. The CUDA Handbook: A Comprehensive Guide to GPU Programming. Addison-Wesley Professional.

Index